The Secret Code
of The Monks

May God reward you for the
love you share.
Kindly yours,
Fr. Otto

The Secret Code of The Monks

Monasticism in History

Rev. Otto A. Koltzenburg, Dipl. Theol.

SAN JUAN
PUBLISHING

SAN JUAN PUBLISHING
P.O. Box 923
Woodinville, WA 98072
425-485-2813
sanjuanbooks@yahoo.com
www.sanjuanbooks.com

© 2011 by Reverend Otto A. Koltzenburg, Dipl. Theol.
Publisher: Michael D. McCloskey
Design and Production: Jennifer Shontz, Red Shoe Design
Editor: Cheryle Dunlap
Proofreader: Sherrill Carlson

Front cover artwork: © Kenneth Zeran
Back cover photograph: *Rev. Otto A. Koltzenburg*
Illustrations: Tracy L. Christianson, TLC Portraits

Library of Congress Control Number: 2011927841
ISBN-13: 978-0-9707399-4-0; ISBN-10: 0-9707399-4-X

First Printing 2011
10 9 8 7 6 5 4 3 2 1
Printed in United States of America

Contents

To my loving parents,
Karl and Gertrud Koltzenburg

Acknowledgements

God and the Blessed Virgin Mary brought rich spiritual and intellectual blessings to years of prayer and research and encouragement as companions on this faith journey. Thank you to the very many people for their strong support through meditation and friendship. Thank you to Msgr. Lopez-Gallo for his spiritual direction. Thank you to Cheryle Dunlap for her many hours of editing and correcting, to Michael McCloskey and San Juan Publishing for including this book in their program, to Linda Monroe and Sherrill Carlson for proofreading, to Ken Zaren for the cover artwork and to Jennifer Shontz for the design and production.

Prologue

by

Msgr. Pedro Lopez-Gallo
Proto-Notary Apostolic of His Holiness

When I was asked by the author of the *The Secret Code of the Monks* to help him obtain the canonical *Imprimatur* for its publication, I had replied that the book, being a factual history of monasticism, did not necessitate a *Nihil Obstat*, according to the norms of the new Canon Law of 1983.

Only books on the sacred scriptures, liturgy, catechism, and public or private prayer need previous approval from the Holy See, Episcopal conferences, or the local bishop.

What I can confirm is that there is nothing in this book that contravenes Catholic doctrine or morals. I appreciate Father Otto Koltzenburg's zeal and encouraged him to pursue this project because this new freedom of expression was a providential gift of the Second Vatican Ecumenical Council.

In the old 1917 Code, there were hundreds of rules concerning the obligations of the clergy and laity, but very little regarding their rights. The new codification modified this *Lacuna Legis*, and this was not only because of the grace and leadership of Pope John XXIII but also a result of the publication of the United Nations Charter of Human Rights, which recognizes, among many other principles, the right to freedom of expression.

After Vatican Council II, the *Index Librorum Prohibitorum* (the list of Prohibited Books) was repealed at the universal level. Before that, the Congregation for the Doctrine of Faith had also abrogated these prohibitions in 1966.

While the Church has not lost her natural and divine right to watch over the orthodoxy of publications, to prevent harm to the integrity of the faith and the morals of its faithful, the ecclesiastical legislation actually encourages pastors to utilize their right to, and make, ample use of mass media.

How very timely it is for the faithful in general that this work on Christian monasticism should appear, now that the Church is undergoing an abominable crisis—one that may be worse that the persecution of early Christian by enemies who tried to destroy it. Today, the poison of sexual abuse of minors is endemic and deeply affects the lay faithful as well as priest and bishops.

On Good Friday of 2005, just prior to the death of John Paul II, Cardinal Joseph Ratzinger proclaimed: "How much filth there is in the Church of Christ, and even among those who, in the priesthood, ought to belong entirely to Him." Last year, on his way to Fatima in Portugal, the Pope said at the press conference on the plane: "The greatest persecution of the Church does not come from the enemies on the outside but is born from the sin within the Church." Then he asked for universal remorse and forgiveness, adding: "Forgiveness does not replace justice."

Remorse alone is not enough—repentance and penance are necessary for the perseverance of the immaculate Bride of Christ that is the Church. Thus, nothing can be better for her healing than when we Christians enter into the dark night and ascend our Mount Carmel, as described by John of the Cross and well-expounded on by Fr. Koltzenburg.

A spiritual apathy has taken over our public and private devotions. Traditional practices of the faithful have diminished to the point where churches have become museums rather than places of prayer. If our mystic saints were alive today, they would exhort us to return to a more contemplative life and undertake fervent meditation resulting in the purification of the spirit. Our souls need to encounter God anew within the realm of quietude.

Our personal darkness has grown to become a clamorous noise. We now all need to absorb the silence of caves and deserts where hermits and monks found themselves. The divine loneliness and solitude will be filled with the celestial melodies that only God can bestow. This is the purpose of Fr. Koltzenburg's book: to teach us to crack the *The Secret Code of the Monks* and learn to live it.

It is a fascinating and dynamic narration that will invite every person from all walks of life—be it the Pope or a taxi driver—to listen and heed the call to enter contemplative mysticism.

Early Christians were motivated by a desire to seek God through a life of asceticism and prayer. The reader may be pleasantly surprised to discover that the old ways of dedicating one's self to God may still exist in this modern day and age.

The drab, coarsely woven habits of Franciscan monks and the simple blue-and-white saris of Mother Teresa's Missionaries of Charity are reminders of a medieval past finding its place in the contemporary world.

Unlike Buddhists and Muslim men and women who also enter monastic lives, Catholic monks and nuns seek God through their total following of Christ crucified. They answered a personal invitation to be celibate and chaste and renounce all personal and private property by living in isolation (like a hermit) or in a community (in monasteries and convents).

Some may interpret this withdrawal from the rigors of modern society as idleness. Nothing can be further from the truth: the monastic life is an intense combination of spiritual, intellectual and laborious activities, as is evident in their long hours of deep prayer, meditation, reading; physical work such as gardening and farming; and their teaching and missionary apostolate. Their artistic talents find expression in sacred hymns, which require high musical skills, and in many other creative activities. St. Benedict called this ORA ET LABORA (Prayer and Work).

The author has researched long and hard to produce this, his labor of love for the Church. It would be redundant to continue with my praises—it is up to the reader to discover the joy and grandeur of this little-known way of life in the Church, which has been the backbone of its spiritual and mystical holiness.

One of the greatest mystical souls of our Church, St. Teresa of Avila, encouraged each one of us to enter happily into the Body of Christ:

Christ has no body but yours,
No hands, no feet on earth but yours,
Yours are the eyes with which He looks
With compassion on this world.
Yours are the feet with which He walks to do good,
Yours are the hands with which He blesses all the world.
Yours are the hands, yours are the feet,
Yours are the eyes, you are His body,
Christ has no body now but yours.

By reading this book intensely, one will feel the need to belong to the esteemed groups of mystics and share in their Beatific Vision in heaven. It is edifying to discover that many others have discovered and enjoyed this secret life with God—from the existentialist Lutheran, Søren Kierkegaard, to committed people in Russia, Greece, Italy, and France. They have all discovered that there is no substitute for the value of prayer.

A glimmer of radiance will enlighten the world. Silence shall prevail and enable us to hear His Voice more intimately through a mystical life of contemplation.

— Pedro Lopez-Gallo, JUD
Proto-Notary Apostolic of His Holiness

Introduction

Each person comes to God in a unique way

Through the centuries the contemplatives, monks and nuns, have been an integral part of the Catholic Church, given a focus to all who want to be close to God. Some time of private prayer and stressing our bond with the Lord is already being a contemplative. The difference of the monk is only that he has devoted his whole life to this unique bond with God, who doesn't exclude anyone, but is always calling people to belong to him and his family.

The monk intensifies this bond, often giving inspiration to many others. He exemplifies that our final calling is to be with God. He either has removed objects or people who would block this access to God or has discovered that these have already been removed by God or by the intermediate circumstances which are in His control. Along with his vows of poverty, chastity and obedience he discovers a greater freedom of the Spirit and trusts the blessings of heaven, since he has left some earthly blessings behind. He is fully aware that the freedom of the Spirit and the trust in heaven are purchased at a great price and he would be unrealistic if he wanted to minimize the sacrifices involved. On the contrary, his personal sacrifices he turns into gifts for God who uses them as he likes, but who uses them always for the benefit of those in greater need of his divine assistance.

The contemplative is willing according to the words of the gospel to go into his own room and to pray to God in secret and he believes that God hears and rewards his prayers. This privacy constitutes the secret code of the contemplative. It is not a recipe, because each person comes to God in a unique way and in a biographical and historical setting for which there is no substitute. No one single book can cover all these ways and settings and therefore a description of the secret code of the monks doesn't and cannot claim to be complete, but to give hints and encourage the reader to also allocate time to prayer and meditation and to take the many examples given as incentives.

These pages also contain the description of a good number of nuns, who have made extraordinary contributions to the secret code of the contemplatives. However, if the title had been: "The secret code of the monks and nuns", it would have been somewhat misleading.

Spiritually men are like a focal lens of a camera and women like a panoramic lens. This means, men are better equipped to focus on just one thing or on one issue (for better or for worse) and women are better equipped to absorb and to respond to as much in their view as possible (and this too can be for better or for worse). Both endowments give evidence and reason to look at the issue of contemplation through the centuries up to the present.

The strength and persistence of contemplation through the ages is actually amazing and reminds us how important this aspect is in the life of the Church. In some eras in history the monks have saved the Church and have made great contributions to human affairs. With wholehearted love of God many contemplatives put their life on the line in the glorification of God and the service of the Church's mission. The sacrifices they have made willingly continue to be a source of encouragement. They have passed the test, have found their reward with God and as saints they are still concerned about all those on their pilgrimage of faith. It has to be considered a blessing to discover them as friends through our prayer, our willingness to learn about them and from them. The incentives they give should only increase with the passage of time.

The knowledge of some historical data and developments is necessary in order to locate the situation in which they lived and made their contributions. Since the first occupation of the contemplative is his connection with eternal life, we discover that the inspiration he gives is of a timeless nature and therefore always worthwhile to be the object of our attention.

May these pages benefit the reader in his or her contact with God's grace and the confidence God wishes all believers to have in Him.

Kindly, Fr. Otto Koltzenburg

The Birth of Monasticism

Reaching out for the treasure of God's love

The quest for Christian Monasticism has been part of Christianity from the start. The special life of the Blessed Virgin Mary in Nazareth is seen as a life of prayer and contemplation, giving herself to the Spirit of God. The thirty years of our Lord, before his public ministry, have often been described as a time of devotion and intimacy with his heavenly Father, the hidden years of his earthly life.

These insights give the believer the awareness that his own life is in God's hands. The believer knows that his earthly life is only part of the story and that the greater part is hidden in the future provided by God. For him the future in the Lord is most important and theologically most urgent. For him the words of Jesus to the rich young man, "Go, sell what you have and give it to the poor, you will then have treasure in heaven," are first of all an invitation to search for this treasure in heaven and to find some freedom from earthly possessions. The treasure may just make him long for heaven and find some solace in this longing and trust in it.

The treasure in heaven may make him more generous towards his neighbor, especially when he sees him in need. The treasure may also strengthen him to share his faith with others and to join them in prayer. On account of it he may also feel the call to leave the world behind or to do like St. Paul, to use the world as though not using it.

The monastic or the monk has made this transition in faith, leaving the world behind and channeling all his energy and love on the treasure in heaven. He knows that this transition includes these other steps of first hearing the invitation, of then gaining greater freedom of spirit, of praising

God and being in His presence. In this freedom of spirit he appreciates the parable, "Consider the ravens: they do not sow, they do not reap, they have neither cellar nor barn—yet God feeds them. How much more important are you than the birds. Your Father knows that you need such things. Seek out instead his kingship over you, and the rest will follow in turn." Jesus addressed this parable to everybody and the monk only applies it in his particular call and the circumstances of his life. This also means that everybody can join him in some capacity even if he doesn't feel a special call to the religious life.

The monk lives in response to the call from God. He is familiar with his family and his social situation from which he began his career, and his own life remains connected with them. It might very well be that his life as a monk is only an intensification of what he has experienced so far. It might equally well be that this intensification provides inspiration for those he has left behind and for others who become aware of it.

The inspiration which the monk gives to others also means that his life is not one of isolation or meant as criticism, but as a source of encouragement and strength in the bonds of faith, hope, and love. If he intercedes for others and his prayer is answered, then both will share in the grace of God's kingdom. There is something basically monastic about our awareness of God's kingdom or as St. Therese of Lisieux put it: "It is especially the gospels, which sustain me in my prayer."

Jesus gave the example and set the tone for this aspect of monasticism in our Christian lives. As the Son of the Blessed Virgin Mary he was bound to grow up in this atmosphere of the closest bond with his heavenly Father. The saving events of the Chosen People, regular prayer, especially the psalms, and meditation, liturgies and pilgrimages to Jerusalem penetrated his being with the presence of His and Our Father. The humble circumstances of his home, the need of studying, especially God's revelation in the Sacred Writings, and the hard work along with St. Joseph made him share the destiny of all mortals; and made him grow in the wisdom from above. The home of the Holy Family can easily be perceived as a model-monastery in poverty, chastity and obedience to God in heaven.

These aspects are also part of Jesus' public ministry. He called his disciples to these virtues for the sake of the kingdom and he even called some away from their marriage. He had left the concern of securing his personal subsistence in God's hands when he began to proclaim the Kingdom and poverty became a spiritual value, but he received support from friends for the necessities of life. And yet the humility of receiving support from others had to go through this radical poverty of relying on heaven's generosity. His disciples had to go through such a transformation of being in God's hands. Once this transformation had taken place the many miracles manifested the power of heaven. The group of disciples around him already had some characteristics which we would later describe as monastic. The setting of Christian communities will always share these characteristics. Even the normal parish community coming together for Mass on Sunday is somewhat monastic. The people separate themselves for an hour from their normal occupation and look up to heaven and its blessings. In worship they let their souls soar to the throne of God and are grateful for the answers to their prayers. If they happen to go to Mass in a monastery they will join the monks and for that time participate in their life.

The history of the Church should foster such participation. The gospels describe the community around the Lord and his interaction with all the people not only up to the very end, but beyond this end in his resurrection and from then onwards. The initial and permanent flame of life and grace coming from the Risen Lord is always the focus of all of Christianity and can never be separated from it.

The Jewish Religion had prepared for this and as a lasting feature of the history of mankind this promise remains with us. Believers cherish this promise and experience its fulfillment in Jesus Christ.

After the Resurrection of Jesus the Church grew tremendously, but it expanded so rapidly in the awareness that we are people of prayer and worship and live in gratitude for what God has done for us in and through his Son and what he continues to do for us in and through him. We will continue to be amazed about this expansion of Christianity in Antiquity despite the obstacles and persecutions it had to go through. Virtually overnight the early Church became an institution, which held its ground in the arena of the world of Antiquity.

Continuing the tradition of the Old Testament the Church established ordained ministers, Bishops, Priests and Deacons as leaders in the parishes. These leaders were bound to lead more closely religious lives through prayer, sacraments and regular liturgical celebrations. Prayer meant that the psalms were a normal portion of their spiritual observance. The people of the Old Covenant, the Jewish people, had established themselves rather well in the ancient world. The Roman Empire had about sixty five million people at the time of the beginning of Christianity and ten percent of these were Jewish.

They were tolerated and accepted as an exception in the fabric of the different societies. At first people believed that Christianity could be tolerated in a similar way, but this didn't work out. There was something puzzling and challenging about these Christians. As Jesus had preached the gospel to the poor and the sinners, so did the Christians. Nobody was excluded from becoming a member of the Church; poverty was no hindrance to believe in God and the sinner only had to convert and ask for forgiveness. In and through Jesus heaven had opened for everybody.

This was most alarming and threatened the historical establishments at that time. If the slave claims to have the same value as the governor in the eyes of God, then the governor may want to teach him a lesson. If the claim of the slave is derived from his religion, then the governor may not like this religion either and persecutions are almost a normal consequence. It became even more puzzling when the conviction of all these new believers grew instead of diminished in the midst of persecutions. This growth of conviction bound the believers only more closely together even when they lost members through actual martyrdom. Those who sacrificed their lives in witness to Jesus strengthened the Church's conviction that Jesus had opened heaven for us. The death of Jesus and the death of the martyrs had become the key which opened the gate of eternal life. This mysterious key had been entrusted to St. Peter, the prince of the Apostles, and the more often it opened heaven, the stronger did this institution, the Church, become.

Throughout the Empire believers came together in groups, assemblies or later parishes as members of this particular Church. This identity was clearly defined and the more the Church was threatened the more clearly did this identity become. Given the strength of character and the loyalty of the people of Antiquity we assume that the bonds established in the Church were equally strong and loyal. Family bonds, bonds of friendship and commitments on the sacramental and spiritual level had to be firm if they had to face the requirement of the possible sacrifice of life.

The code, which ran through these bonds and commitments, was the inner awareness that God only waited to reveal his final glory to his followers. Even our sinfulness is no final obstacle for this revelation of his glory, since Jesus came to save sinners. We naturally assume close-knit communities and people with a tremendous spiritual identity being part of the Church at that time. The martyrs became such shining examples because they increased the enthusiasm of faith in an unheard of and unparalleled way. People felt in their hearts that they still belonged to them and that love grew through them. The Church had become quickly a spiritual reality for which there was no merely human explanation and no substitute.

In its outward appearance this institution continued the Old Testament: Scripture and Tradition, teaching about God, liturgy, ordained ministers and so on and added those of the new: Baptism, Eucharist, Penance and so on. The writings of the New Testament gave a firm foundation very early, confirming the authority of God inherent in this community.

Seen from within this transition to the Church came about quite naturally and with certitude, which could only originate in God's revelation. The teachings about the Blessed Trinity and the role of the Blessed Virgin Mary were inherent from the beginning and only had to unfold and be explained when these questions arose. Faith communities like those of St. John in Ephesus or those of Antioch met as assemblies in which believers felt the final fulfillment we gain in Jesus Christ, although they had to wait for the actual time of its arrival.

The Church had to be a missionary Church because of the awareness that God doesn't want to exclude anyone from the final fulfillment. We have to appreciate the attraction of the Church in the various societies of the Ancient World. Somebody may have been a slave and was addressed by a member of the Church as somebody whom God loved even to the point of Jesus giving his life for him. He was invited to participate in prayer gatherings in which they celebrated the sacramental presence of the Lord, worshiped him, invoked his second coming and already shared the unity given by the Holy Spirit.

They called each other brothers because God had established a brotherhood of an even greater intimacy than all earthly relationships. Separations between rich and poor, educated and uneducated, governors and governed, nations and kingdoms had been ultimately absorbed in and through Jesus Christ. The basic requirements of mutual love and respect could fairly easily be met because God's promises were so close and almost tangible. If members failed to meet some expectation and committed a sin then they could obtain forgiveness and be fully reinstated. Close bonds brought such forgiveness more easily to a good end, especially in the awareness that we are all sinful through Adam's fall and called to rejoice all the more in the love of our Redeemer. Overall the fabric of the Church was established quickly and very well to the great surprise of the general public and the official establishment in Antiquity.

The appeal of the Church gave evidence that God was active within her and that believers in turn had to remain close to him in their hearts. And this is not always easy.

The newness of Christianity in the world of Antiquity also brought about something new by way of the persecutions and martyrdom of Christians. Through their way of looking at the human person from God's point of view the Christians challenged the culture and the establishment around them and this challenge incited persecutions, which then in turn resulted in acts of violence against them.

Despite their suffering believers experienced the persecutions and the martyrdom of many of their members in a totally different light: Jesus Christ had called them to believe in him and to give witness, even if this meant to offer their very lives for him in sacrifice. At the moment of this extreme sacrifice they were aware and convinced that they would meet Jesus in eternal life and participate in his divine glory, which would not come to an end. Their death experience was paradoxical: Instead of looking at it as a departure from the world they sadly had to leave behind, they were filled with the inner joy of God's grace. Finally, the new life had begun and the joy of heaven took hold of them. All the love of the Lord which they had celebrated in the sacraments of the Church had come to this culmination in the Risen Christ, who favored them to come to him in this way. The sacrifice he required was not given sadly or grudgingly but joyfully, filled with trust, confidence and peace.

Consequently the martyrs were honored by the Church. Their memory was respected and cherished. The stories of their ultimate witness to Christ became part of the tradition of the Church. They had followed the teaching of the Gospel, found their fulfillment in and through it and confirmed the spiritual and theological identity of the Church. In and through them the teaching of faith proved to be true and continued and increased the inner strength of the faith communities. Persecutions could be sporadic and with greater or lesser intensity across the vast Roman Empire, but the theological experience of these remained constant and became part of the spiritual treasure of the Church.

Jesus Christ had given the example through his own redemptive death on the Cross and convinced his followers through his glorious Resurrection. His presence was continually felt by believers and they were willing and eager to meet him. The martyrs did so at the point of their death. The many experiences of this utmost intensity of meeting God led to ever greater recognition and respect of Christianity and it became obvious that a spiritual reality had come forth which was unparalleled in history and for which there was neither an explanation on the mere historical level nor a substitute. Christianity had to be accepted as this unique formidable power of the history of the world.

It was Jesus Christ, the eternal Son of God, who had called all these people and only Jesus Christ could bring human beings to this point of sacrifice, martyrdom and death, because of the salvation of mankind, which had begun in and through him. The sense of divine joy and glory prevailed in the midst of the struggle of the Church on earth. In prayer, meditation, contemplation and the liturgical celebrations believers were always able to renew this divine joy and glory prevailing over them, because the treasures of heaven are inexhaustible. The observances of physical or spiritual poverty, chastity and obedience even increased their sense for the treasures of divine blessings.

This attitude found in the early Church quite naturally led believers to spend more and more time in prayer, meditation and contemplation. The efforts of these had to begin with individuals, who first decided this on their own and were happy when they could experience and also witness to an increased intimacy with God. In order to engage in their efforts they stepped aside from the larger community or the parish, spending more time in personal prayer and adoration. Being away from the community didn't mean that they isolated themselves or assumed an attitude of superiority; on the contrary God calls believers into unity and through their prayers and contemplation the spiritual bonds with others actually intensified. This was similar to the martyrs who brought people closer to God. The hermits did the same.

This is why we observe these developments simultaneously: Martyrdom and Hermitism coming about side by side in the early Church. In the way God could call someone to become a martyr for the gospel he also could call someone to become a hermit for the gospel. His grace would flow through both these channels. The hermit had been a full member of the community and he accepted his call from God, in order to be closer to Him and to let his life speak about this closeness.

It is essential for the understanding of Hermitism and Monasticism that they originated in the lessons of God's Revelation and brought the hermits, later the monks and many other believers into a closer bond with God. Different vocations draw from the same source of God's abundance.

Martyrdom made the Church aware in the most drastic fashion that

Christianity had entered the history of the world as a spiritual power that was not always welcome. It is insufficient to believe that the struggle only had to do with the Roman Empire and its interest to defend its power and position. People at the time of the Roman Empire were deeply penetrated by the values of paganism. Their faith was strong that it had been the gods who had achieved their victories for them, gave them good weather, abundant harvest, a stable government, wisdom and protected them from calamities. In the sentences against the martyrs this faith showed its power and we shouldn't underestimate it. Before their execution the martyrs were asked to sacrifice to the gods. Such sacrifice would have spared their life. When they persisted and refused such sacrifice their faith in Jesus Christ had to be strong, overcoming all human anxiety and fear of death. The struggles involved also explain that the transition from paganism to Christianity was real and often had to be purchased or validated at a great price. Jesus had gone before and they followed him.

Similarly the early hermits followed Jesus in solitude, prayer and the hardships and sacrifices connected with such a life-style. Their reward and their consolations were spiritual. They were able to confirm their faith that Jesus had called them and that they remained close to him throughout their earthly existence and would be able to join him in heaven and receive the beatific vision promised to all believers. Their lives were in agreement with the general thrust of Christianity and made its own contribution to it. Their efforts may also have been needed to strengthen the spiritual identity of the Church at large. If for example they joined the community for the celebration of the Eucharist on Sunday then people would recognize them as these hermits who spent the week in prayer by themselves on the outskirts of town. Bishops and other leaders of the community may not always have agreed with them, because they didn't really fit their plans of administration and the activities of the parish. They may have provided a challenge for many to also consider giving more time to God in prayer. From a Christian point of view such a challenge is healthy and calls people to the awareness that our lives should be in close contact with heaven and its blessings and that they shouldn't evaporate in the business of merely earthly preoccupations and aspirations. The depth of understanding and following the gospel has to be real and go through the struggles and tests imposed upon it by the personality of the individual believer, by the circumstances and the traditions, which brought these conditions about.

In God's providence Jesus Christ came in the fullness of time. Besides his divine intention to give his life in sacrifice for our salvation he suffered his death because of the circumstances of the religious and political establishment of his time. What is true for the Master is also true for his followers.

Besides the background of the Jewish Religion, Christianity made its advance in the world in late Antiquity (0–500 A.D.), which was dominated by the heritage of the Greek culture and religion. This particular heritage could be proud of a history of over 800 years and their faith-realities—belief in gods guiding our destiny as mere mortals—had a remarkable spiritual power. It wouldn't be helpful for our investigation to underestimate this power. Although Christianity proved stronger and more convincing the transition from one to the other wasn't easy and needed a real conversion in order to happen. The common language of most people at that time was Greek, something like English in our modern world. Information and ideas were transmitted and shared in this language and the New Testament has come down to us in this language as well.

By way of natural talent and endowment the Greeks were very much interested in Religion and wanted to worship the gods properly and reverently. St. Paul observed this as we know from his discourse on the Market-place in Athens (Acts 17:22 ff).

We may consider one example from this long tradition of the Greek Religion. The poet Sophocles (490–406 B.C.) described our relationship with the heavenly powers in his dramas or tragedies. Human beings are like nothing in comparison to the gods and heaven doesn't have to justify its action towards mortals. This can bring human beings into a terrible bind. One of his characters, Antigone, gave an honorable burial to her brother, which the king had forbidden. Respect for the gods and for the deceased required from her to do something against the wishes of the ruler. This brought her into a tragic bind, since the king threatened and finally imposed the death sentence on her. Love for her brother and the recognition of the rights of the gods prevailed at the cost of her life. Her self-evaluation was: "My part is to love and not to hate." The stage-productions of the poet were liturgies for all the people, who recognized and rejuvenated their faith through these. The attitude of Antigone in regard to the divine is typically Greek, penetrated by a sense that heaven is in control of our destiny and that we have to respect it.

PART I

Late Antiquity

Sophocles

"My part is to love and not to hate"

T he poet and statesman Sophocles wrote 123 theatre plays, designed to witness to his own conviction and to celebrate his own faith along with his people. These many productions were liturgies and were followed by the people with a sense to participate in the divine coming down to them in these. We might consider that their attitude is also part of our own faith and yet it takes a real conversion to the gospel to make this transition from the one to the intimate bond we enjoy in Jesus Christ. The prayerful person in Antiquity had to give time and attention to this transition and be convincing through the life he led. The hermit could very well be such a prayerful person who provided a point of reference not only for members of the Church, but also for people in this large pagan environment.

St. Paul in his discourse on the market in Athens wasn't even all that successful. Some sneered at him and called him a magpie. And yet God is patient with human beings and gives time to cooperate with his grace in freedom. The reaction of the Athenians to St. Paul shows the strength of their conviction and that they wouldn't let themselves be won over all that easily. Hermits and contemplatives come to the help of missionary activity to live out the depth of our faith, which ultimately remains invisible to outward observance and is a matter of the heart. In recognition to our topic, there is something hidden and secret in our faith.

The poet Sophocles and many others of Antiquity described a whole range of human beliefs and commitments and we may do well to respect this. In the extraordinary success of Christianity we easily bypass this paganism of Antiquity and shrug it off as something of little importance or value. At the time of the early Church, the encounter between the Greek culture and Christianity was real and this non-Christian heritage had to be taken into serious consideration; otherwise we would fall prey to it. To some extent Christians could go along with the ancients, make them wish and long for the truths of the gospel and prepare the step for them to join the Church. Often this companionship before conversion can be merely spiritual, done in prayer and silence, hermits and monks giving the lead. From God's point of view we might even be astonished how much can be accomplished by prayer and meditation alone, apart from work and active involvement. Also from this angle we can admire and support the hermits and contemplatives.

Besides the many stage-productions, nourishing the faith of the people and making them susceptible to accept Christianity, the Greek culture had developed an intellectual landscape of extraordinary richness and depth, which by its very nature lent itself to meditation. The hermit or monk could display the attitude of the philosopher although he was specifically directed towards the presence of Jesus Christ; and yet there is a similarity on whose account early Christians were open to take this intellectual landscape into consideration. In this attitude the hermit or monk also confirms this experience that the proclamation of God's kingdom may very well be prepared through patiently witnessing to the eternal, and that prayer has to join preaching in order to go to the depth of peoples' hearts.

Socrates

He accepted his death in the belief of the immortality of the soul

One of the highlights of the Greek intellectual landscape was Socrates (469–399 B.C.). He lived his whole life in Athens and his concerns revolved around the well-being of the city and its citizens. His basic education was common to people of his age and status in society, studying music, geometry and gymnastics. However, he also liked to work and practiced the art of sculptor in his father's workshop. He gave this up when he believed called to be available for the education of the Athenian youth. His aim was the moral and intellectual reform of his contemporaries. Although he spoke of a divine call he may just have followed his conscience, but in this he believed responsible to higher ideals and truths, which we discover and once we have done so, also have to follow. He was very apt to convince his people first of their ignorance in regard to the principles, which should be the basis of their endeavors, and the goals of their activity. Many people who didn't like to be convinced of their ignorance didn't like him and they responded by opposing him; except for young people who were pliable enough to cope with a put-down, because they enjoyed the irony of it; besides this, they could use this method on their parents, proving their ignorance. This infuriated them especially against Socrates. Once this basic human ignorance had been established Socrates concluded correctly that there must be basic truths like justice, goodness, order and the immortality of the soul.

His method didn't leave people in the lurch in regard to basic values, but they were forced to look deeper into themselves, acknowledge their mere humanness and the need to rely on principles not of our own making. He was convinced that we are empowered to recognize the need and the foundation for good moral conduct and that we are capable to follow the norms which we have found. From this point of view he provides incentives later for the Christian in his search for reliable ethical norms. On account of his educational approach he was accused of sidetracking the youth and alienating them from lawful authority.

He was sentenced to death and he had to drink the hemlock. He was composed at the time of his death and we assume that this was the case, because of his inner conviction of the immortality of the soul. Believing that our life goes on also after we leave this world is a great consolation for human beings and this belief gains its greatest determination in our Christian faith asserting the Resurrection of the dead and life everlasting. Socrates began a tradition of research, which has remained a part of mankind's search for the truth, and he was a well-known figure at the time, when Christianity began its great expansion in Antiquity.

We naturally assume that many contemplatives were interested to study this school of thought in order to appreciate the Christian heritage even more and in order to be able to explain their faith to non-Christians of their time, if they should get in contact with them. Socrates has an immense impact on mankind and remains one of the great ones. The Danish scholar, Søren Kierkegaard (1813–1855), took Socrates and his Irony as a starting point for his own intellectual career in his dissertation "The Concept of Irony with constant reference to Socrates", confirming the importance of this Greek scholar in the nineteenth century.

Socrates didn't leave any writings of his own; his insights are known through his disciples, Plato and the historian Xenophon (450–354 B.C.)

Christians receive the truth through God's revelation in the Old and New Testament and the teaching Magisterium of the Church and yet they are free to broaden and deepen their understanding of the faith through independent research. This is part of the basic attitude of believers who want to continue with an open mind on their faith journey. Far from alienating us from the gospel, such research makes it possible to see Revelation and ourselves in a new light and to find that God has been and is active in human hearts where we at first may not have expected it. We can be happy to discover how open the early Christians were towards pre-Christian and non-Christian dispositions and achievements of the human mind and heart. They were glad to discover and to confirm what is commonly human and then to transpose or convert it to the proper Christian understanding of the divine truth. Through this openness they were able to be true missionaries, who brought about a heartfelt conviction in their contemporaries. They understood that Christianity is a leaven in the world, penetrating the given milieu from within. When for example they learned that Socrates was able to stand still for a night and devote himself to think through a question, then they could transfer this attitude to one of prayer and contemplation and use it for their own approach in their love for Jesus Christ. The scholar had given an incentive for deeper meditation. Such a transfer was not only true for the contemplatives, but also for the theologians of the Church.

Plato

Showing a way to find our ideas and our ideals

The second great thinker of Greece and a disciple of Socrates was Plato (427–347 B.C.) He was also born in Athens and enjoyed an educational upbringing in a very favorable intellectual atmosphere. At the right time, at the age of twenty, he came to know Socrates and fell under the spell of this genius. His discipleship and friendship lasted until Socrates' death in 399 B.C. Before that time he had already devoted himself to study poetry and the spiritual and religious myths of Greek tradition. After 399 B.C. he joined a group of Socratic disciples. He traveled to different parts of Greece, Egypt and Sicily, where he tried to influence the ruler to adopt a new form of government. His influence failed and he was put in jail and sold as a slave.

Like his master, Socrates, he learned the hard way how difficult it is to suggest something new. Fortunately, a friend ransomed him and he could return to Athens and continue his teaching and writing career up to the time of his death at age 80. He perfected the style of presenting his thoughts in the form of a dialogue like in the Phaedrus, Protagoras, Phaedo, and The Republic. The Symposium invites the reader to be engaged in it. Through conversation we come to know our human condition. Given our limitations we are like being in a cave with our back turned towards the opening. We get a clue that there must be real light and understanding, but we may not even be able to endure these. By consistent efforts we come closer and our conviction grows that eternal truths are real, that we got to where we are only because of them and that we long to realize them in us. We naturally love what is good and beautiful. We may have to strive until our love is mature to reach what is really good and beautiful. We may have to undergo long training and even suffering until we can endure the purity of the eternal ideas of the good and beautiful. These are greater than our understanding of them and yet after our training and suffering we may be able to step out of our cave and endure the light of the sun. Centuries later St. Augustine used this description for our appreciation of the revealed truth about the Blessed Trinity and the love, beauty and goodness we find in God. The philosopher's method lends itself very well to meditation and prayer and gives us the notion how easy it was for the prayerful person in the Christian era to respect these ideas of the pre-Christian world. Besides this, the school of Plato and those of many others prepared the way for people who wanted to be together to pursue a common spiritual goal.

Aristotle

Through our research we discover God's intention for his creation

T he third of these big three of Greek Philosophy was Aristotle (384–322). His father was the court-physician of the King of Macedonia, a position gained by inheritance, and we assume that Aristotle was familiar with medicine through his family background. His propensity was the investigation of natural phenomena also when he became a disciple of Plato at age eighteen. Even when learning about ideas from his master he was determined that these had to agree in some way with our observations. He discovered and believed in scientific research and on account of his realism he became the most influential philosopher of mankind.

Early Christian theologians like the martyr Justin and Gregory Nazianzen were familiar with Aristotle. In the year 342 he was hired by the king of Macedonia to educate his thirteen year old son, Alexander, later called the Great. He held this position until 335 when Alexander started to conquer the then known world. Aristotle then returned to Athens to teach and write there. He included in his writings physics, even zoology, and metaphysics. He became the founder of logic. After the death of Alexander the Great in 323 B.C. the Macedonians had become unpopular in Athens and he left for his country estate at Chalcis; there he died a year later in 322, from an illness which he had endured for a long time. His very practical description of how we gain knowledge of things was virtually rediscovered by St. Thomas Aquinas in the thirteenth century, making it obvious how influential he is and has remained so for almost two thousand four hundred years. Different from Plato his research lends itself to discover God's greatness as the Creator and Protector of everything he has made. For him and his followers it is natural to honor and love God in witness to the design of creation he has entrusted to us. When this is combined with God's Revelation the preparation of Salvation of the individual in Christ is well established.

Aristotle gives a lot of incentives to meditate on his insights in the light of the gospel and when Christianity came on the scene in the world of Antiquity, almost dominated by the influence of Greek thought and culture, the contemplatives did so. Aristotle, like his teacher Plato also was the head of a school. The king of Macedonia had been very generous to him and he could establish a great library, so that many disciples could grow in wisdom. These places of learning were instrumental to bring about many others in the same vein. Especially as the Greek culture continued to grow and spread over the centuries any advance of the human mind and spirit were connected with places of learning.

Many places of study were firmly established at the start of Christianity and increased the intellectual and spiritual curiosity of Christians and their interaction with their contemporaries. The martyrs gave witness that our lives have to conclude and then really begin in the eternal salvation brought to us in and through Jesus Christ. The hermit or the contemplative is giving the same witness in his own situation. Like the martyr he also wants to live in the assurance of his own salvation, but also increase the faith of those who come to know him or of those who have known him all along. He applies the life-style of the scholars and thinkers and makes it useful for his own closeness to Jesus.

His reading of Scripture, his prayers and the celebration of the sacraments are not empty routine and repetition, but a way to internalize God's word and make it more and more his own. As far as other writings help him he will accept these and possibly transform them into a Christian understanding, something that happened with extraordinary and God-given skill as Christianity began to unfold. God probably uses the contemplatives so that the Church keeps the focus given by the Lord pure and simple. The gospel mandates of chastity, obedience and poverty are used for the same purpose, namely to keep the focus given by the Lord pure and simple.

We have to recognize that these schools of thought of the Big Three of Greek Philosophy led to many foundations of a similar kind throughout the world of Antiquity.

Alexander the Great not only conquered the world of his time but also exported Greek culture, customs and wisdom. When a couple centuries later the Romans became prominent the religion, poetry and science continued on under this new leadership. The transformation through Christianity happened by God's design in this environment and had to undergo the struggle.

Those who became believers in Jesus Christ had to leave their pagan background behind, but they were respectful and happy for those things they could accept like the philosophical insights, which could be adopted from a Christian point of view. Other things didn't agree with Christian principles and had to be avoided.

The first Christians experienced the political and social order around them as being hostile to their faith, even as dominated by evil. The establishment required their subjects and especially those employed by the government to sacrifice in the public temples, which also proved their loyalty to the state. Christians couldn't do that and certain professions like soldier, schoolmaster, or state officials were not accessible to them. Even the private life was a sphere where suspicion could arise.

There were gods for every occasion and situation: house and garden, the family, food and drink, health and illness.

Non-Christians observed certain rites and when Christians failed to do the same, then they could be denounced to the authorities and suffer persecution. In many instances to be Christian was precarious and dangerous. They felt deeply the words of Jesus: "In the world you will suffer persecution." By nature their prayer was sincere and penetrated by the greater glory of the Lord in the midst of their endurance. They experienced that their perseverance and their obedience to God could put them into a bind or into a dilemma and when they trusted in God nonetheless, they felt his divine blessings, which were of a spiritual nature. They also experienced that for this blessing the earthly advantages which they could have enjoyed, if they had been unfaithful to Christ, amounted to very little and ultimately to nothing. On the practical level they looked upon the recommendations of the gospel like: "My little children, be on your guard against idols" 1 John

5, 21 in terms of what they knew so well. The conversion to the faith had and continued to cost them so much, so that they were daily familiar with the price of our redemption and the association with Jesus was close and they could feel it. Martyrdom, where and when it happened, increased this closeness with Jesus and had an impact on the prayerful disposition of those left behind. The Church has always felt blessed in a spiritual sense by this kind of witness. The focus on heaven, eternal life is increased by this witness and believers have to take it to heart. When they do, they will be more committed to prayer and gain a greater awareness of the gospel.

The sinister interpretation is possible that the contemplative tries to get away from the possibility of persecution and hides in a safe corner, but he would only fail the test of faith. The contrary is usually the case: When the circumstances require the contemplative to give witness and to even sacrifice himself for God, then he will rally his strength to do so and he might even experience this strength as a gift from above. We are bound to assume this link between martyrdom and contemplation. Both arise from this divine impact of God's Revelation on the human soul. The contemplative rightfully deduced the need of a struggle against worldly principles, even if such worldly powers are not sinful, as St. John wrote in his first letter: "Love not the world, nor the things that are in the world. If any man loves the world, the love of God is not in him. For all that is in the world is the concupiscence of the flesh, and the concupiscence of the eyes, and the pride of life, which is not of the Father but is of the world. And the world passes away and the concupiscence thereof. But he that doeth the will of God abides for ever." 2, 15–17.

The contemplative accepts the struggle as a God-given opportunity to be more closely united with Christ. He may do so joyfully in his conviction, that the martyrs did even more for God, but the Lord may reward him with the assurance that his devotion is equally precious in his eyes. Given the faith of this assurance also makes it obvious that the faithful normally appreciate the contemplative, later the ascetic and the monastic. The variety of gifts are at work for the benefit of all and the contemplative can naturally assume that his gift of prayer finds some recognition in the hearts of other members of the Church.

As mentioned the basic structure of the Church was established rather quickly after the death and Resurrection of the Lord. Given the historical circumstances members of the Church cooperated willingly as brothers and sisters in Christ. The basic openness towards people from all walks of life and all classes of society was a unique feature and brought about a warmth of brotherhood not felt in previous history. This and the eternal promises or better the promise of eternal happiness and glory had created a spiritual atmosphere hitherto unknown. As mentioned, there was belief in life after death as the case of Socrates points out, but this belief couldn't match the one made possible through the Risen Lord. In this new belief Christians gained a greater freedom to deal with the teachings and attitudes of their environment and the heritage that had led to this without giving up their unequalled identity as followers of Christ. The martyr was absorbed by this freedom and this grace made possible in and through God's Revelation. He also was a man of his day and age and had dealt with the then prevalent mentality. He had been willing to engage in a conversation with others and possibly bring them also to the faith in Christ.

The era from the beginning of Christianity up to the sixth century we describe as late Antiquity and we observe that the mind-sets of the big three had grown in influence. Neo-Platonism and Stoicism tried to bring people to adjust to unchangeable ideas and truths; others recognized the harmony of the cosmos and believed in the eternal recurrence of the same and still others like the Cynics liked to poke fun at the establishment, trying to convince everybody that we know very little and that our efforts as human beings may be an object of scorn and contempt.

As Christianity began to unfold, these spiritual powers present had to be taken into account and had to be carefully examined. This examination naturally led to greater self reflection and deepened the believer's awareness for the need of prayer, contemplation and the worship and the sacrifices to be made in their service. This doesn't mean that these spiritual powers of the non-Christian, pagan environment became a source for contemplation, but that they were used as incentives. Christians discovered how much these people did for their conviction and said to themselves, "If they do already so much, then we should make even grater sacrifices for the truth we hold dear." If Christians claim that their religion is valid also from a philosophical point of view, then they are also interested to describe this claim through intelligible explanations and through the life they lead. This necessary comparison between paganism and Christianity challenged the believers to be all the more true to their name.

St. Justin

He combined his philosophy and his belief in Jesus Christ

Saint Justin (100–165) was a student in philosophy, rhetoric, history and poetry. He admired the Stoic philosopher Musonius who had died about the year 100. Saint Justin described that Musonius developed the right ideas about ethics and even offered his life for his conviction. Justin himself came to know Christianity when he was an adult and had to compare its teaching with the knowledge he had obtained before his conversion. He had acknowledged the religious aspirations of pagan religion and their practices and from these he made his transition to the faith. Through his research he was able to describe this transition and witness to it. He realized that the schools of the pagan world endeavored to be also religious institutions with the help of their philosophy and discipline. He concluded that the true religion ought to lead to even more learning and the exercise of all the virtues than the false one. It is most likely that Justin came from a Greek family. He is a typical example of the Greek mentality to be very much interested in the search for God, and to be very devoted to Him once He is found.

Even after his conversion Justin was very much concerned about the debate with non-Christians and promoted this debate through his school of philosophy, which he opened in Rome. Justin tried to convince others of the truth of Christianity. In his words, "It is our duty to make known our doctrine, lest we incur the guilt and the punishment of those who have sinned through ignorance". As a Christian philosopher he traveled in various lands where he held disputations with pagans, heretics and Jews, and finally settled in Rome, where he founded his school. It was there that he argued with a member of the Cynic philosophy, who was opposed to him and who denounced him to the authorities of the state; they in turn put him on trial as an enemy of the state and sentenced him to death. His willingness to die for the faith gave evidence to how much the truth of Christianity prevailed in him. His martyrdom occurred in the year 165 during the reign of Marcus Aurelius.

The saint is especially remembered for his defense of the faith, also known as his Apology. Christians were able to point out their high ethical standards and accomplishments and the often practiced celibacy among them and that their religion deserved to be recognized. The saint's institution for Christian learning and his own fervent practice of this religion could give an example of what was later perceived as a monastery without the term being used for it yet. Academic endeavors and the use of our reason led the saint to greater intimacy with God in prayer and brought him to the point of giving his life in witness for the truth. He strengthens our conviction about this proximity between prayer and martyrdom. In the way that contemplation can lead a person to give his life for the truth, so also the martyrdom of those who have gone before us makes the Christian more fervent and serious in his prayer. He may simply conclude: "If the martyr gave his life for Jesus Christ, then I might be called to spend as much time as possible in prayer on earth and worship him, so that I am truly ready to come to him in heaven when he calls me." The exercise of this readiness may also include the recommendations of poverty, obedience and chastity for the sake of the kingdom. We also assume that this exercise began with private commitments in the family circle and was performed with various degrees of intensity and allocation of time. Something similar applies to martyrdom. Not everybody was ready to give his life for God; many tried to dodge the issue, soften the impact of the demand of the truth and try to die a natural death. Human nature remained the same also within Christianity.

Marcus Aurelius
Emperor and Philosopher

*A*t the time of the death of St. Justin the head of State, or the Emperor, was the philosopher, Marcus Aurelius (121–180). He was a Stoic and a great proponent of the teaching of Stoicism. This school of thought is penetrated by the interest in spiritual control. St. Justin shared the attraction of this teaching. The Emperor and Philosopher's "Observations of Self" are meditations which include his awareness of the divine. He knew that we bring forth what is truly human if we are connected to the divine. Without the presence of this power our own efforts become insignificant. "What power is given to the human being? He has the power to do only the things which obtain divine approval and to accept everything, which the divine assigns to him." (XII) In order to be ready for the presence of the divine, the meditative person looks into himself, "Work at your inner self. There is the fountain of goodness, an ever flowing fountain, if you continue to dig in it." (VII, 59) His relationship to the divine is in the control of his reason:

"One person prays: How do I obtain the favor of the beloved? And you: How do I overcome the desire for it?" (VII, 40) He believes that his emotions shouldn't get in the way of his inner peace. Typical for his stoicism he endeavors to maintain this inner peace, "Among the most useful truths pay attention especially to the following two; first that the things outside of our self are not in contact with our soul, but are immovably distinct from it and therefore any disturbance of the peace of your soul comes about through your imagination, and secondly everything you see changes quickly and will soon have disappeared. How many changes have you already observed? Consider without interruption: the world is changing and life is an imagination." (IV, 3) We can easily understand that St. Justin had been in agreement with such sentiments as expressed by Marcus Aurelius, but also that he found that the real inner peace has to come to us as gift from Jesus; and yet the words of the philosopher can very well be used to support our appreciation of the gospel and to lead to it. The saint made this transition and he along with the many martyrs of his time paved the way for this increase of devotion.

Many martyrs of the Church are known only by God. From the earthly point of view their lives are a secret which is in God's hands and yet they have contributed to the growth of Christianity and those who were close to them simply had to follow their example of perseverance, even if they were not called by God to become martyrs for the faith.

Origen

He worshiped God through a wealth of spiritual experiences

One of those who followed this contact between heaven and earth in an extreme degree was the Christian writer Origen. He was born in 185 and died in 254. At times Christians could live in peace, follow their trade, pray and worship without interference, raise their families and look with confidence upon the end of their life and upon the glory which follows. But then persecutions could arise in a city or in a region of the Empire and these couldn't be predicted. The early years of Origen in Alexandria in Egypt were blessed with such peace. He was highly intelligent and charming and his father, Leonides, highly esteemed his gentle disposition and his purity of heart. He favored and supported his excellent literary education in this sophisticated and advanced city. Origen thrived in this atmosphere of learning and piety. His heart was always expanded to the truth of the Gospel and the joy in heaven's blessings. He knew that his life had to be directed to these and that nothing should take their place.

Suddenly when he was barely seventeen years old a bloody persecution of the Church broke out in Alexandria and his father was thrown into prison, waiting for his execution. Besides Origen there were six younger boys in the family. It is hard to imagine the anxiety, worries and concern for the future of his family going through the heart of this family man. Wouldn't there be sufficient reason to cave in just a little and to get himself out of trouble for the sake of his family? Wouldn't God be forgiving and understanding, since he had already taken upon himself the responsibility for a large family? Sometimes during persecutions it was rather easy to obtain a document of having sacrificed to the gods and then be released. There was an added pressure upon martyrs who owned an estate and Leonides' estate was substantial. Their property was confiscated by the government and the family was left destitute. Despite these grave concerns Leonides remained firm and his son, Origen, wrote him a letter of support, expressing his love and admiration and his sincere desire to join him in martyrdom. However, his mother didn't want him also as a martyr and forced him to stay at home. She hid his clothes, so that he couldn't go out of doors.

At the time Alexandria along with the other parts of Egypt were ruled by the Greek portion of society. The Jews formed a powerful and very influential minority. The bulk of the population was the indigenous Egyptians, dominated by the first two mentioned sections of society. Leonides belonged to the Greeks.

We have to admire Origen's willingness to join his father in martyrdom. It confirms his conviction that those who suffer death for Jesus' sake will join the saints in heaven. His faith was firmly established and our judgment would be unfair to think of it only as some youthful enthusiasm. We assume that he maintained his conviction until his own end. Leonides did die a martyr and his substantial possessions were confiscated by the government. This left his family in poverty and they had to suffer and work hard in order to survive. Loyally and faithfully Origen stepped up to the plate and supported his family. Because of his great talents he was able to make money by teaching younger students and even by selling his manuscripts. He was also blessed in that a wealthy lady admired his talents and was generous to him and his relatives. When such needs arose the Christians would join even more closely together and grew in their faith.

When his younger brothers became older they in turn could help and contribute for their survival. Once these first hardships had been endured and surmounted Origen was able to devote more time to contemplation and ascetical practices. He and other solitaires of his time engaged in these from the Christian point of view. Our lives are hidden now in Christ and will be fully revealed and blessed in heaven. The instinct of sexuality was included in this view and Origen like other contemplatives consented to the procedure of self-castration. This was done in an interpretation of Mt 19, 12 "some have freely renounced sex for the sake of God's reign". We have to consider that this procedure was more common in Antiquity like the Ethiopian Eunuch mentioned in the Acts of the Apostles and doesn't deserve to be looked upon as totally out of the question for Christians. Origen believed himself to be called to a celibate life, but later he didn't favor the practice of self-castration for the contemplative.

For the topic of the secret code of the monks, Origen qualifies as an early highlight. From his prayerful disposition and his sincere interest in the eternal his entire human existence remained at this cross-section where man is face to face with God and nothing else can take its place. We assume that he developed his interest through other contemplatives who interpreted the gospel as a call to remain in God's presence as much as possible. On a practical level we assume that there were already hermits towards the end of the second century. Later hermitism became a movement which attracted thousands of people first throughout Egypt and later expanding to other parts of the Near East, until it finally found acceptance in all of Christendom.

Like many other people entirely devoted to prayer he let God direct his future, which became a source of meditation over the centuries. Because of his education in Greek culture and philosophy he was interested to let the light of Christ shine in this environment. Similar to St. Justin almost a century earlier in Rome he taught Theology to people who wanted to advance academically in their understanding of the truth and either make a transition from a pagan background to Christianity or be able to explain their faith in terms of Greek thinking. Origen could do this for them and he was highly respected and acknowledged. However, his school was not under the direct supervision of the bishop of Alexandria. Usually the bishop respected him as well, but there could be occasions of suspicion and possibly envy. People came to him who were at first only interested to become Christians and Origen left them total freedom to join the Church or not. Some of his students became so fervent that they were willing to become martyrs at times of persecution. Origen encouraged them and accompanied them to the end, also taking the risk of martyrdom himself.

In either 218 or 222 he was even invited by the mother of the Emperor, Julia, to visit her in Antioch and to explain to her and in the Church she attended his theology. Origen enjoyed such excursions also for his own continued education as he had enjoyed visits to Rome, Greece and later to Arabia. His faith was put to the test from within the Church. At age 46 he again visited Palestine and was ordained to the priesthood in Caesarea by the local bishop and by the bishop of Jerusalem, who both supported him as a prominent teacher of theology. His own Bishop, Demetrius of Alexandria, felt greatly offended by this ordination outside his diocese. He unleashed a storm of opposition against Origen. Two councils were held, one banished him from Egypt and the other deposed him of his priesthood. Persecutions from within the Church are always most painful, especially if the one persecuted believes in his heart that he followed God. His ordination should have confirmed for everybody that Origen was deeply committed to the teaching and the discipline of the Church, but this was obviously not the case. He had to swallow this bitter pill and rally his strength to found a new school in Caesarea. Once again he continued to attract young men, who were impressed by his wisdom and found their way to wisdom itself through him. He was the first who developed an overall system of theology, which has continued its influence through the centuries, inviting readers to become contemplatives in the presence of the One Eternal God.

Towards the end of his life the persecution of Decius (250) was raging and Origen was imprisoned and barbarously tortured. Despite his hardships he wrote letters giving strength to believers and encouraged them to remain strong in the midst of trial. He was threatened to be burned at the stake, but the authorities didn't follow through with their threats. He was set free, but he had suffered so much that his health was severely impaired and he died about the year 254 at the age of sixty nine. He was buried with honor as a confessor of the Faith. Some of his sentences were condemned by bishop conferences, but it seems that these condemnations were never formally approved by the Holy See.

Even modern theologians like Hans Urs von Balthasar and Henry Lubac consider him orthodox and it is possible that he will one day be enrolled among the saints of the Church. We can pray for this. Although he was a great teacher his philosophy and his theology are at the service of prayer and contemplation and strengthen the reader to focus on eternal life. He also witnesses to this lively exchange of ideas between Christianity and paganism without compromising his conviction in the superiority of the Church's teaching and mission in the world.

Very painfully Origen experienced the power of the bishop, who expelled and deposed him and he was fortunate that another bishop had watched out for him. The frustration of Origen was often part of the sacrifice which the hermits had to make.

The bishop was the head of the community; all the offices, their functions and the services they rendered were well prescribed and the bishop had the power to assign their tasks to different people. Women would also make their influence felt. The monastically inclined individual may not have found his place in this fabric of Church life. He could have made some compromise and accept a position through which he felt he would fit in, but he would have felt a certain emptiness and lack of response to the call of God in his heart. If he wanted to be faithful to his inner call, then he had to accept this alienation and recognize in it an intensification of the gospel in him.

When he decided to go his own way, then this was not intended as a protest against the Church at large. He may have chosen the life of a hermit, because he firmly believed that he would acquire his own salvation more assuredly in this way. He was convinced that this would bring him to a greater undisturbed contemplation and a mystical vision of heaven. For this step he had to renounce the world, including his faith community, give up his occupation on the social level and accept the practices of the hermits.

This meant that most the time was spent in prayer, spiritual reading and the celebration of the Sacraments, Eucharist and Confession. During the second century the faith communities had already become larger and were more able to afford this "loss of members", who wanted to devote their life to prayer and contemplation. Bigger parishes were also capable to support these "monks", respect them and to believe in the validity of their call from God. Origen shared their ideals, although he had to follow his vocation as a theologian and teacher of the faith, especially for those highly educated individuals who had to be addressed on their level.

At the same time, he and the hermits renounced sex for the sake of the kingdom. This was a normal development, since he wanted to be free from the intrusion of sexuality without being opposed to the vocation of marriage for other people. Genuine Christian spirituality always requires such liberation even amidst great sacrifices. Without such sacrifices our access to God's reign would be too cheap and our appreciation of its value would decrease instead of increase. The many early martyrs, the hermits and the contemplatives were able to describe the value of God's reign through the lives they led. Origen had participated in all three aspects and his witness has spoken to many people throughout the centuries. When he began to teach he was concerned to take his interest of hermitism along with him. He stated: "You can be alone with God even in the theatre." This is possible for a strong mind like him, but others are in greater need of separation from the world so as to be also physically alone with God. Origen's statement also shows his familiarity with hermits and his continued spiritual kinship with them. As a teacher he also did something similar to the hermits in the desert.

People in Antiquity had a great sensitivity that areas are dominated by certain spirits. Jesus used this same expression when he talked about evil spirits who live inside a man. In their understanding a city or a region was in the control of a spirit and human beings who did harm to others may only have acted as the agents of these evil spirits. The martyrs had learned this lesson the hard way. The teacher of theology addressed people who in his understanding were enshrouded by the spirit of paganism and the education he provided acted as positive liberation from these spirits of heathenism. In a similar way the hermits were interested to bring even the desert into the control of Jesus Christ.

Without this presence of the Lord they considered the desert to be inhabited by evil spirits. The consideration was very likely that the desert was barren and poor because of these evil spirits living there. The hermit therefore chose these deserted spots to drive them out and to bring the life and light of the gospel, so that even the desert could rejoice in the salvation brought by God's messengers, in this case the hermits. This aspect also supports the great enthusiasm for the life of the hermits not only at that time, but also later on in different parts of the world. People being in contact with the hermits and supporting them believed in this personal protection brought to them through the lives of the hermits. It was through them that the evil spirits were removed further from the cities and they owed them a debt of gratitude for the conditions they endured for the spread of the gospel. If they had seen the modern desert-monk, Charles de Foucauld, who died in 1916, they would have looked upon him from this angle, namely to bring the glory of Christ into this remote region of the Sahara desert. Charles de Foucauld shared similar sentiments in the twentieth century. Origen shows not only this link between martyrdom, hermitism and the teacher of theology, but he establishes this insight that all three live from the same source and present God's grace in different aspects.

The harsh treatment he received from his Bishop Demetrius of Alexandria also shows that neither the teacher of theology nor the hermit in the desert received the automatic approval of the hierarchy. Spiritually Origen had exercised a greater freedom of expression towards paganism and the hermits exercised a greater freedom in regard to their situation of prayer and both could be regarded with suspicion. Bishop Demetrius of Alexandria elevated the discussion to the level of dogmatic theology, claiming Origen to be heretical. The fact that he incited an entire bishop-conference speaks about his power and his vindictiveness, but not necessarily of the truth. Origen was firmly committed to God's revelation and it wasn't really necessary to unleash a storm of opposition against him.

Many hermits and contemplatives could live in a similar twilight of following God's call but not being truly respected by the hierarchy of the Church. God's call isn't always as simple as we would like it to be, but the contemplative has to wade through prejudices and even opposition within the Church. He may even find his vindication only in heaven and his witness is all the more convincing because of it.

It is difficult to asses the number of the hermits at the end of the second and the beginning of the third century, but if we consider that a century later St. Anthony alone gave spiritual direction to over 6,000 then we may deal with rather large number of people devoting themselves to this life-style. As in the case of the many martyrs so it is also in the case of the many hermits that they are known only to God and we may meet them in heaven around God's throne.

Hermitism

Alone with God, but not disconnected from others

Hermitism began in Egypt. It is the land where the desert is close at hand, often not far from the cities and villages. It is also the land where the Israelites had been called away from the land of slavery and the early hermits made an exodus in order to be closer to God. For them their life was also a call from God. Their simple and frugal life, for example weaving mats for their livelihood and living with very little shelter was "their Exodus" from this world so that in their faith and in their hearts they could already join the many saints and angels in heaven, increase their bond with heaven's glory and make the separation between heaven and earth as little as possible.

The glory of the Risen Christ gave this inspiration and they felt privileged to take it to heart. In this light we also have to appreciate the enthusiasm of these early hermits. They were not isolated and disenchanted individuals left in the lurch by an overly active and busy society. They were people full of enthusiasm, exploring and promoting the joy of salvation. They had discovered the pearl of great price, had sold the entire field of the world to purchase it and they were happy that the value of this pearl increased day after day and year after year.

In the vicinity of the different cities the hermits lived within earshot of each other. They were free to visit and to talk about their faith and pray together. On Saturday or Sunday they came together for the Eucharist or they went to the nearest parish to participate at their service. They engaged in normal human interaction, learned from each other and made each other strong in their vocation. Although they lived separately as hermits they rejoiced in the greater unity brought about by the Holy Spirit. There was a spirit of friendship, shared faith and destiny prevailing over them. Paradoxically the Holy Spirit works in this fashion time and again. Where we see and often experience isolation he sees and establishes spiritual and sacramental bonds, which are even stronger than earthly ones. The gospel mandates of poverty and chastity were easy for the hermit to establish. He simply refrained from wealth and conjugal love.

For the third gospel mandate: obedience a second person was needed. Usually it was on older hermit who had proven his faith and his perseverance for a number of years and who was willing and capable to act as spiritual advisor. The hermit being obedient to him was happy to receive his instructions about the psalms being prayed on a regular basis, about the history of salvation, the gospels, the letters of the New Testament and the book of the Apocalypse. If he was well educated in the wisdom of the Greeks he could use this for illustration.

The younger hermit would receive a lot of incentive and material for meditation and prayer. People in Antiquity were very apt to know things by heart and they could recite most of Scripture from memory and the younger hermit would naturally develop a strong desire to also know all these valuable lessons by heart. Things kept in memory were already treasures and he was grateful for them. The more the experienced and the younger shared these spiritual treasures the more grew the spiritual bond between them. The young hermit may very well have started with youthful affection for his master and teacher, but he was led to an inner wisdom in which this affection also matured and in which he gained greater spiritual independence.

The early hermits considered obedience to be the mother of all the virtues and they were familiar with the saying: "Obedience is that which opens heaven and raises man from the earth." This also means that obedience was elevating and not used as discouragement or a put down. An individual feels in his heart whether a recommendation or a command makes him stronger or weaker, happy or unhappy.

The individual hermit was able to judge this for himself without making his own judgment the criterion of his obedience, which then could turn against him. The touchstone had to be the wisdom of God being at work in both, the older and the younger one. At a certain juncture they might even have decided that the younger could advance to another teacher and continue in his vocation through him. But such a transition shouldn't be done willfully or haphazardly, because both wanted to continue in the unity given by God. By way of legislation this obedience wasn't as firmly fixed as in later monasticism, but by way of content it had a God-given purpose and stability.

The vocation the hermits were engaged in after all was a life-long commitment and we would have the wrong impression if we thought of it as suffering from constant ups and downs and the flow of merely human emotions. These men of Antiquity discovered a call from God and it was impossible for them to think that God would toss them on a sea of ephemeral likes and dislikes, advantages and disadvantages or success and failure. The transition to another master or teacher was made in responsibility before God and the ideal was that such transitions would come about without any hard feelings on either side. They continued on the same road of salvation and they were responsible for each other. The joy of salvation remained their trademark and it shouldn't lead to anything of an oppressive nature. Things they had learned they could share with others. Some sayings gained greater value because of their spiritual depth and they led to collections of the "Sayings of the desert Fathers". The hermit's life was not a ready recipe in which one format fits all, but one filled with enthusiasm and where human beings were accepted in the home of believing souls. We assume a steady increase of the number of hermits in the third century and even a movement into this particular presence of God.

St. Anthony

People knew that paradise had started in his soul

I n this way we may look at St. Anthony who lived from about 250–356. He was born at Coma in Egypt. Historically we are more familiar with St. Anthony on account of the biography written about him by St. Athanasius, Bishop of Alexandria, who lived from 295–373. He was a contemporary of St. Anthony. He was personally interested and inspired by this famous saint, who had so much influence upon the Christians. Sayings of St. Anthony, some sermons and basic directions for the life of hermits have come down to us through the writings of St. Athanasius. We also do well to assume some ecclesiological interest of the Bishop of Alexandria in his description of St. Anthony. His narrative makes the hermit's life palatable for the Church and even gives him as an example for all. The bishop expresses his admiration for the saint and witnesses to his belief that the saint belongs to the Church and that not only he, but also all who follow him should be accepted.

According to his biography St. Anthony was the son of a well-to-do farming family, whose farm was very fertile and prosperous. When he was only twenty years old his parents had died and he was left with this large estate and had only to take care of a younger sister. During Mass he had heard the words of Jesus to the rich young man, "Go, sell what you have and give to the poor, you will then have treasure in heaven." He believed that God had spoken these words to him directly and followed exactly as they were said. He sold his inheritance, provided for his sister and went away into the desert for prayer. There he found an older hermit who had lived there from his youth. St. Anthony attached himself to him. We may assume that this older hermit had lived there for quite some time and made the point that this life was acceptable and worthy of imitation.

By joining an older hermit and learning from him, St. Anthony confirms the insight that there already existed a tradition of these early monks, and that he wasn't the first one. We can certainly admire and respect these many first contemplatives who followed a call from God and renewed this single minded adherence to the Gospel in this fashion.

They were believers who like the saint had grown up in the various cities and villages of Egypt, had increased their prayer and let it dominate to the point of going off by themselves. St. Anthony also attests to the simplicity of their Christian faith. He had grown up in the sheltered atmosphere of his family and had not joined in the public education and entertainment of his contemporaries. His devotion was single-minded and not mixed with the wisdom and culture of the Greeks.

This is important for our inquiry, because it stresses the insight that the hermits began their vocation on Christian fare and were not in need of outside influences or incentives. Comparisons with these are of value by way of historical research, but we have to assert that hermitism and later monasticism developed from the gospel and all the religious practices of the Church and has to be understood first of all on an exclusive Christian foundation. The gospel bore fruit in monasticism and monasticism is derived from it and is not in need to borrow from non-Christian sources. However, the similarities explain how much practices of devotion lodge in the depth of the human heart and that the gospel corresponds to the essential human aspirations and leads them to an even closer bond with God.

St. Athanasius described that at the time when St. Anthony went into solitude there were many fervent persons who led retired lives in penance and contemplation near the towns. Already Origen had pointed out in 249 that these ascetics abstained from flesh-meat no less than the disciples of Pythagoras. The word ascetic comes from the Greek and simply means practice or training. By way of austerities St. Anthony qualifies as an ascetic. He used to eat about six ounces of bread soaked in water and sometimes added a few dates. In his old age he added a little oil. In his younger years he visited several hermits and stayed with them for a while until he believed himself sufficiently equipped to live by himself, alone with God.

Well known are his spiritual struggles. In a vision he saw the whole earth thick with snares (like the devil's snare in Harry Potter) and he called out to God: "Who, Lord can escape them all?" A voice answered him, "Humility, Anthony!" When he lived in a tomb, demons attacked him in the form of wild beasts and left him almost dead. This conflict inspired the modern artist Salvador Dali to make models of them. The struggle continues even if it takes on different forms. In 285 he withdrew across the river Nile and lived on a mountain near Pispir, now called Der el Memun for the next twenty years. During these years he never saw any human being except a man who brought him bread every six months. However, his singular holiness was attractive anyway and people tried to come to him. Hermits settled in the vicinity to be closer to the saint and through him closer to heaven. In 305 he agreed to become their spiritual guide.

This formation was already a settlement, which later would develop into monasteries without the term being used for it yet. In a sense it was more like a laura, because the monks prayed and meditated mostly by themselves. At its height the settlement had about 6,000 monks and we can admire his faith to take on the spiritual responsibility for them. He became the focus of a movement and we can understand that later he received the title of Father of Monasticism, but this term doesn't really apply to him especially in a legal sense. His primary goal was solitude with God and after giving instructions to the monks for some time he again withdrew even further into the desert between the Nile and the Red Sea, where he spent the last forty five years of his life. During these years he wasn't as strict and allowed people to visit him and also preached to them. He went to Alexandria to strengthen the Christians suffering from persecutions.

In 339 he had a vision of mules kicking down the altar and he was aware of the harm the Arian persecution would cause in Alexandria. His vision materialized two years later. In 355 the bishop of Alexandria begged him to come and preach against the Arians. His words were simple, "God the Son is of the same substance with the Father and the Arians are not different from the pagans who worshipped and served the creature rather than the Creator". At the age of 105 he had gained a unique dignity and his holiness shone forth. People were awestruck in his presence, knowing that God was in him. Even pagans wanted to see the man of God. Heathen philosophers were astonished at his meekness and his wisdom. In his very existence he had given the lesson that the humiliation of the Cross is the greatest demonstration of God's infinite goodness. He died a little later alone in his solitude on Mount Kolzim near the Red Sea. He asked his disciples to bury his body secretly, because he didn't want any cult to develop on his behalf. People believe that his remains were discovered in 561 and later brought to Vienne in France. For out topic: The Secret Code of the Monks St. Anthony is a wonderful example how a single phrase from the gospel becomes instrumental to provide a code for a whole life. The recommendation of the gospel to dispose of his earthly treasure and to accumulate his treasure in heaven made a contemplative out of him and the direction of his life was set.

He spoke only Coptic and no Greek and his vocation didn't depend on the wisdom of the Greeks, but solely on God's revelation. However, he willingly talked with pagan philosophers and was interested to make them aware of the spiritual values inherent in Christianity and the vocation of the monks. Some of his sayings and a sermon about the duties of the spiritual life and the warfare with demons have been preserved for posterity. Other sayings go back to him and display his dignity and spiritual elevation. One of his letters, originally written in Coptic, was translated into Greek. He didn't write a rule for monasticism, but certain recommendations concerning the life of monks reflect his sentiments.

Throughout the centuries he has received the highest recognition and respect not only as a great saint, but also a man who fostered the sense of believers directing their whole life towards God, especially those who make the promises of the religious. When he gave away his inheritance he placed his young sister under the care of virgins living in community and these women can be considered the counterpart of the monks, following the same ideals as the hermits. Later the groups of independent hermitages were called Lauras and in the West they are represented in some way by the Carthusians. St. Anthony continues to be an inspiration.

One of the great researchers of early Church history was John Henry Cardinal Newman (1801–1890). He described St. Anthony as follows: "His doctrine surely was pure and unimpeachable; and his temper is high and heavenly, without cowardice, without gloom, without formality, without self-complacency. Superstition is abject and crouching, it is full of thoughts of guilt; it distrusts God and dreads the powers of evil. Anthony at least had nothing of this, being full of holy confidence, divine peace, cheerfulness and valorousness, be he (as some men may judge) ever so much an enthusiast". These qualities described so well by Cardinal Newman make it obvious that the hermit and later the monk is called to be a man of gentleness and moderation. For St. Anthony the inner disposition of the contemplative is immediately connected with heaven. For him the virtue of discretion was most important for attaining perfection. He can still teach us today how to respect this inner sanctuary in each and everyone. Without this awe of the soul and for the soul of our neighbor our communication tends to become rude and lack the quality of kinship felt in the heart. St. Anthony's elevation of spirit can again become contagious in a world where human interaction has become mundane and flat. Through this tendency modern forms of communication increase tension and conflict instead of decreasing them. Never before have human affairs led to so much controversy as in our modern world, in which we try to bring peace through controversy. Seen from this angle the hermitism of the ancients is very much needed and able to create or recreate this typical Christian peace of mind, which our modern world is no longer able to give. Few names have exercised on the human race an influence more deep and lasting, more wide-spread or beneficent as that of St. Anthony and we can be happy where and when his ideals are being renewed.

One crucial historical change took place during the life-time of St. Anthony and the story developed that he accepted the focus of this change as a visitor. It may be just a story that the Emperor Constantine the Great (about 280–337) came to consult the greatest saint of his era (besides his own mother, St. Helena) or that he sent a letter or ambassadors to do this for him. According to the story friends of the saint expressed their astonishment about this occurrence, to which the saint replied, "This is not as amazing as that the Son of God came to visit and live with us poor mortals." Even if it is only a story it describes very well how much St. Anthony was penetrated by the glory of heaven and that there is nothing on earth to match it, not even the Emperor.

Constantine the Great

He believed he had gained a great victory in the sign of Christ

Constantine the Great had an impact on monasticism because during his reign Christianity began a new era and people had to respond to this change also by way of contemplation. He was born in Nisch, now Serbia. His father was a Roman General, who was elevated to the rank of Caesar and in 305 named Augustus. His mother St. Helena was of humble birth, possibly the daughter of an inn-keeper. His father called Constantine to his court in 305 and Constantine was able to distinguish himself in Britain before the death of his father the following year. There he was proclaimed Caesar by his troops. Factions in Rome led to his being proclaimed Augustus, although he was busy to defend his frontier against the Germans. In 312 he had to take his position by marching on Rome and he had to fight the usurper, Maxentius, whose army was possibly five times as big as his (100,000 troops against 20,000). A vision had assured him that he should conquer in the sign of Christ, and his warriors carried Christ's monogram on their shields. Constantine was victorious and Maxentius died in the Tiber.

Constantine was most benevolent towards his enemies and showed gratitude towards the Christian religion. Christian worship was henceforth tolerated, edict of 313. Constantine was able to stabilize his position in Rome but he was even more interested to get a firm grip on the Eastern part of the Empire. This was also due to the more theocratic mentality of the populations there and his interest in monotheism versus paganism and also because the economic conditions in the East were better. He achieved his goal in 324 when he defeated his opponent Licinius, killing 25,000 men. The following year Licinius was condemned to death and executed. Under him Christianity became the religion of the state, but paganism continued to be tolerated.

The Empire began to respect Christians in the military and as state officials. This caused great consternation and anger among the pagans. Formerly they had been the masters and their religion had dominated and now their position had become precarious and even subject to suspicion. At an earlier time even Christians, like St. Justin, didn't believe that such a thing could ever happen. The mentality of martyrdom was too deeply ingrained in them and they were convinced that Christianity is a religion of suffering and death with the outlook on a glorious resurrection.

Now, Christianity received one privilege after another: immunity and freedom from tax and from compulsory service for the clergy, the right of the Church to inherit property and Sunday as a day of rest and worship, and the right to live celibate lives. Constantine acted not only as a smart politician, but also followed his conviction. He was certainly strengthened by the example of his mother, whom he respected very much. Some of his ideas were syncretistic, mixing the old and the new, even bishops tried this by praising him as an angel of God and as a sacred being, but Christianity continued to assert itself. Even after his conversion he was brutal by causing the execution of his son, Crispus, his first wife, Fausta, and his brother-in-law Lisinius along with his son.

Along with his harshness he recognized the care the Church gave to the poor and to children, who before that time had little or no protection. He brought his own children up as Christians. He himself received baptism when he approached his death. This was done more often in Antiquity. People believed that they would go straight to heaven if they were baptized shortly before their death, because all their sins were forgiven through this sacrament. His older son leaned again towards paganism. His younger and more favorite son became Arian, closed all the temples and even began persecutions of pagans and what he considered "heretics". His policies had even ramifications on the Inquisition at a much later time.

Constantine's mother, St. Helena, deserves mention for this historical change. She became a Catholic only at the age of sixty two or three, but until her death at age 80 she led a most devoted life. She regularly attended and assisted at Mass and was very generous by building and adorning many churches. She showed a great concern for the poor and for people in distress, like soldiers and people condemned to the mines. Through her intervention she freed many from oppression, prison and banishment. She embodied this Christian attitude that we have to take every opportunity to increase the awareness of God's kingdom. Her stays in the Holy Land were pilgrimages, elevating her spirit to the glory of the saints and it was there that she spent her last days on earth. Later the Holy Land became a place for many monasteries and convents to some extent following the example of the Empress. As her son set new policies favoring the cause of Christianity, so St. Helena set the tone for an atmosphere in the Empire, in which the faith could thrive and prosper. Christianity is not a system of legality, but a religion where human beings can be at home with God and St. Helena welcomed people to this home.

The many martyrs of almost three centuries of Christianity had clarified the point that the transition to this home with God has to be purchased. When the Empire changed to be pro-Christian people could join the Church rather easily and it seemed to be rather cheap to be Christian. The Church historian Eusebius was extremely enthusiastic about the beginning of this new era, when the Church had obtained recognition, freedom and public respect. We can understand his enthusiasm, but we also have to be realistic about the fact that some of the exuberance would neglect the seriousness of the scandal of the Cross especially in times when things go well.

It is in this light that we acknowledge a surge towards hermitism and monasticism in the Church. As the martyrs had given their life for Jesus, so also the hermits and later monks were willing to devote their earthly existence totally to God even when this didn't require an actual death. The reward already began in their prayer, because God was close to them and gave them the right connection between heaven and earth. This happened not only in Egypt, but also in other parts of the Roman Empire where people belonged universally together. This universality has never been easy for the Church.

By God's grace monasticism could spring up in the Western part of the Empire as well. One of the early supporters was St. Hilary of Poitiers in Gaul, who was not a hermit, except to some extent for some years he had to spend in exile. He was born during the time of Constantine the Great at the beginning of the fourth century in Poitiers and died there in 368. He belonged to a noble family, but he grew up as a pagan and received a good education in liberal arts. He had a strong desire to clarify the question of religion and discovered that polytheism was unsatisfactory.

This opened him up to monotheism and the reading of the Bible brought about his conversion. He had been married before and had a daughter named Apra. It would have been nice if the son of Constantine the Great, Constantius had stayed within Catholicism and safeguarded the unity of our religion, but this was not the case. He succeeded his father as Emperor, but not as a Catholic. He became an Arian, not believing in the eternal divinity of Christ. As St. Anthony had argued, this was a relapse into paganism. Constantius' policies led not only to Hilary's banishment to Phrygia, but also to St. Eusebius' banishment even to Upper Thebaid in Egypt.

The years in exile deepened prayer and meditation for them and fostered a greater appreciation of theological learning and monasticism. When he finally returned from his exile he could renew his friendship with his most illustrious disciple, hermit and monk, St. Martin of Tours. He had encouraged St. Martin in seeking solitude and St. Martin was grateful for his support. Both had discovered that the witness of faith is nourished in contemplation and for both the idea of hermitism or monasticism was a grace given by God. For St. Martin it had been a blessing to come to know St. Hilary and to enjoy his approval of his unique call to contemplation and we find that his call came with the typical independence of God's grace in a different part of the Empire.

St. Martin of Tours
He saw Christ in the beggar

St. Martin was born about 316 in Sabaria, Pannonia, now Hungary. His father was a military tribune and was transferred from Hungary to Pavia in Italy, when Martin was still young. When he reached adolescence he was enrolled in the army as well. He was touched by grace and strongly attracted to Christianity, which was favored in the camps since the pro-Christian policy of Constantine the Great. Because of his personal holiness he was considered a soldier-saint. From Italy he was sent to Amiens in Gaul, the scene of the celebrated event of the cloak. On a winter-day as he was riding out of the city he saw a beggar, half-naked shivering on the side of the road. Martin divided his cloak and gave one half to the beggar. The following night the beggar appeared to him in a dream as Jesus Christ, saying to him: "Martin". As a consequence of this vision he "flew to be baptized". He was released from military service at Worms on the Rhine, from where he went to Poitiers to become a disciple of St. Hilary.

He visited his mother and converted her and some others to Christianity. The Arians in Pavia had the upper hand and publicly scourged him and he had to leave the country, because of his Catholicism. On his return he learned that St. Hilary had been banished because of his faith and he went to the island of Gallinaria for the sake of prayer and contemplation. In 360 St. Hilary was permitted to come back and Martin followed him and was able to live as a hermit for ten years on a piece of property which St. Hilary had allotted to him.

Many other hermits became his disciples, so that St. Martin became the first leader of a monastic community in Gaul, now called Liguge. This community was a real laura, which means hermits who only come together on occasion. He left his retreat in order to preach in different parts of Gaul. In 372 he was elected Bishop of Tours against his will.

He wanted to live as a simple monk and therefore didn't reside in the busy city, but in a monastery, which he founded outside. Yet his influence spread throughout the country and he was respected as a saint already during his life-time. He died Nov. 8, 397 in a remote part of his diocese.

St. Martin gives a wonderful example of Western Monasticism. His call from God made him a contemplative and solitary and given the proper instruction from St. Hilary he would have been happy and content to remain in this state for all of his life. It wasn't his interest or choice to attract disciples, but they came anyway because of his holiness and spiritual strength. He responded and invited them into his company. He believed that they had been given to him by God and God didn't want him to refuse them, but to accept them as brothers. This development also shows something mysterious about Christian brotherhood. They are brought together by heaven's grace and bound together in the Lord.

Their union is in God by way of faith, prayer, study and the sacraments. It has begun on their earthly journey and will be accomplished in heaven. The contemplative also knows that there is no earthly substitute for this unity, which will be finalized only around the Throne of God. It is also from this angle that we can understand St. Martin's reluctance to accept the Episcopal dignity. As he had branched out from his solitude to accept brothers, so he also branched out to accept the leadership of his diocese and even far beyond its area. Even for the administration of his diocese and other missions he liked the company of brothers. In conjunction with his singular call he knew of the unity, which God wishes to bring about for believers.

When he was made bishop of Tours he started a monastic settlement, Marmoutier, close to Tours, which was similar to his first one; this means it was a congregation of hermits. Along with St. Martin they in turn were willing to answer needs in the world and therefore they could remain distinct from any secular occupation, but neither ignorant nor indifferent to the concerns of the Church at large. Being open to active work does not mean that any activity would stifle the presence of God's grace. We have to recognize that for St. Martin conversion to Christianity meant to begin a life of contemplation.

Like the martyrs before him his very life had to become a witness and being a hermit was best suited for him. We can assume that this turn to permanent prayer came already in his youth when he was looked upon by others as a soldier saint, which might have been as early as the year 332 or 334, contemporary to St. Anthony although far away from Egypt. When later he became a bishop he quite naturally linked these two aspects: leader of the flock and being a monk. This combination became most fruitful and life-giving for many centuries to come. Without some contact with society the life of the hermit can become a burden and lead to distress instead of the joy of the spirit.

Under all circumstances we are enabled to rely on the Holy Spirit to breathe new life into the hearts of those who turn to him. In the first part of the fourth century the Holy Spirit could breathe where the hermits were, whether in Gaul or in Egypt, and fill their hearts with enthusiasm and new life. That is why these settlements could attract so many young men and women to give their life to God in prayer. In the case of St. Martin we have to give credit to his religious experience (about 337) at the time of his conversion, which he interpreted as the beginning of his worship of Jesus Christ, who is above time and place. It is also this experience, which gave rise to his fame as a spiritual hero and a popular saint through the centuries.

As in the case of St. Anthony it has to be concluded that this private revelation stands out and that the later development has to be brought back to this source. He was contemporary to both St. Anthony and St. Pachomius even though his vocation came a little later in time and fully developed later on. For this reason he deserves to be taken into consideration along with them. When he became bishop of Tours in 371 he was able to expand the idea of hermitism to monasticism by establishing the abbey of Marmoutier close to his Episcopal See.

St. Pachomius

Envisioned many monks coming together in a monastery

St. Pachomius had a similar background as a conscript in the Emperor's army as St. Martin, but his army-experience occurred in Egypt. He was born as the son of pagan parents in Upper Thebaid about 292 and died about 346. He was ordered to join the army at age twenty or in 312. The young recruits were conveyed down the Nile River more or less like slaves and treated harshly. Fortunately they were treated with kindness and compassion by Christians. Pachomius was grateful and considered their spiritual motive for their generosity. As in many other cases so also in his their love drew him to be interested in Christianity as well. Upon his discharge he became a catechumen and was baptized. Naturally this led him to be exclusively in the presence of the Lord and he sought out an old hermit, Palaemon, wanting to become his disciple. Along with the promise to follow the evangelical counsels he received the habit. They would do some manual labor, which was accompanied by interior prayer, and sometimes pray the whole Psalter together in one day.

At times he went alone into the desert of Tabennisi for meditation. There he was asked by a heavenly voice to build a monastery, in which many would join him. He reported his experience to his master Palaemon and he believed him. The idea was different from the well-respected hermitism and cannot be traced back to it. We do well to appreciate these two vocations as distinct, although they have always recommended each other, overlapped and used in conjunction. We also do well to join Palaemon in believing that Pachomius' experience was genuine and not just a way of improving the living conditions of the hermits. Palaemon helped him when he began to construct his first monastery, but he remained a hermit. This venture didn't change Palaemon's vocation, but he trusted that God called others to the way mapped out by Pachomius.

From God's view there is a real call for some people to become monks and to live in a religious community. Pachomius received this revelation and followed this intuition. At the same time contemplation was part of God's plan for the monks in a religious community or a monastery. After all the very word monk designates someone who is alone and he has to consent to this portion of hermitism in his life. The concerns for the community can also become a burden and he may have to be willing to be with God alone.

Pachomius' idea was greatly blessed. Shortly afterwards his oldest brother John became his follower and word got around that every man could come and be a monk. His sister wanted to share the same ideal and through her Pachomius started a monastery for women. The women followed apace and also single-mindedly focused on prayer.

Pachomius began to serve his brothers by doing chores for them, so that they gained the conviction how serious he was about his invitation to this new life with him. Once they had benefited from his humility and patience they were able to trust that God had also called them. Given these virtues the enterprise grew rapidly, possibly too quickly. Three or four monks lived in one room or cell according to the trades they practiced, like fullers, weavers, bakers, carpenters, architects and so on. Later they had ships bringing their goods down the Nile. Pachomius had a great sense for organization with a superior general, regular visitations, general chapters and a centralized government, similar to what the Cistercians or Mendicants did eight or nine hundred years later.

Unfortunately his organization turned out to be more like a military or barrack system and lacked the family-style so important for the monasticism beginning with St. Benedict in the Middle Ages. At the time of his death there were over three thousand monks in his seven monasteries and a large number of nuns in two monasteries for women. These large numbers also verify that this vocation is genuine and part of the Catholic Church.

Theologically St. Pachomius was very strong in his belief in the Blessed Trinity and he opposed Arianism. In the fourth century his foundation suffered severely through interior stress and the attacks of Barbarians. Monks who had to flee for their life brought their ideals to other parts of the world and their sufferings became the seed of new monasticism elsewhere. His rule set the standard for monasticism.

The heart of Catholicism, namely Rome, deserves attention also in regard to monasticism. The twelve Apostles had the experience of the group around our Lord and Savior, Jesus Christ, and this had penetrated their very being and had given them their identity as missionaries, shepherds of the faithful and administrators of the sacred mysteries. They had continued regular religious observances, the feast-days of the liturgical calendar after their transformation through the death and Resurrection of the Lord and coming together for the sacraments and prayer had always been their focus and the focus of those who belonged to the communities.

The Roman mentality had a long tradition of the father of the family setting the tone, protecting and guiding those entrusted to him. Quite naturally this was absorbed into the Church, the leaders being called Father and in the case of the Pope, the Holy Father. This particular tradition reached back to St. Peter and continued henceforth not only for the Holy Father in Rome, but also for all the bishops of the Church. Those who worked with him and acted on his behalf were first of all bound by sacred vows and promises made to him. These very bonds were spiritual and had to be continually nourished through prayer.

It was in this religious atmosphere that they could blossom and bear fruit. Those who exercised various ministries could drift away from the spirit and become mere functionaries or even become negligent in their service; then they had to be brought back into the fold and into full communion and be careful to follow the intention of the shepherd. Especially St. Peter through the martyrdom he had suffered for the Church grew in importance and intensified the responsibility of those who cooperated with his successor or with some other bishop. When the Church was under persecution and pressure the prayerful commitments increased and at other times they could deepen in gratitude for the peace granted by God. Such ups and downs are part of the faith in its history and the Church only has to be aware of it and remain constant. Those who cooperated with the Holy Father or with some other bishop knew that they belonged together. They wouldn't consider themselves without such belonging. This sense of the group has always been a God-given reality. Through its very foundation by Jesus Christ the Church intensifies its life by being in close contact with him. It is always Jesus who builds the Church on the foundation, which St. Peter and his followers provide.

As mentioned, martyrdom miraculously strengthened the love between heaven and earth. Those who had close relatives or even parents who had died as martyrs felt this strength in their soul and it gave the incentive to follow their example of total commitment even if martyrdom was not required of them. We pointed out the case of Origen, who at the beginning of the third century sent his father a letter expressing his gratitude for the martyrdom he was expecting and intending to join him in this, but was prevented from it through the objection of his mother.

St. Eusebius

Accepted his exile as a means of salvation

owards the end of the third century we have a similar case, St. Eusebius of Vercelli. He was born in Sardinia about 283 and died in Vercelli in 371. While he was still an infant his father either died as a martyr or died when he was incarcerated because of his Catholicism. He also had a sister. After the death of his father his mother resettled with her two children in Rome and gave them a good Christian education and we can be certain that the children grew up with a clear awareness that their father had given his life for God and this made a lasting impression upon them. If their father was in heaven because of the strength of his faith then they were obligated to also exercise a similar strength in their faith. In the religious atmosphere of the eternal city Eusebius was able to appreciate the priests and teachers of the faith and to deepen his love for God, our Father in heaven.

As explained, the community spirit was strong and many prayer meetings and liturgical celebrations were conducted in groups which could easily develop into proper religious communities, even if they didn't use the title for it. This view is traditional in the Church, for example it was held by the spiritual writer Spreitzenhofer in Vienna already in the nineteenth century.

We assume that Eusebius found this community spirit in Rome when he was growing up, excelled through his love of God, his intelligence and leadership skills. This might have happened as early as the beginning of the fourth century and when he was of age he was ordained lector. He was able to become the head of a religious community, being penetrated by contemplation and lead others in the same constancy and growth in prayer. Although there are no definite dates for this because of the lack of historical documents we can assume that this happened already about 320 or a few years afterwards. This leaves us with a very early date for a religious community in Italy and we recognize the justification for such a topic as: The development of monasticism in Italy. This prestige as a leader of a religious community also agrees with the fact that the clergy and the people of Vercelli recognized his talents as a leader when he went there later on and when he was unanimously chosen for their bishop.

It agrees further with the witness of St. Ambrose of Milan (340–397) that Eusebius was the first in the West who united the monastic discipline and the life of the clergy. It would have been a natural development that he was head of a religious community and when he became a bishop that he involved the priests of his diocese with monastic vows. His success as a bishop evolved from the fact that he made his priests feel at home with contemplation, channeling all their energy first on the love of God and from there they were able to serve the faith community with distinction. The model of the Eastern monks was well known and in such a fertile religious ground as Rome it didn't take–to speak in modern terms–rocket science to transfer the basic requirements of monasticism: poverty, chastity, obedience and life in common to this environment.

In the case of Eusebius we can accept the notion that his interest in the ideals of monasticism had a theological foundation. There is no witness of a private revelation for this as for St. Anthony, St. Martin or St. Pachomius, but we may do well to assume some privileged closeness to the grace of God in his life, because he was totally committed to the orthodoxy of the faith and had to pay a heavy price for his conviction. Whatever happened, his conviction about the divinity of Jesus Christ was firmly established in the midst of great opposition and he knew that his salvation was connected with it. His work as a bishop went far beyond that of a contemplative giving himself to prayer in seclusion, but his endeavors were always in touch with the truth.

Some time after the official recognition of Catholicism within the Roman Empire a new, serious struggle came about for the Church. The adherents of Arianism didn't believe in the perpetual divinity of Christ or to put it simply: The Holy Spirit came late upon Jesus Christ, at the time of his baptism in the Jordan, and left early, before his death; in this way a mere human being died, but not God, the Son of the Father. This shift, as St. Anthony observed, brought the old paganism back on the scene and renewed the former encounter between orthodoxy and opposing forces.

Arianism had begun in about 323 when a priest, Arius, from the diocese of Alexandria, Egypt, believed and taught his Christological heresy, as mentioned that Jesus was not the eternal Son of God. Consequently he was excommunicated after the Council of Nicea in 325 and the orthodox faith was phrased in our Creed. Arius continued to preach and teach his opinion and found a lot of people who joined him including many bishops who wanted to be avant-garde, promoting the future. Arius and his entourage were extremely effective in their advertising techniques. His heresy was composed to the tunes of popular songs and sailors all along the Mediterranean ocean sang these songs and like a wild-fire the message spread. Simple words like, "There was a time when he, Jesus, was not" caught on quickly; people discussed these questions of Christology in the market places and many found the songs and their content very good. The number of people advocating Arianism grew rapidly through portions of the Roman Empire and they couldn't be ignored. Especially when even prelates were in favor it was just looked upon as a movement of modern Christianity, which could take the place of the old. We appreciate the means of communications of the Roman Empire and witness that these could also be used against the truth. The heresy persisted for several centuries and caused prolonged suffering for those faithful to the Christian teaching.

St. Eusebius was one of those who had to suffer, especially when the Emperor, Constantius, had become an adherent of Arianism. In 355 Pope Liberius asked Eusebius to go to a Council in Milan and settle the difference between Arianism and Orthodoxy. This council had drawn up a condemnation of St. Athanasius of Alexandria, the fearless champion of the true faith. Eusebius couldn't do this. He insisted that Athanasius hadn't done or taught anything wrong and that he should first be heard before being condemned. The Catholic bishops were in the majority at this council, but the Arians were stronger, because they had the support of the Emperor, who was enraged at Eusebius. He wanted his execution, but softened his verdict by sending him into exile. St. Eusebius accepted his fate as a spiritual martyrdom. He even developed the desire to end his life in suffering for the kingdom of God. A portion of his exile he spent among the monks in Thebaid, Egypt. When the Emperor, Constantius, died towards the end of 361 the saint was able to return to Italy and continue his work as bishop. We are convinced that his time in exile and among the contemplatives in Egypt also strengthened his adherence to monasticism and his trust that the truth grows in our hearts the closer we are to God's grace. He was also delighted when he met St. Hilary in Italy, who in turn had supported the contemplative settlement of St. Martin, and could cooperate with him to further overcome Arianism in the Western part of the Church. This Trio of Western contemplation also give witness how quickly and how early the basic need for monasticism had made it across and had been accepted in Italy and France.

St. Athanasius
Enthusiastic about the Desert Saints

We also have to include St. Athanasius (about 297–373) in this development of Monasticism in the early Church. He was a monk at heart, although he became famous as a bishop and as a defender of the true faith. He was born in Alexandria in Egypt and received an excellent education in Greek literature and philosophy, rhetoric, law and the teachings of the Church. Besides his great interest in learning he was very much attached to prayer and made friends with the hermits in the desert and especially with St. Anthony. He said of himself, "I was his disciple." He was ordained deacon at age 21, became the secretary of the bishop and already produced his famous treatise on the Incarnation. He had to fight Arianism, which had started in his diocese, and shortly after the Council of Nicea, when his bishop died he succeeded him, although he was not yet thirty years old. He visited his huge diocese and fostered the bonds of friendship with the monks in his territory.

The members of Arianism continued to harass him, thinking, "If we get him out of the picture, then we can take over." Their goal was obviously to put an Arian bishop in his place in Alexandria. Already in 335 they accused him of having murdered someone, but Athanasius didn't pay much attention, because he knew that the supposed victim was alive and well, even though in hiding. Other charges were brought against him and at one point even the Emperor, Constantine was displeased with Athanasius and banished him to Trier in Belgian Gaul, now Germany. Through God's mysterious design of salvation and sometimes secret code of providential guidance this "monk" and friend of the hermits of the Egyptian desert lived in the second capitol city of the Empire in the far North-West, where monasticism would grow so powerfully in subsequent centuries. His exile there lasted for only two years until the death of Constantine and the bishop of Trier granted him generous hospitality. We assume that he could not only practice contemplation there but also give an impression of his first hand experience of hermitism in Egypt.

Not only did the message travel fast, but the messenger himself was transported and explained meditation through the life he led. He wrote the biography of St. Anthony and we have to emphasize that he was in exile in Trier while his hero of hermitism was still alive. It is more than conjecture to imagine that his heart was filled with enthusiasm for the greatest desert-saint and ran over in witness about him. Trier was an early stronghold of Catholicism, because it was considered the second capital of the Empire next to Rome. God can use a person as a letter and explain an issue better through him instead of using words.

Later on St. Athanasius was banished again and again and again, a total of five times and he spent seventeen years in exile, usually as a simple monk, but he was able to write his treatises of theology during these 'quiet' years. His writings became cherished treasures of orthodoxy in the Church. In his heart he combined the monk and the bishop and it is only natural that both, monks and bishops, can depend on such a great example and model of their Christianity. He also makes the point that one shouldn't be thought of without the other, unless one wants to bypass the challenge of the Cross in the life of the Christian. He also affirms the insight that hermitism and later monasticism developed as a consequence of the gospel-spirit, the true intention of the believer and the application of this call from God. Hermitism and monasticism are in agreement with the eternal life God offers to us and therefore they are timeless, even if the expressions for them have to undergo changes in history. We also affirm that hermitism and monasticism began rather early and were well underway and established in the first part of the fourth century with St. Eusebius indicating a smooth transition from clergy working together to monks following simple guidelines for their prayer as the source of strength for their pastoral involvement in the city and their common life.

St. Basil
There is service in Contemplation

In the Eastern part of the Empire we find an even more pronounced inclination towards monasticism through St. Basil. It grew early in his inspired understanding of the source of spiritual brotherhood. He lived from 329 to 379. St. Basil was a man of fine human qualities, warmth of heart and an extraordinary sense of unity given by the Holy Spirit. His close friend St. Gregory of Nazianzen gave a wonderful description of their friendship in one of his sermons: "Basil and I were both in Athens. We had come, like streams of a river, from the same source in our native land, had separated from each other in pursuit of learning, and were now united again as if by plan, for God so arranged it.

I was not alone at that time in my regard for my friend, the great Basil. I knew his irreproachable conduct, and the maturity and wisdom of his conversation. I sought to persuade others, to whom he was less known, to have the same regard for him. Many fell immediately under his spell, for they had already heard of him by reputation and hearsay.

What was the outcome? Almost alone of those who had come to Athens to study, he was exempted from the customary ceremonies of initiation for he was held in higher honor than his status as a first-year student seemed to warrant.

Such was the prelude to our friendship, the kindling of that flame that was to bind us together. In this way we began to feel affection for each other. When, in the course of time, we acknowledged our friendship and recognized that our ambition was a life of true wisdom, we became everything to each other: we shared the same lodging, the same table, the same desires, the same goal. Our love for each other grew daily warmer and deeper. The same hope inspired us: the pursuit of learning. This is an ambition especially subject to envy. Yet between us there was no envy. On the contrary, we made capital out of our rivalry. Our rivalry consisted, not in seeking the first place for oneself but yielding it to the other, for each looked on the other's success as his own.

We seemed to be two bodies with a single spirit. Though we cannot believe those who claim that "everything is contained in everything," yet you must believe that in our case each of us was in the other and with the other.

Our single object and ambition was virtue, and a life of hope in the blessings that are to come; we wanted to withdraw from this world before we departed from it. With this end in view we ordered our lives and all our actions. We followed the guidance of God's law and spurred each other on to virtue. If it is not too boastful to say, we found in each other a standard and rule for discerning right from wrong.

Different men have different names, which they owe to their parents or to themselves, that is, to their own pursuits and achievements. But our great pursuit, the great name we wanted, was to be Christians, to be called Christians."

This enthusiastic description of the friendship of the two students, later monks and finally bishops also gives evidence of the qualities of St. Basil and that he didn't mean monasticism to be a cold, barren atmosphere, but one filled with the love of the Spirit. St. Basil's whole life and career speak to this effect. He grew up in a family of ten children and when he was still young his father died and afterwards the family moved to an estate at Annesi in Pontus, on the banks of the Iris. The family owned quite a bit of land. As a boy he was sent to school at Caesarea and came to know and love the bishop there, Dianius, who was like a father to him. When he later continued his studies in Athens he greatly excelled in the most important subjects of that time: rhetoric, grammar, philosophy, astronomy, geometry, and medicine. Having successfully completed these he returned to Caesarea and began a career as a teacher. St. Gregory said of this return: "There was now no other need left than that of spiritual perfection". As an adult he renewed his friendship with Bishop Dianius, who had been the object of his admiration as a boy, and it seems that the bishop now baptized him and ordained him Reader.

The whole family was very devoted to God. His grandparents had proved their witness to Christ during times of persecution and had spent seven years in exile. They had led the younger generation to the conviction that our true home is in heaven and the grandchildren greatly benefited from this insight. After the death of his father his mother adhered even more to her religious observances through regular reading of the Wisdom literature of the Bible and praying the Psalms. The oldest sister, Macrina, was betrothed to a young man when she was twelve following the general customs at the time, but the young man died before the wedding. She refused another marriage and drew closer to God. Instead of getting angry and lashing out, she grew in interior wisdom and humility. She even taught these virtues to her younger brother, the great St. Basil, when he had become a little arrogant as the successful student from Athens. He accepted her religious instructions and owes some of his holiness and fame to her. Under these conditions there arose the desire of forming a religious community on their estate in Pontus. They established this accompanied by considerable generosity to the poor. Basil may have encouraged them to take this step, but he also benefited from their commitment and it must have helped him to embark on his own vocation as a hermit and a monk. Macrina impressed him. Since she never had a husband on earth she was betrothed to God.

For the sake of a firm foundation for his vocation he visited monasteries in Egypt, Palestine, Syria and Mesopotamia. When he returned he was filled with admiration for the austerity and piety of the monks, and he founded a monastery in his native Pontus, not far from his mother and sister. He had also studied the writings of Origen and admired their depth and wealth. His experiences and his great learning empowered him to develop a program for

Monasticism. He believed it to be an integral part of the life of the Church and his further development speaks to this effect.

His own bishop Dianius died in 362 and the new bishop, Eusebius, called Basil away from his retreat, ordained him priest and gave him an important place in the administration of the diocese. In ability for the management of affairs Basil so far eclipsed the bishop that ill-feeling arose between the two. Some people might go so far as to call it jealousy. "All the more eminent and wiser portion of the church was roused against the bishop", wrote Gregory, and to avoid trouble Basil again withdrew into the solitude of Pontus. However, in 365, he was restored to his former position. He proved to be a man of unusual powers and in 370 he succeeded to the see of Caesarea. "His election," says Gregory "was followed by disaffection on the part of several suffragan bishops, on whose side were found the greatest scoundrels of the city". Jealousy can easily develop into animosity and open hostility.

Despite the discomfort this caused him he devoted himself to his office. He drew up a summary of the orthodox faith, paid visits, sent messages, gave interviews, instructed, reproved, rebuked, threatened, reproached, undertook the protection of nations, cities, individuals great and small. He was a cool, persistent, fearless fighter in the defense both of doctrine and of principles. He showed a marked interest in the poor and the afflicted. He built a magnificent institution named after him: Basileiad. In this house care was provided for the isolated stranger, the sick poor in need of medical treatment and unskilled people received industrial training, so that they could find a job. He preached forcibly about the social obligations of Christians, especially those who are wealthy. He himself was a practical lover of Christian poverty by way of simplicity of food and clothing and austerity of life. The saint had to undergo sufferings of many kinds: a painful estrangement from his friend Gregory of Nazianzus, Bishop Anthimus of Tyana became an open enemy, Eustathius of Sebaste became a traitor to the Faith and a foe as well, his brother, Gregory of Nyssa, was condemned and deposed, the Arians gained power after the death of the Emperor Valentinian and his own health was failing.

The Goths began to invade, Antioch was in schism, and Rome doubted his sincerity and the bishops refused to be brought together as he wished. As Newman put it: "The notes of the Church were obscured in his part of Christendom, and he had to fare on as best he might—admiring, courting, yet coldly treated by the Latin world, desiring the friendship of Rome, yet wounded by her reserve—suspected of heresy by Damasus and accused by Jerome of pride." By personal virtue he attained distinction in an age of saints; and his purity, his monastic fervor, his stern simplicity, his friendship for the poor became traditional in the history of Christian asceticism. Throughout, Basil was steadily pursuing to effect unity in a disturbed and divided Christendom. St. Basil died on the 1st of January 379 at the age of fifty. His death was regarded as a public bereavement; Jews, pagans, and foreigners vied with his own flock in doing him honor.

His personality and the broadness of his involvement in all spheres of the Church's activity explain the goals for his rule for monasticism and the influence he exercised upon it. He preferred the life in common over the life of the hermit and his reason was theological: God didn't create human beings as isolated and wild beings, but he created them soft and gregarious. God's intentions for human beings are best pursued in community.

The most basic rules for the community are found in Scripture and in its application. Of course, the questions arising for human beings are infinite in number. St. Basil applied his regulations to the monastery. He linked monastic life and service for the Church at large very skillfully. Monasteries in the cities had to be willing and endowed to help people in need and to educate students. He liked to turn monasteries into center of true Christian Spirit, which were able to give witness to their faith. The communities of monks would give an example and lesson in applied Christianity to the society surrounding them. His endeavors created a particular type of monastery, which is still prevalent in the Orthodox world to this day. His general idea of monasticism and the rule he wrote for them created a standard which cannot be bypassed or ignored, if monks are willing to let themselves be transformed to gospel values in imitation of our Savior.

By coincidence or God's design St. Basil had also as a classmate in Athens the son of Julius Constantius, the half-brother of Constantine the Great, Julian, who was later known as the Apostate, because he fell away from God's Revelation. Julian was even two years younger than Basil and yet could pose as representative of the royal family. Being so close to earthly greatness could have made Basil look up to power and prestige instead of choosing the humility of the gospel and maybe that his sister had to remind him of God's call for him. And yet being friends with someone connected with the political establishment also reminds the religious that this is part of our destiny as historically conditioned beings, whether we happen to be monks or lay-people.

Julian, the Apostate

The struggle between paganism and Christianity continues

In retrospect we would wish that Julian had recognized and in some way followed Basil's inspiration, but this didn't happen. Julian was born in 331 and after the death of his uncle Constantine in 337 there was a struggle for power in the royal family in which several of his kinfolk were killed and he and his older step-brother Gallus barely escaped this massacre. Julian was brought up in the faith, but the brutality he had to go through sowed bitter hatred in his heart against the murderers and later against Christians in general.

You cannot be a murderer and a Christian at the same time. Julian had a sincere interest in intellectual pursuits and applied himself to grasp neo-Platonic philosophy, but this got mixed up with magic and mysteries, which didn't open his soul to be receptive to the purity of Christian principles. His step-brother Gallus made a name for himself in military campaigns in the West and even received the title Caesar, but became rather brutal and was beheaded in 354. This made things only worse for Julian, who went to Athens in 355 to continue his studies. It doesn't seem that his Christian class-mates were able to change his mind, because he joined Hellenism and was initiated in the Eleusinian mysteries.

He had converted from his Christian background and began to advo-cate paganism as opposed to Christianity. Like his step-brother he was also presented to the army in the West as Caesar and was extremely successful in campaigns in Gaul and Germany and also as an administrator. His troops admired him and enthusiastically proclaimed him Augustus. He became Emperor in Constantinople after the death of Constantius in 361. He dropped all outward appearance of being Christian and entrusted himself to the pro-tection of Zeus and demanded from all cities to reopen the temples for pagan worship and to restore the sacrifice of animals on the altars. For Christians this was abhorrent and they felt that the Emperor had become an open enemy.

He revoked all the titles and rights to land and property and the revenues granted to the Church since Constantine the Great and the Church had to repay the subsidies and grants it had received from the former government. His anti-Christian policies were of short duration, because he died in a battle against the Persians only one and a half years after he had taken office in 363. St. Basil was not personally affected, because he was building up his monastery in Pontus and yet the events showed him as every believer how easily the opposition to Christianity can arise and that we never really have a final historical transition from paganism to Christianity.

We assume that the story of his classmate, the Emperor, Julian the Apostate, alerted St. Basil very much in regard to Theology which he had to defend against the Arians later. In various forms and degrees paganism has always raised its head and threatened Christianity. This threat can be renewed in our modern world through some trends in psychology, which promote the mere enjoyment of basic instincts instead of elevating them in the service of the Spirit. When finally many monasteries were established in the cities, including Constantinople, they were able to implant this Christian Spirit in their midst and be there as places of worship, witness and reminders of our common call from God.

Revelation in the Old and the New Testament and the fast growth of Christianity led to the call to hermitism and monasticism quite naturally through the "instinct of faith". Those who followed this instinct or in some way were reminded of it couldn't really dodge it. This is similar to all believers, who know what their conscience tells them, even if they at times should deviate from it. The more outstanding individuals only shed light on what is happening universally.

St. Jerome
Temptation is part of who we are, but finds healing in Jesus

This was also the case with St. Jerome, who was about twelve years younger than St. Basil. He was born about 341 in Stridon on the confines of Dalmatia and Pannonia (Hungary, a Province of the Roman Empire). His native language was Illyrian, but he was well-trained in Greek and Latin literature and became a master of these languages. We assume that his early upbringing in the faith through the example of his family, prayers and customs of devotion was excellent and left a deep impression on his soul. These remained present to him although they were overshadowed for some time.

His father paid attention that he received a good education and sent him to Rome, when he was old enough. His great sensitivity proved itself in his ability for languages and his talent for poetry developed along with his studies. His main educator in Rome was a heathen, who along with the classical literature he taught caused Jerome to forget or to suppress some of his childhood-piety. All the emotions which had been united in the pious simplicity of the child were disjoined and developed into a severe rift in his soul. This led to great distress. And yet, he was free to move about in the city and with his friends he liked to visit "the tombs of the martyrs and apostles, going down into those subterranean galleries whose walls on either side preserve the relics of the dead".

We can feel the attraction to be a friend of the martyrs and also the appeal which the pre-Christian literature and philosophy had for him. To bridge this gap between these two forces had to become a major concern for him. The appeal of carefree pre-Christian indulgence became very real for him, but he didn't become engrossed with this life-style; instead he became a catechumen and was baptized by Pope Liberius in 360. This intimate, sacramental contact with the center of the Church attracted him very much and made him wonder whether he too could be involved in it. However, at first he decided to travel so as to improve his studies.

He went to Trier in Gaul, the capital north of the Alps, which had famous schools and there began to undergo systematic theological training. It was also in Trier where he had a serious conversion experience.

This in turn made him more committed in regard to his vocation. Having heard that Bishop Valerian of Aquileia was very accomplished in educating his seminarians and his clergy he joined them from 370 to 373 and formed close friendships, especially with Rufinus. These years of his close association with the clergy guided him and some friends to entrust themselves even more to God in solitude and contemplation. It appeared to be a natural transition for them. Four of them planned to seek this life in Antioch and arrived there in 374. Two of them were struck down by illness there and died. He himself suffered from a severe fever and in its heat he thought of being before the judgment seat of Jesus Christ, who asked him: "Who are you?" Jerome answered: "I am a Christian." And he received the reply: "Thou art a Ciceronian: for where thy treasure is, there is thy heart also." This experience led him to spend four years alone in the wilderness of Chalcis. He had become a hermit. He fasted and prayed and suffered much from ill health and even more from strong temptations of the flesh. His only companions were scorpions and wild beasts.

We still have to admire the frankness in which he described his temptations: "Many times I imagined myself witnessing the dancing of the Roman maidens as if I had been in the midst of them. My face was pallid with fasting, yet my will felt the assaults of desire: in my cold body and in my parched flesh, which seemed dead before its death, passion was able to live. Alone with this enemy, I threw myself in spirit at the feet of Jesus, watering them with my tears, and I tamed my flesh by fasting whole weeks. I am not ashamed to disclose my temptations, but I grieve that I am not now what I then was. I often joined night to day crying and beating my breast till calm returned."

Worded differently, he often was at that point when his emotions and the power of the imagination could have overpowered him and taken him where his innermost spirit and his understanding didn't want to go and he hailed so loud to the wind and rescued his self-respect and the better portion of himself. In his tears at Jesus' feet he learnt that divine grace is more than an emotion and he made this transition of trust in God. This confrontation and this conflict are part of the Christian message and they do not really exist outside of Christianity. Through his endurance of this struggle St. Jerome gives evidence to us that he belongs to the great ones of the Spirit of mankind. Very much like Søren Kierkegaard in the nineteenth century he makes the point that the essential for man is in the heart and its encounter with God alone. The hermit is suited to this encounter and God can call him to this situation, even if he opens other avenues for him later on. No outward observance or ritual is a substitute for this.

By way of digression we also have to understand Christian marriage in this light. We don't have to worry that Jerome would have gone to Rome and find one of these girls for himself and have some fun. He suffered these temptations of the flesh, but he didn't seriously consider to fall into these, because this wouldn't have been of any use to the girl he could easily find, nor to him who had been grasped by the eternal Son of God. The struggle was that Jesus Christ became the bridegroom of his soul. In Christian marriage the man or the wife takes the place of Jesus Christ as the bridegroom of the soul. Each partner is first of all responsible to Jesus Christ and the partnership he has established.

The struggle to obtain this clarity and depth of Jesus Christ being present in and for each other can be even more severe in marriage and when the partners have succeeded in the struggle they will equally feel at home with the Lord. Sexuality can express this feeling of being at home very well. If it doesn't do this, then it becomes a phantom which only leads to greater and greater estrangement. In Christian marriage sexuality is at the service of the Spiritual bond, established by the Bridegroom of the Soul, Jesus.

By way of second digression we can also perceive true Christian friendship in this light. The friend represents Jesus Christ and there is no need for any sexual expression. The result for St. Jerome was that the spirit just dominated and he was extremely sensitive to the value of Christian friendship, because he appreciated the unity God wants to establish for believers. He was not cynical or discouraging about friendship, because he knew that God is interested to connect an eternal value with it.

St. Jerome went through this crucible of solitude and it became part of his identity. Then he rejoined the endeavors of the Church at large. "When my soul was on fire with bad thoughts," he wrote to his friend Rusticus in 411, "as a last resort I became a scholar". He studied Hebrew: "I turned to this language of hissing and broken winded words. I thank our Lord that I now gather such sweet fruit from the bitter sowing of those studies." Asceticism and studies became important for him. Although he was ordained to the priesthood, he never celebrated the Eucharist, because he believed himself to be called to be a monk and a recluse. To further his studies he went to Constantinople to learn from St. Gregory of Nazianzen in 380, whose close friend St. Basil had died the previous year. Immediately a friendship developed between the two and Jerome benefited greatly from this Master of Sacred Scripture. In 382 he returned to Rome.

Pope Damasus employed him as his secretary and asked him to revise the Latin version of the gospels (Vulgate) and the Psalter. Besides his official duties he fostered contemplation among prominent women of the Roman society. They experienced this same call to be closer to God, to be in the world, but not of the world. Their aspirations corresponded to those of Jerome. People were impressed by his personal holiness, learning and honesty. And yet he liked to speak in extremes of black and white and he was extremely sensitive. He was outspoken and often satirical and sarcastic and chastised vices in others, but also in himself. We recognize that he had come on the scene in Rome as a personality with extraordinary erudition, spiritual appeal and the aura of holiness. His sudden leap to publicity as the secretary of the Pope also speaks to this effect. This also connected him with influential people in society, especially the women who accepted him as their guide for their search in prayer. People of this era were very receptive and willing to spend more time in prayer and some of his students became outstanding in this regard. We are indebted to the saint through whose extensive writings we are familiar with them. Without St. Jerome there wouldn't be any records left of these important developments of true trademarks of Catholicism.

St. Marcella, St. Albina, and St. Asella
Helping the Sick and the Poor

St. Marcella, her mother St. Albina and her sister St. Asella, deserve special mention. Marcella's husband had died shortly after their marriage and she didn't want to remarry, although the consul, Cerealis, proposed to her. Instead she was interested to imitate the contemplatives of Egypt and the East, who were well known before St. Jerome came to Rome. In a very short time several communities sprang up in the city. The time was ripe for the establishment of these monasteries. She continued her correspondence with Jerome also when he had left and we are fortunate that sixteen of his letters still exist, making recommendations for religious living together. She remained in Rome until the city was sacked in 410 by Alaric, the king of the Goths. St. Melania the Elder didn't remarry either after her husband, Valerius Maximus, prefect of Rome, died, but she was the first one who went from Rome to Jerusalem and built a monastery for fifty nuns. Her granddaughter, Melania the Younger joined her many years later.

St. Paula followed a similar pattern of widows who gave their life to God. Especially her daughter St. Eustochium remained close to her. Together with St. Jerome they visited Egypt to come to know the life of the monks and anchorites and then established a monastery in Bethlehem. St. Paula had learned Greek from her father and also studied Hebrew and was able to assist St. Jerome in his translations. St. Fabiola was also influenced by St. Jerome, but she had a different interest for her religious life. Her first husband made married life impossible and she obtained a divorce; she was then forced to take a second husband, who later died. She did public penance and was readmitted to communion by the Pope.

These were the first Christian public hospitals in the West. We have to acknowledge the theological intuition of the saint. By her faith and the teachings of the gospel she was aware that Jesus was suffering in the poor and the sick and in helping them she came closer to God. Contemplation can stand out by itself, but it can also be applied in this way and it takes a saint to make this true application. These women made a great contribution for monasticism and the religious life.

The mentioned journey to Palestine and Egypt took place in 385, one year after the death of Pope Damasus, which left St. Jerome free to follow his inclination to live as a monk. He even had to cope with gossip accusing him of scandal in connection with St. Paula, but the victories he had gained in his struggles can assure us that his intentions towards the nuns were impeccable and above reproach. This is confirmed by the fact that he settled in Bethlehem by himself in a cave and his reason for this location was also theological. He was interested in spirit to have a place ready for Mary and Joseph, if they should come again to Bethlehem to look for a place to stay. The mystic believed in the birth of Jesus not only in a stable, but also in the refuge of his heart. Before he had settled in Bethlehem he had already written his fine apologia.

He found some years of peace. He was impressed by the spiritual wealth he met there: "The illustrious Gauls congregate here, and no sooner has the Briton, so remote from our world, made some progress in religion then he leaves his early-setting sun to seek a land which he knows only by reputation and from the Scriptures. And what of the Armenians, the Persians, the peoples from India and Ethiopia, of Egypt, of Pontus, Cappadocia, Syria and Mesopotamia? They throng here and set us the example of every virtue. The languages differ but the religion is the same; there are as many different choirs singing the psalms as there are nations." We notice the saint's skill as a writer and his Catholic mentality to bring all people together in this praise of God. In this setting he felt closer to heaven: "The apostles and martyrs pray even more for us after their victories." He consoled St. Paula, upon the death of her daughter Blesilla: "She now prays to the Lord for you, and obtains for me the pardon of my sins." He felt close to God because of his purity of heart which he had obtained in penance and contemplation. As a monk he sought this union with God and was aware of the clarity and simplicity in which it is achieved, readily admitting his own weakness and insecurity, saying: "There is no safety if a man sleeps near a serpent."

He went to extremes in his fight for his understanding of the truth, being opposed to Origen and yet accepting very much from his teaching, sacrificing his long friendship with Rufinus in his zeal for the truth and even alienating himself from St. Augustine, who had to use the utmost patience to calm Jerome's nerves. St. Jerome stands out as a witness for the contradictions of the human heart and the victory won by God's grace. Even the monk in a cave is a challenge to fathom the depth God has created in man. He and his era confirm the vibrancy the call to religious life had brought about and they strengthen our awareness how much it is at the heart of the Kingdom of God.

Historical events also take hold of the saints. Germanic tribes had been on the move for almost a couple of centuries. Already in 251 the Emperor

Decius fell in battle against the Goths. They became an even greater threat to the Empire. They in turn were beset by the Huns in the fourth century, were first accepted by the Romans, but then rose up against them and beat them in a decisive battle already in 378 and over thirty years later were able to plunder Rome in 410 under the leadership of Alaric, who died shortly after this victory.

Many refugees fled to the East and St. Jerome wrote of them: "Who would have believed that the daughters of that mighty city would one day be wandering as servants and slaves on the shores of Egypt and Africa? That Bethlehem would daily receive noble Romans, distinguished ladies brought up in wealth and now reduced to beggary? I cannot help them all, but I grieve and weep with them, and completely given up to the duties which charity imposes on me, I have put aside my commentary on Ezekiel and almost all study. For today we must translate the words of Scripture into deeds, and instead of speaking saintly words, we must act them." The saint was committed to do what God asked of him and showed the strength, but also the flexibility of his faith. Despite these historical disturbances monasticism proved itself and often became a stronghold for stability, physical and spiritual.

As noted the examples of Egypt had been readily accepted in Italy in the fourth century and even more so in other parts of Northern Africa. It became natural for smaller groups to join together for the sake of prayer and community life.

St. Augustine

The Grandeur of Salvation is channeled in a personal way

The most powerful figure for Monasticism in Northern Africa and later for the entire Roman Catholic Church was St. Augustine, Bishop of Hippo. He was born on November 13th, 354 in Thagaste in Northern Africa (only thirteen years after St. Jerome) and died on August 28th, 430 in Hippo, the city, where he was the bishop. He had to deal with the monasticism as it had developed before his time.

Although St. Augustine is one of the most prominent doctors of the Church in regard to theology and philosophy and his influence can hardly be underestimated, we also have to respect him in connection with the monastic movement. His natural disposition, his struggles, the warmth of his heart, his sense of true Christian friendship, his love for community and his affection for brothers who live in unity stress this point. He was able to foster monasticism from the bottom of his heart. His mother, St. Monica, tried to make a model-child and model-Christian out of him from his early childhood, but he strayed. He later found out that the gracious teaching, which she had given him, lodged deeper in his heart than the things he did for a while and the things he believed for a while. Intelligent and successful as a student he also enjoyed the company of friends who liked to do fun things, even if they didn't agree with Christian norms. The theatre-plays of the fourth century pagan culture were often indecent and yet the witty student enjoyed them nonetheless. It even seemed to increase the closeness with friends. Later in life he regretted it.

To make his enjoyment complete Augustine was involved with a girl and he had to confess to his mother, that this girl was pregnant, and that he was the father. He was only eighteen years of age, when his son, Adeodatus, was born. The name Adeodatus, given by God, was well chosen, for the saint was later aware, that God remains good, even if human beings try to escape his will. This child was actually a great delight for his father and mother and St. Augustine loved him dearly. He also proved very intelligent as he was growing up and St. Augustine was very happy about his progress. He stayed at his father's side, eager to learn from him and join in his debates when he was of age. The care he received from his father also shows St. Augustine as a man, who had a sense of family-bonds and bonds of friendship, such as would naturally develop in a monastery. St. Augustine developed his career as a teacher and professor of rhetoric up to the fall of 386, when he was thirty two. His mother had prayed fervently for his conversion and he resigned his professorship and he went with his mother, his son Adeodatus and some friends to the country estate, Cassisiacum.

He devoted himself to the pursuit of true philosophy, which by that time was inseparable from Christianity for him. His son was fourteen years at that time and was wise enough to join the search for truth. He had grown up in this exciting intellectual atmosphere of his father and his friends. His mind had early adapted itself to understand what they were talking about and equally early he was able to put his own observations and suggestions into words. His mother had also come along to Milan and there would have been the opportunity for the parents to get married. Augustine's mother, Monica, favored this, hoping that through this sacrament the grace of God would enter her son's heart.

No reason is known, why this didn't happen, but we can suppose that there was a major one. Adeodatus' mother withdrew from her "family left her son with his father and returned to Carthage". Augustine felt this separation deeply and witnessed about it: "She was stronger than I and made her sacrifice with a courage and generosity which I was not strong enough to imitate." She probably went into seclusion in a monastery and offered her life to God, affirming the truth of the deeper dwelling of God's grace in the human heart. Augustine was happy to have his brilliant son at his side and was a good father to him. He gladly accepted his contributions to the discussions and called him: "that boy, the youngest of them all" and acknowledged his participation in his essay, called "The Teacher". Augustine even felt a kind of awe about him as he told in "The blessed life": The grandeur of his mind filled me with a kind of terror."

Adeodatus prepared for baptism along with his father and his father's lifelong friend, Alypius. Through the sacrament the son of sin became the child of grace in the unfathomable richness of God's design. All three received baptism at Easter 387. Adeodatus died the following year in the sixteenth year of his life, before he could get into trouble like his father. Of course, we also have to admire St. Augustine, who has endured comments about his youth for over one thousand five hundred years.

St. Augustine experienced a calming of his passions and was able to make the great resolution to choose wisdom for his only spouse. In the fall of 387 St. Augustine had already lost his mother, who died on their return journey from Italy to Africa.

Knowing her in God's hands made him even stronger in his dedication to eternal life and in himself to seek refuge in prayer. As in the case of St. Anthony we can assume a private revelation which drew him towards contemplation. He had heard children playing and one child saying: "Take and read, Tolle, Lege". He interpreted these words as directly said to him by God, namely to take Holy Scripture and read it. What he had begun in Cassisiacum he planned to continue in Africa, namely to retire to the family estate there and to make it suitable for a monastery.

His trip home was delayed until the following year 388, after the death of the tyrant Maximus (August, 388). The first agreement of his group was to live in poverty, prayer and the study of religion. He did not seek to be ordained and even avoided this, but the people wanted this to happen and he accepted the priesthood in 391 against his will, consenting to God's call. Later in 396 he became the bishop of Hippo, a position he held for thirty four years. He continued to live together with brother priests in a monastic setting, attached to the Episcopal See. The monastery and especially the city even proved to be a strong protection against the invading Vandals towards the end of his life. They surrounded the city, which was well fortified and able to withstand a siege for eighteen months. At the beginning of August in 430, St. Augustine became seriously ill and he died on August 28th of that year.

As one of the most prolific geniuses of mankind, his spiritual and intellectual impact remains constant through the centuries, which only enhances his influence on monasticism for the entire Church. As mentioned, St. Augustine didn't initiate monasticism in Northern Africa. It existed before his efforts and the improvements, which he brought to it, have to be evaluated from his way of seeing "room for improvement".

His own development, the strength of prayer as he had experienced it through his own mother, Monica, the inclination of his mind, his awareness, that "our hearts are restless, until they rest in thee, O Lord" and his faith in the brotherhood of believers, besides his work as administrator and bishop paved the way for giving direction to monasticism. As he pointed out in his Confessions, he was familiar with St. Anthony, whose life-story had already become part of Christian literature at the time St. Augustine was growing up. After his conversion he knew how to respect this great saint and to incorporate his example into his own idea for the life of the monk. Throughout his life St. Augustine had a penetrating sensitivity for the gift of friendship, which was part of his understanding of monasticism.

He knew that Jesus had called his Apostles friends at the Last Supper and that Christian friendship was a gift from him to be cherished. The time to collect his thoughts along with his mother, his friends and his own son in Cassisiacum served to prepare him for his understanding of the truly contemplative life. The years of philosophical research and meditation bore even greater fruit in Christian meditation, in which the soul already participates in the gift of eternal bliss as offered in our salvation. Once he had become a priest in 391 he was even more committed to call his brother priests to this bond of prayer. We might consider this a courageous step, namely to combine priesthood and being a monk. He was not only courageous enough to propose this combination, but also able to explain his ideas about it and to give incentives for their realization, through his theology and ecclesiology.

He gladly accepted the description of the early church in the fourth chapter of the Acts of the Apostles: "the believers were of one heart and one soul" and applied it to the priests living in community. The ideal as described in the Acts could hardly be realized in the Church at large, but the small group could give a convincing example for the Church. His recommendations for the religious life became influential for many monasteries especially those who worked closely together with a bishop, but they were also adapted for women religious, so that convents of nuns followed his insights as well.

Like St. Jerome so also St. Augustine has become an open book which everybody can read. In his Confessions he opened his heart to all who seek God and showed God's grace at work. God gave him freedom to deviate from the truth, to learn from his mistakes and to return to his divine and everlasting love. Even the sin of lust became an occasion for him to realize that nothing merely earthly can compare to the bond given to us in Jesus Christ. His philosophical endeavors have become a timeless lesson about human insights and God's revelation. His adherence to Manichaeism describes a danger which comes up again and again. Manichaeism looks at the confrontations we experience: good and evil, spirit and matter, old and young, life and death, created and uncreated and so forth and proposes solutions to these enigmas. In our modern mentality we have created different confrontations like rich and poor, female and male, developed and underdeveloped, new and old, boom and bust and so forth and we propose solutions to these enigmas, which are similar to those of Manichaeism. Like St. Augustine we also have to work through these and find our way to God's revelation.

This is even more so because Buddhism has similar view as Manichaeism and requires a solid Christian dialogue, if we want to qualify as a world religion. Without the proper qualification we easily lose what we have as did St. Augustine in the beginning. From this angle the saint is up to date, deserves our attention and also deserves to have monks willing to follow in his footsteps. His code for the monks can speak to us as well. He used the language of Platonism, but the Christian meaning of this language was decisive. Throughout the ages it remains a challenge for believers, that the terms they use don't overpower the meaning they feel in their heart. The saint was victorious in this struggle and makes it possible for later generations to obtain similar victories. He also was a man of the Western Part of the Roman Empire and inherited its sense for organization so important for Westerners, including the Catholic Church and her monasteries.

St. Augustine experienced towards the end of his life that migration of people bring about a movement which also involves the quiet monastery. The Vandals, Germanic tribes, moved South at the beginning of the 5th century and via Spain they crossed over to Northern Africa in 429 and used

Carthage as their stronghold to dominate the Mediterranean Ocean. After St. Augustine in 455 they even plundered Rome. Unexpectedly the world changed and monasticism also had to cope with this change. The description of the code of the monks has to be realistic and always reckon with things unforeseen and yet being part of a plan not in our grasp.

Quite often it is an advantage for a monastery to be located close to or even within a city. It provides a focus for Christian identity and enhances missionary influence. At times of historical upheaval or of migrations like those of the Vandals a monastery in a remote area may have a greater chance of survival. The monks in cooperation with God's grace make this choice and can rely on God's providence for the place most conducive for them. At the mouth of the river Rhone, Marseille, along the coast there are a number of Mediterranean islands and one of these, Lerins, became a habitation of monks.

Honoratus and Cassian

God wants us to be at home with him in Prayer

This island-monastery had been founded between 405 and 410 by a monk named Honoratus. He was born about the year 350 and died in January 429 at the age of 79. He had converted to Christianity from a pagan family, as did his brother Venantius. Their conversion led to a serious endeavor to be with God. Nothing should separate them from him, which in turn involved the question of becoming hermits or monks. Naturally, the two embarked on a pilgrimage from Marseille in 368. A more advanced contemplative, Caprasius, was their guide.

He was able to teach them on this pilgrimage about hermitages and monasteries in Palestine, Syria and Egypt and they could discern, whether this was God's call for them as well. Becoming a hermit or a monk can be discovered, because everyone has to take God's Word to heart and make it his own. He may learn that he becomes more connected with heaven and his longing grows. He can observe this in another hermit or monk, who is his teacher. This was the goal of the two on their pilgrimage with their guide. Sadly to relate, Honoratus' brother Venantius died on this trip in Achaia and Honoratus had to cope with his death. Paradoxically it increased his conviction of the short duration of our life and the ever greater need to entrust not only the soul of a beloved brother, but also our own to God, who takes life at his own choosing. He and his guide returned, but they stopped in Italy and visited Rome.

Once arrived back in Gaul, Honoratus settled on the wild island of Lerins with the intention to live there in solitude. Disciples joined him and they developed a settlement for religious, which eventually grew into a monastery. Later the monastery became rather illustrious on account of accomplished ecclesiastical writers and a number of bishops originated from there, who in turn founded monasteries. These became centers of culture and science, especially during the decline of the Roman Empire in the fifth and sixth century. Honoratus also wrote a rule for solitaries, but it has not been preserved.

Contemporary to Honoratus was John Cassian who was born in Provence about 360 and died in 433. He was the son of wealthy parents and received a good education. Similar to Honoratus he also wanted to discern his vocation of a monk and set out with a friend, Germanus on a pilgrimage in 380. First they went to the Holy Land and became monks in Bethlehem, but they stayed there only for a while. They wanted to deepen their understanding and went to Egypt, the heart of contemplation at that time. They entrusted themselves to Archebius as their teacher and lived among the hermits and shared their mission to pray for the whole world and to draw together in the Spirit. These years were very informative and Cassian collected the material for his later writings, his rule and his Conferences on the Egyptian monks. They lived there until the year 400 when Cassian was forty. He then sought out St. John Chrysostom in Constantinople as his teacher, especially in Scripture.

St. John Chrysostom (347–407) in turn had been a hermit under St. Basil the Great for four years and had been a solitary for another two. By the time Cassian arrived he was the Patriarch of Constantinople and very much under pressure in this city of High Politics and resented by the Empress Eudoxia. In 403 thirty six hostile bishops condemned him. The Pope sent five bishops to come to his aid, but they were imprisoned and St. John Chrysostom was sent into exile. For a short time this exile was revoked, but only to be renewed by the Emperor and made even worse by sending him father away at Cucusus, Armenia, where he eventually died. His 238 letters from exile, his 88 homilies on John, 90 on Matthew and 32 on Romans survived him and have established his fame as one of the great saints. Cassian could stay with him until his departure into exile and then go to Rome to defend him, which didn't help, but proved his innocence. He arrived in Rome in 405.

Cassian continued his monastic life and after 415 he was able to establish two monasteries in Marseille, one for men and another for women. This also means that he was very receptive to follow the examples of Constantinople and Rome, namely to have monasteries in the city. And yet first of all he was deeply committed to the fact that the hermit or the monk has to train the inner man. It has to be taken into account that the historical, political, biographical or any other situation of the monk, impact his inner life, but these influences do not ultimately determine his fate of salvation. The monk will find access to his inner freedom and the joy of everlasting glory if he addresses the obstacles to God's grace and his own imperfection in childlike trust, confident that God calls him in love, understanding his imperfections and helping him to deal with them well. These obstacles are universally human and the monk is not becoming hysterical if he notices them and addresses them. Neither does he impetuously try to find a quick solution to a problem.

If he tries to solve all his problems today, then he might not know what to do tomorrow and he is getting bored. Human nature is not that way; only human beings imagine that it could be thus. As a monk of over thirty five years of experience Cassian knew how to spiritually cooperate with human nature and yet he pointed out a list of obstacles of perfection: gluttony, impurity, covetousness, anger, dejection, boredom (ennui), vainglory and pride. We take this list as fruit of his meditation and prayer and as a help to encourage our soul and to make it firm in the presence of the divine.

It should not be taken in the way of dissecting modern psychology, which very often tears human beings apart instead of giving strength and protection in the midst of spiritual trials. The monk may include psychology, but his expertise is trans-psychological, spiritual, sacramental and theological. We can be sure that Cassian wouldn't fall prey to our modern pan-psychology in which secular forces devour the spirit of man. Cassian also makes the point that monasticism is universal, because he underwent a long training in the East (Egypt, Palestine and Constantinople) and continued in the West (Marseille) without disruption of his contemplation. He wouldn't see the need to make a strict separation between East and West. The grace of God is one and human beings may channel it differently according to their nature and temperament.

Cassian developed a program for monasticism, its habits and lifestyle. He wanted to describe his observations of his stay with the monks in the East and make these available to his hearers and readers. Succeeding generations took his writings to heart, appreciated their value and made use of them. One was St. Benedict. Those who taught Cassian had been influenced by Origen, who in turn remained influential for the future.

Unfortunately St. Augustine considered Cassian to be semi-pelagian (Do we need God's grace to exercise the virtues leading to salvation?) and Cassian was never declared a saint in the Catholic Church, but he is considered one in the Orthodox. Both Cassian and Origen are theologically in a tough spot after their death, but they remain classical teachers of divine truths through the centuries and we should be grateful that God gave them as gifts to the Church. We can also appreciate that Cassian dealt with virtues needed by all believers and not just by monks. Achievements but also struggles experienced by all bind us together and enhance the life of the Church and Cassian did it very well.

As can be expected once the paradigms of hermitism and monasticism have been set they automatically find followers from city to city and country to country. St. Augustine was able to enlarge monasticism far away to the East from Egypt and the same happened to the North of Palestine in Lebanon and Syria. The word about hermitism and monasticism spread from town to town. Some men or women learned about it, came together in groups for prayer and began a monastery of their own. In the fourth century Syria already belonged to the sphere of influence of monasticism from Palestine. Paganism required greater sincerity from the Christians in the exercise of their religion and many responded with love of God and prayer. We also find the observation confirmed that enlightenment is granted in the most humble and simple circumstances. God speaks where human beings live a simple life.

St. Simeon

Closeness to God on a Pillar

Like St. Anthony in the desert, so also St. Simeon the Stylite came from a humble background where he received his call from God. He grew up as the son of a shepherd and was a shepherd boy himself for some time. At age thirteen about 402 he heard the beatitude in the Church: "Blessed are they that mourn; blessed are the clean of heart." He believed that God had spoken these words to him directly and he wanted to make them his own.

He asked a hermit about it and the man explained to him, that he would find the happiness promised in these beatitudes through continual prayer, watching, fasting, weeping, humiliation and suffering. In addition to these words and their explanation he received a vision about the construction of a pillar and he knew that this was meant for him. Since there were already monasteries in the area he applied to one of them and was accepted, but his heart was set on the most sincere asceticism, following the explanations of the hermit.

He learned all the psalms by heart and many parts of the New Testament. These nourished his soul and he could pray them continually. He tried to live in two monasteries, which were well established, but his singular piety didn't really fit in, so that he had to live by himself. He moved to the foot of a mountain. Twenty six times during the forty days of Lent he imitated our Lord without eating or drinking. His fame spread and many people came to see him, but also to ask for his prayers and his counsel. To gain greater privacy for his devotion he built a pillar and lived on top of it. This pillar had to become higher and higher, because people climbed up on the side in order to see him.

Miracles of healing occurred and he had to deal with multitudes of people coming to him. He gave two homilies each day and through him many people from Persia, Armenia and Iberia were converted to the faith. The Emperor and the Empress revered him as a saint and listened to his counsel. He became well known in Europe as well and especially Rome endorsed him very much. Pictures of him were drawn or painted and distributed to the faithful. These actually enhanced the use of sacred images in the Church and our willingness to be motivated in our faith through them. His example also shows that the Holy See was very much involved in his cause and the asceticism connected with it. We are not obliged to follow such an extreme penance but are encouraged in our faith by it nonetheless.

The pillar-saint gives this vivid impression that ultimately our life is in God's hands and his example like that of many others through the ages has made this most obvious. The shepherd-boy and Pillar-saint St. Simeon the Stylite and the many hermits and monks reinforce our awareness that the movement they represent was basically a lay-movement and was not initiated by the clergy. We have to acknowledge this as a reality in the Church, that the impulse for new life has an unexpected source. We can also be grateful that the Holy See was sensitive and accepted this impulse very well. St. Simeon the Stylite died in 459. He was contemporary of St. Patrick, but totally independent from him. St. Simeon also exemplifies the impact hermitism and monasticism had acquired in his society and in his era.

Simultaneous to this great saint of Syria there came about the Christianization and the consequent monasticism in Ireland. Abbots became the leading men and their prayer turned Ireland into the island of saints (no sinners, because the Irish repent before they sin); their fervent devotion was combined with study, so that it also became the island of scholars.

St. Patrick
Called by God

The beginning of Christianity and monasticism in Ireland depend on their greatest saint, St. Patrick. He was a monk at heart. Born in 387 at Kilpatrick, near Dumbarton in Scotland of a Roman family of high rank, his mother Conchessa was a near relative of St. Martin of Tours. When he was sixteen years old in 403 he was captured by Irish raiders and sold into slavery. He had to tend sheep on the slopes of Slemish and he spent most of his time in prayer. He said about 100 prayers a day and about as many at night.

Like St. Augustine he opened his heart in his "Confessio" and described the pain he felt through the sudden and total separation from his family and friends. He had a very sensitive nature and was worried that he hadn't known God well enough up to that time and had not listened attentively to his priest explaining the faith. Basically he had been a carefree youth like most, but he accepted his slavery to draw all the closer to God. He had to engage in interaction and conversation with his Master, the family and the clan and quickly acquired a perfect knowledge of the Celtic language. He was still young enough to learn this "sweet tongue" like the natives. We admire the ability of the youth to go along with the people, to learn to love them, but not to get side-tracked into their paganism. He kept his heart pure. We also admire that he didn't become despondent, but kept his spirit intact through his contact with Jesus. This ordeal of his youth lasted for six years and we would understand if he had lost hope, but paradoxically the love of God grew more powerful in him.

As other great mystics he also received some private intuition or revelation, a voice telling him to remain strong, because he would soon gain freedom. His increased inward contact with Jesus became so powerful that he believed that a ship was waiting for him. He had to travel 200 miles to come to a harbor where a ship was waiting. After some additional prayer he was able to go aboard and leave Ireland. And yet, these six years of slavery had made a believer out of him. Instead of a carefree youth he had become a contemplative.

He perceived himself as being in God's hands. His closeness to God led to miracles respected by others and he was happy to join his family and they were delighted to have him back again. The years of captivity and the people he had lived with for so long had acquired a place in his soul and in a vision they cried as if with one voice: "We beseech thee, holy youth, to come and walk among us once more." This couldn't be accomplished immediately and directly, because the Holy Spirit had to direct his steps.

The first requirement therefore was to turn to God in prayer and first he joined the monks at Lerins, off the coast of Cannes in France for three years, from 412 to 415. He became a monk and remained one also when he helped Bishop Germanus at Auxerre for fifteen years. We conclude: Without monasticism Patrick wouldn't have become a great missionary, either. The mission of the Church is intimately connected with the contemplation and the monasticism within it. Without these the Church is superficial and a meaningless noise. During his years with Bishop Germanus he was ordained and asked to join the bishop on a mission to Britain, but Patrick's heart was set on Ireland.

Germanus consecrated him bishop and when he finally landed in Ireland in 433 he had been a contemplative for over 25 years, if we include his years as a shepherd. He came to Ireland as one who loved the people and spoke their language, but who had to rescue them from paganism and establish them in the truth. The Pope had entrusted him with "the mission of gathering the Irish race into the one fold of Christ". Some time after he had offered his first Mass in Erin the barn he had used was turned into a Church and a monastery was built on the place. St. Patrick gathered disciples and many of these became monks or nuns consecrating their lives to prayer. When, for example, the chieftain Secsnen had converted, his son wanted to remain at the saint's side and St. Patrick was glad to accept him into his company. Others were obligated to lead Christian lives in their families, which they did willingly, since marriage-bonds were solid by their very nature. The saint had to hold his ground against Druidism and often be in danger, but his success came from his intimate union with God, reinforced in his contemplation.

Earlier history records that St. Patrick consecrated about 350 bishops, which would also strengthen the notion, that the community life was strong. Daughters of a converted chieftain founded a monastery for women at Clonbroney. Quite often vocations of monks go along with vocations of nuns in a given territory and their circumstances.

The saint's call to intense contemplation are attested from the places he used for solitude and retreat like the island Lough Dergh, known as St. Patrick's Purgatory or the 4,000 foot high mountain in the far West of Connaught, facing Crew Bay, in pagan times known as Eagle Mountain, but later as Croagh Patrick, i.e. St. Patrick's mountain. Like Moses, St. Patrick stayed there for 40 days to obtain special blessings and mercy for the Irish people. Like St. Anthony in the desert he also had to endure the attacks of demonic powers. It probably would take a modern artist like Salvador Dali to give an impression of the attacks, but we do well to accept them as part of the growth of Christianity. In his biography or "Confession" he pointed out that he had to bear insults from unbelievers, to hear reproach of his going abroad and to endure many persecutions even unto bonds, but that he was ready to give his life to the Lord. Despite his sufferings he was happy, since: "Sons and daughters of Scottish chieftains are seen to become monks and virgins of Christ." This was one fruit of his prayer and his penance, namely companions, who followed him, were devoted to him and were encouraged in the bonds of prayer. His apostolate in Ireland was less than thirty years, but he was blessed to have converted the nation to Christianity and he could be proud that he had baptized and confirmed thousands of people.

Through him monasticism became an outstanding feature of the Church in Ireland. As making sacrifices was part of St. Patrick's life, so it became part in the attitude of later generations. Monks of these later generations made the sacrifice of leaving home for the sake of Christ and became instrumental for the Church in central Europe. St. Patrick died in 461. He also affirms the similarity of the contemplatives who enriched the Church with new life, namely that they were in touch with God's grace also through private revelations they received and that through these they were ever more deeply penetrated by the gospel. It wasn't preaching that brought him to this bond with God, but a message or a word that was meant just for him. We have to reckon with special graces God is granting to individuals and it may take some time until they enter the main stream of the Church. Also in the case of St. Patrick it is remarkable that the Holy See acknowledged his missionary fervor and made him a special envoy for the work in Ireland.

The century of St. Patrick was also significant for the Roman Catholic Church. As mentioned the King of the Visigoths, Alaric had conquered Rome in 410 and this event signaled that the Emperor and the Roman Empire had become weak. The Emperor had moved to Ravenna already six years earlier, because Ravenna was a more secure place for him. The Church was left as the main institution in the city of Rome. In fact, the Emperor Honorius (395–423) was not able to withstand the Visigoths. Almost the same situation came about when the Huns invaded the Eternal City in 452. The Emperor Valentinian III was equally helpless. Only Pope Leo the Great (440–461) was able to negotiate with Attila, the king of the Huns and achieved that the city was not destroyed. This accomplishment of the Pope also increased the prestige of the Papacy. People respected the office of the successor of St. Peter and the Church was able to survive the collapse of the Western Part of the Roman Empire when the Germanic ruler Odoacer (434–493) took over in 476. Although he was defeated in 489/490 and killed in Ravenna in 493, the events brought about a new era of Western Civilization. The Germanic populations proved their strength and their viability for centuries to come. By way of sophistication, political and cultural skills the Roman cities were much more advanced, but they were not able to withstand these populations on the move. The Germanic populations had been driven West and South by the Huns and their advance was expressed through military operations and occupations of portions of the Roman Empire. It had been almost natural for the Romans in past centuries to look upon Germanics as subjects and to try to keep them under control. Now the tables were turned and the Germanics showed their strength.

We have to admire the way in which the Pope looked upon this change; not as a threat, but as an opportunity to open the Church for these people. For him they were not uncivilized nations who had to be kept at bay, but fellow human beings in need of the gospel and potential brothers and sisters in Christ. The Pope also recognized their inner spiritual determination which would be life-giving to the Church once it had been transformed from paganism to Christianity. His missionary spirit and his positive attitude in the midst of tragic historical changes are most remarkable. This also shows that he acted as spiritual leader and the Successor of St. Peter and not as the representative of the Roman Empire, trying to maintain his political influence. The Germanic populations were deeply religious and in need to have their spiritual aspirations be enlightened by God's Revelation. Typical for their mentality is that they are loyal to one leader. In the religious sphere the Holy Father was able to match their interest, because of the leadership he provided.

The words of Jesus to St. Peter in Mt 16, 18 "I for my part declare to you, you are Rock, and on this rock I will build my church, and the jaws of death shall not prevail against it" became more and more important. The leadership the Pope provided rested on the Word of God and was more dependable than any earthly institution. A new fusion had come about between this Germanic mentality and God's Revelation and the Church continued to prosper in this union. The fact that this union would be abused for the sake of earthly power in later centuries should not discourage our appreciation of its initiation. When human beings abuse religion for personal gain, then they are sinful and have to repent.

The original intention was religious and we have to acknowledge this truth. Later interpretations have looked upon the Church as merely an extension of the Roman Empire, but we find that these interpretations do not match the actual historical circumstances. Pope Gelasius I (492–496) developed the theory of the two powers: The spiritual power is independent from the secular and both have to be obedient to God's laws. We also understand that the Holy See was so supportive of Monasticism, because the contemplatives are serious in their search for the spiritual and want to rely almost exclusively on God. The Holy Father and the bishops had great interest to strengthen monks and nuns in their vocation and this in turn benefited the Church at large. Monasteries continued to thrive and their number increased in this era of the end of Antiquity and the beginning of the Middle Ages about 500 A.D.

PART II

Middle Ages

he historical changes at that time created the need for greater unity also for the monasteries; but unity works best when it is found as a gift from God and it usually doesn't come about when it is imposed by laws or policies. People are naturally drawn to the bonds of love given by heaven and they shy away from restrictions, even if they are well intended. Quite a few rules had been created to guide monasteries and there was the danger that these were just regulations lacking the fresh and invigorating breath of the Holy Spirit.

St. Benedict

Warm of Heart

ne monk, St. Benedict (480–possibly 560), stands out as the giver of a rule for monasteries, where the Spirit can breathe and give encouragement to those who seek God. In our view it is significant that the Holy Father, Pope Gregory the Great (590–604) wrote his biography. The Pope was very impressed by the miracles and visions of the saint and he showed him as an example of holiness and spiritual power. He dedicated a whole book to this holy man of God, Benedict, and wanted all the faithful to share his admiration and devotion to him. The Pope skillfully publicized the life of the saint, but didn't necessarily follow the directions of the rule in his guidance of the Church. Despite this discrepancy we are grateful to Gregory the Great for his enthusiastic story, because without it we would know almost nothing about the life of this remarkable man.

St. Benedict and his twin sister, Scholastica a nun, were born about the year 480 as children of a Roman noble of Nursia. The parents were well-to-do and interested in a good education for him. When he was of age he attended schools in Rome and pursued his literary studies there until he was almost twenty years old. He was fully aware of the dissolute and licentious lives his companions were living and it seems likely that he was in danger to go down the same path. He himself was deeply affected by the love of a woman, but he didn't do what St. Augustine had done over a century earlier. He made a choice between sin and sanctity and the latter won in his heart, although it was purchased at a great price. In an almost Socratic fashion he maintained his sanity and stability. At the right time he made the sovereign decision to leave Rome, "instructed with learned ignorance and furnished with unlearned wisdom" as St. Gregory described it. He left his books behind, abandoned his father's wealth with the intention to serve God alone.

As St. Gregory put it: "He drew back his foot which he had already set forth in the world." He had a servant accompany him, who did basic chores for him. He found the company of virtuous men about 40 miles from Rome in Enfide and joined them in their devotion and love of God. A miracle, which he worked, drew attention to him and he escaped alone, leaving even his servant behind. He came to Subjaco, trying not to remember the evils of the great city of Rome and he believed that it would be better for him to live alone, poor and to support himself by his own work. A monk, Romanus, advised him to become a hermit.

This he did and lived in a cave above a lake. Romanus visited him often and supplied him with food. Benedict advanced greatly in interior wisdom and in maturity of mind and character. The monks of the contemplative settlement about him came to know and respect him greatly and when their abbot died, they approached Benedict and asked him to be their abbot. Benedict couldn't really trust them and their different way of life, but he consented against his will. They were not serious to take his advice and to follow his guidance and even tried to poison him. (Of course, they might have thought that he was very holy and on his way to heaven and they might want to speed the process). His working of miracles became more frequent and people were attracted by his sanctity. Once again he could be the abbot for those willing to belong to him. For them he built twelve monasteries with twelve monks and a superior in each one and he himself remained the abbot for all of them. They also began to accept boys to be trained in a school which they established.

The course was now set for him to write his famous rule. It is written for laymen searching for God, who wish to deny their own will, put on the strong and bright weapon of obedience in order to fight for the Lord, Christ, our true King. The emblem of the rule is: Pray and work, ora et labora. Work is the means to goodness of life. The great disciplinary force of human nature is work; idleness is its ruin. Through the rule he wants to bring people back to God by the labor of obedience. Work causes all growth of goodness. Through the weariness of labor the monks overcomes temptations and the enticements of evil. God's grace cooperates with the one who works. The religious life as envisioned by Benedict is essentially social. The life of a hermit is possible only for those few who are advanced in self-discipline. The hermit exemplifies that ultimately our lives are directed towards God alone and the vertical direction of our lives shouldn't be ignored. In his wisdom St. Benedict combines the vertical and the horizontal aspects of our faith.

His rule is intended to regulate the life of men who live, work, pray, and eat together. The government is paternal through the elected abbot. Much of the rule is legislation of the social and domestic organization in this communism of possessions. Worldly ranks are suppressed, "No one of noble birth may be put before him who was formerly a slave". The use of goods should be in accord with the gospel and the vows of poverty, obedience and celibacy. Each individual receives what he needs. The monastery should be in a position to give alms, not to seek them, to relieve the poor, to clothe the naked, to visit the sick, to bury the dead, to help the afflicted and the stranger. In St. Benedict's time the poor came to him to get help to pay their debts or to receive food.

The Benedictines vow to stay in one place, stabilitas loci. Before the abbot makes decisions he listens to an open debate of the brothers, aware that he and they are bound together for life. Work, self-denial, and prayer should bring people back to God. There is a guideline for prayer, but the community may modify it, only all the psalms should be prayed once a week. Life is incomplete, unless penetrated by prayer, realizing the presence of God, through which the spiritual is joined to the merely human. Through the prayerful care of the heart we perceive Christ in others: to serve the sick is to serve Christ and to receive a guest is to receive Christ. The monks are bound to common prayer,through which God consecrates the community. The chief work of the monks is the worship of God, the source from which all other works find their inspiration. "Our prayer should be short and said with purity of heart, except it be perchance prolonged by the inspiration of divine grace. The obedience to the rule helps the monks as they hasten to their heavenly country." Regeneration is not reached by solitude, nor by austerity, but through man's social instincts, his obedience and work. To avoid evil neither the body nor the mind should be overstrained.

Pope Gregory gives the impression that St. Benedict taught himself and that the rule is a result of his meditation, but the saint was more connected and freely used other sources and made them his own. The abbot of a monastery in the neighborhood, the deacon Servandus visited Benedict often and reported about his guidance of his community. He also witnessed to the vision of cosmic glory, which St. Benedict received. In his rule the saint simply assumes regular contact of the monks with people outside. For example he included a chapter about guests coming to stay for a while in the monastery. We assume that he was well informed about the flourishing monasticism in Gall, the monastery on the island Lerins and those in Burgundy.

St. Anthony was well known through the biography written by St. Athanasius, which includes this basic intention for the monks: "In answer to the question of a monk, what he should do to please God, the abbot St. Anthony responded: 'Whatever you do or say, look for everything for guidance in Sacred Scripture.'" And St. Athanasius added this comment: "He, St. Anthony, learned asceticism from the Bible." St. Benedict followed this recommendation and found many regulations in the Bible, for example the love of neighbor and his up-building. He was concerned not to teach anything which would be contrary to God's law. He was very much influenced by the rule of St. Augustine and the human warmth found therein.

The supreme goal of the community is in agreement with Acts 2, 44f and 4, 32–35 to live together in unity, with one heart and soul to be united in God. His rule describes brothers, who are personally poor, but united in love and not a Church distinguished in a hierarchical order. The description he gives of the Abbot as Father giving his life for the well-being of souls belongs to the most beautiful witness of this office in the history of monasticism. Every effort should lead to the reestablishment of the ideal community of the Acts of the Apostles.

The Spirit of Origen pervades his rule as well, which reminds us of the beautiful description given by Hans Urs von Balthasar: "After the vase was broken into thousand pieces and the name of the Master had been stoned to death and thrown out, the sweet smell of the oil filled the entire house. There is no thinker in the Church who is as much present everywhere although invisible like Origen." This applies first to Cassian, who was familiar with the Spirituality of Origen, which had such a tremendous influence on the monks of Egypt. Both, Origen and Cassian were of importance for the rule of St. Benedict.

Another source for his rule was the so-called Master Rule. In 1933 the Benedictines Justo Perez de Urbel OSB (Silos) and Augustin Genestout OSB (Solesmnes) discovered simultaneously the dependence of the Rule of St. Benedict upon this Master Rule (Regula Magistri). This means that the saint also used the Master Rule substantially for his own purposes and made it his own. The scholars are not blaming the saint of plagiarism, because he is already in heaven and no lawyer can sue him for a settlement. The scholars had to make this honest assessment and point out that the Rule of St. Benedict already stood in a given context and tradition. This in turn doesn't diminish his rule, but rather secures its environment and may even enhance its influence.

St. Benedict knows the monk as someone who searches for God. This is also basic for all Christians and the pious seclusion only provides the setting for it. This very broad view also has the advantage that it can be applied to all kind of circumstances. It proved to be a real advantage for monasticism, because it fit many historical, social and geographical situations.

St. Benedict remained in Subiaco until 529 when his growing influence aroused jealousy and in order to save his followers from persecution, he withdrew to Monte Cassino. There was an old chapel dedicated to the God Apollo, which he tore down and built an oratory dedicated to St. Martin and he began to establish a monastery there. Its location close to a great highway brought about increased communication with the outside world: friends, abbots, nuns, bishops and nobles. Despite his singular devotion to God the saint and his monks were not isolated.

The monastery became a protector of the poor. His monks would take on any kind of work adapted to their circumstances: teaching, studying, taking care of souls, farming, practicing an art or music. No work is foreign to them as long as it is compatible with the life of the community and the Divine Office.

During the later part of the year 546 Totila, the King of the Goths, visited St. Benedict. The saint scolded him: "Many great sins have you committed. Give over your sinful life. You will enter Rome, go beyond the sea, reign for nine years and in the tenth you shall leave this mortal life." Totila was impressed by the saint's prediction and people believe that he wasn't as cruel as he had been before. Abbot Sabinus came for a visit to the saint after December 17th, 546 and told Benedict about the triumphal entrance of Totila in Rome and about the capture of the city. It is generally assumed that Totila conquered Rome on December 17th. Totila's visit is the only date in St. Benedict's life we know for certain. Before his death he was privileged to have a vision of God and he knew of his approaching end. The earliest date of his death is 547, but it is possible that he lived until 560. Perhaps the most striking characteristics in St. Benedict are his deep and wide human feelings and his moderation.

Through his biography we also know about his twin sister, Scholastica, a nun as devoted to God as her brother and very effective in her prayer.

Also in the case of the Rule of St. Benedict the Holy See proved to be instrumental of favoring its success. Through the efforts of Pope Gregory the rule was very much accepted in the quickly growing Church of the Anglo-Saxons and the Franks. They welcomed the rule as the "Roman" one and honored St. Benedict as a "Roman Abbot". Quite often the rule was adapted and implemented as the circumstances demanded. By its very moderation it was never intended to dominate, but simply to be of service for all those, men and women, searching for God in contemplation.

In 580 Monte Cassino was pillaged and burned by the invading Lombards and the surviving monks had to flee to Rome. The information seems to be reliable that the body of the saint was translated to Fleury in France. In Rome the monks lived according to the Rule of their founder, but it was within the city. They were only able to return to Monte Cassino in 718 and rebuilt the abbey, when the Abbot Petronax, a native of Brescia, was entrusted with this task by Pope Gregory II. Thirty years later in 748 Pope Zachary exempted the abbey from Episcopal jurisdiction.

This exemption assigned to the Abbot the dignity and the rights of a bishop and made him directly responsible to the Holy See. It was and still is beneficial both to the Holy See and to all Benedictine Abbeys throughout the world, once the paradigm of Monte Cassino had been set. Benedictine Abbeys only breathe and flourish freely in this exemption from the local ordinary. Theologically this is extremely significant. Bishops should learn contemplation from the monks, because this is their expertise and calling from God. Monks should not depend on busy bishops with their eternal administrative paroles. Throughout the centuries this decision of Pope Zachary has proven to be most life-giving, inspired by a deep sense of Catholicism.

The same sense for true Catholicism was at the heart of Pope Gregory the Great when he initiated the "second" mission to England. Christianity had existed in England through the presence of the Roman Empire, but the Romans were used to look upon the Northern Populations from the point of view of a Superior Civilization. By the fourth century Christianity had been integrated into their fabric of society, but this didn't mean that the Non-Romans could easily become their friends; except, Christians are bound by their faith to look upon all as brothers and sisters in Christ. The Christian-Roman, St. Patrick, had done so in regard to the Irish.

However, by the time of Pope Gregory (590-604) Christianity had disappeared from most of the country through the decline and collapse of the Empire. The Picts, Anglo-Saxons and Germanics from Frisia had expelled the Christians, who had fled to Wales and to Bretagne (France). Pope Gregory, the first Monk-Pope, who had turned his family-estate into the Monastery, St. Andrews in the line of St. Benedict, had recognized the spiritual potential of these new English people, possibly through English boys he had seen on the slave-market in Rome. He had a personal interest in bringing Christianity to these pagans. He even had to overcome the resistance of bishops in Bretagne in respect to the English mission. They didn't want to be bothered with this additional burden of proclaiming the gospel to "Germanic non-Christians" and the Pope had to do it his way. He sent monks from his monastery, St. Andrews in Rome, as missionaries to England, in order to bring them into the fold of Christ and his Church. The Pope, who was farther away, saw the potentials and the bishops, who were rather close, did not.

Through his contacts Pope Gregory knew of the interest of the English to become Christian as he wrote in a letter: "News has reached us that the nation of the Angli greatly desires to be converted to the faith, but that the bishops in their vicinity pay no heed (to their pious wish) and refuse to second it by sending preachers." Theologically, the mission was well prepared when the forty monks under the guidance of St. Augustine set out from Rome in 596. Gregory the Great was the first Pope who turned to the Germanic populations. He also had a genuine sense of accommodation: Accepting pagan customs and filling them with a new Christian content.

St. Augustine of Canterbury

Mission to England

Through familiar outward celebrations people were enabled to find the inner joy in Jesus Christ. Spirit filled transformation instead of external indoctrination worked marvels for the mission. St. Augustine of Canterbury (he died in 605) and his companions first approached King St. Ethelbert of Kent and on Christmas the following year he was permitted to baptize him along with 10,000 people. The success was overwhelming and soon included Wessex and Northumberland. We appreciate that the contemplative spirit of the monks enabled them to bring the gospel to these people in a way that was not an imposition, but a gift which they could make their own.

At the same time the monks were able to continue their observance and to make people interested in the religious life to become contemplative men or women. Monasteries became a vital part of the Church. People naturally accepted this combination of the cloister as the focus of religious identity and practice and their own participation in the sacramental and devotional life of the Church. The monastic movement was part of Christianity. This success also gave evidence that Christianity revived after the decline of the Roman Empire and monasticism proved its strength because it stands for the eternal in the midst of historical developments and changes.

The gentle presence of the Benedictine Rule fostered the establishment of many monasteries as religious, cultural and educational centers throughout the kingdoms of England. We admire the men and women who felt the call from God to the religious life and filled a nation with the fervent spirit and the love of God. In prayer their souls surged towards heaven and they were happy to include everybody in this upward movement. A new era of history had begun and monasticism was privileged to be at the head of this movement. We also respect King Ethelbert of Kent and many other political leaders who favored the cause of religion in the realm and its close connection with monasticism.

Many monasteries had been built in Ireland earlier and about the time when England rejoined the Church the Irish monks were willing to make further sacrifices for Christ. One such sacrifice was to leave home and to offer this up to the Lord in gratitude for his love and also as a penance. Some went to another place in Ireland and finally some went abroad. Often they made such moves in a group under a leader.

St. Columbanus
Counseled by God

One of these leaders was St. Columbanus. He was born in 543 in West Leinster, Ireland, and died in Bobbio, Italy on November 21st, 615. This means that he was born during the life-time of St. Benedict. From childhood on Columbanus was well instructed in the faith and cherished a great love of God in his heart. He was very handsome and girls were easily captivated by his beauty. This caused temptation for him, which he had to conquer, if he wanted to follow his true vocation. An older woman advised him to flee from all occasion of sin and to retire from the world. He followed her advice and went first to the monastery of Bangor on the coast of Down, embracing the monastic state.

When he was about forty he believed that the voice of God counseled him to preach the gospel in foreign lands. Again we have to reckon with a private revelation. With twelve companions he first sailed to the coast of Scotland, moved on to England and arrived in France in 585 and they settled in the Vosgese Mountains.

Old habits are hard to break and family and home form part of the identity of a person, whether he follows in the footsteps of his parents or whether he enters a monastery.

When the monks came from Ireland and settled in this foreign country, they brought their spiritual and social background along and transported it into this region. Even when they kept to themselves as contemplatives, their very presence made them known and they witnessed to their way of life, their prayer and liturgy, by erecting a house for worship, into which people could come, if they wanted to. If only they kept the doors open and let people experience for themselves the divine office and other celebrations, then they were already active as missionaries. To witness to their faith was part of who they were as believers, who knew of God's all-embracing love of mankind and the need to have this message of salvation brought to everybody. Even though France had been Catholic for centuries, there were ups and downs in the strength of the faith of the people and those who led them, so that the monks could consider themselves to be missionaries as well. The people there were struck by their modesty, patience and humility. Also the king of Burgundy, Gontram, was impressed by their faith. He was gracious to them and granted them the half-ruined Roman fortress of Annegray. Catholicism in the region had come to an ebb through the invasion of barbarians, the negligence of the local clergy and the accompanying indifference, vices and impiety. The saint and his companions had set out into an unknown future, but the inspiration proved to be true.

Being uprooted from their faith through the historical circumstances and their own weakness, the people experienced a hunger for religion when these men were in their midst. Columbanus' sanctity and the miracles he worked drew crowds to his monastery. He himself loved solitude and often withdrew further into the forest with just one companion as his messenger to spend more time in prayer. Many disciples wanted to join him and his companions and they got a second building, (a castle) at Luxeuil and they started a third foundation deeper in the forest at Fontaines in 590. Later from Fontaines alone further 50 monasteries were founded. We can see the sudden attraction religious life had. St. Columbanus also started the observance of perpetual praise of God; several choirs alternated in constant prayer and praise of God in the Church, today we would call it 24/7. He also wrote a rather strict rule for his communities.

The Frankish bishops became angry at him (and possibly also a little jealous) and because they held absolute authority, they assembled to judge him. The cause of dispute had to do with the difference of the date of Easter. The saint didn't appear, lest "he might contend in words". His call from God was more important to him than to win or lose an argument. Even the royal household was set against him through Brunehault, who was in charge. He and his Irish companions were taken prisoner, but Providence helped them to escape and to be on their way, first to Metz, where they found hospitality.

They then moved on to Mainz and from there to the Lake of Zurich. Persecution wasn't lacking there either and they continued on to Bobbio, in Italy, between Milan and Genoa in 612. Here Columbanus felt obligated to oppose the Arians and built up the faith of the people through his preaching. On a visit to Rome he had received relics from his Holiness, Pope Gregory, to be used in his new foundation at Bobbio.

Here we can also witness the Holy Father's support of monasticism. For some time he was able to live more in retirement and prepare for death. The mysterious presence of God's grace in his heart had brought about his closeness to heaven and a mission, which had impacted many people and engendered a tradition for religious and generations of the faithful grateful for his sanctity. The influence he had had in Gaul remained. He had given the example for this kind of missionary journey for the sake of Christ, leading monks from Ireland to the Continent. He had also endeavored to be in good standing with the ruling nobility of the country. He had suffered disappointment and even failure, but his intention was pure.

If the ruling class is faithful to the gospel, then the people will be strengthened in their faith and exercise their religion willingly and enthusiastically. Disappointments can be overcome and forgotten and the basic intention can resurface and prevail. From his youth he had sought the life of a monk and the regulations found in a monastery were second nature to him. Consequently his rule presupposes a suitable organization and doesn't see it necessary to establish it. From this angle some questions of organization have to be settled along with it.

At the beginning of the sixth century what we know as Antiquity had come to an end. The Roman Empire had been a very impressive enterprise and had shown great strength as a political power. At its appearance, Christianity seemed insignificant in comparison and the persecutions were often meant to eradicate this intrusion into the sphere of power. The many martyrs for the faith made it glaringly obvious that they were inspired by the Resurrection of Jesus Christ. The death of the martyrs became the birth of Christianity. Monasticism lives from the same mystery and inspiration. It originates in the secret call from God in the heart of the monk (or nun), whether he lives as a hermit or in a community.

The witness of the martyrs was so convincing because of this inner strength they had and the witness of the contemplatives exercised the same convincing power as it unfolded. By the sixth century Monasticism had become an integral part of the life of the Church. It had become indispensable. Society and the Church needed this intense focus of Christian identity, so easily lost in the shuffle of life. In Europe the spread of Christianity, its building of tradition and customs went hand in hand with the establishment of monasteries. As we can be astounded about the growth of Christianity in the midst of persecutions, so we can also be astounded about the rapid growth of Monasticism in an environment, in which paganism persisted along with Christianity.

This struggle is part of human nature. The contemplatives at the beginning of the Middle Ages paved the way for the success of Christianity in this struggle. Believers are obligated to recognize this persistent and ever-present struggle and to foster the victory of God's love. The monks let this victory happen. They also show that God's love is above nature and not polemical against anything God has created. They deflect the opposition they experience, because of the security they have found in Jesus.

Europe had become very fertile ground and many monasteries could be built, because of this enthusiasm and attraction. Even when monks were martyred by people opposed to them, like St. Kilian, Kolonat and Totnan in Wuerzburg in 689, the attraction of monastic life only increased. The spirituality of the monks also increased the loyalty of the countries to Rome. In England 33 kings and queens ended their life in a monastery and 23 kings and 60 queens are venerated as saints.

This cooperation between the nobility and the monasteries greatly contributed to the stability of the Church and of Society. There was a vibrant and steady growth in the seventh century and the generations found their home in this Christian culture, which included the monks and nuns. Some peace radiated from these many centers of the Spirit and many monks could let their lives speak for the eternal truth. In their soul our mere human existence gained a new quality, unknown before.

Given their training in the monastery, their focus on contemplation and their obedience to the rule made them first of all monks, people being in touch with their heavenly homeland already in their hearts. This could remain so for them for the rest of their lives. Nothing more was needed to achieve their salvation in Jesus Christ.

Bede

Experienced the Gentle Strength of God's Grace

The illustrious Venerable Bede may serve as an example of such a life in the monastery. He was born in the territory of Wearmouth in North-umberland, not far from the Monastery of St. Peter and St. Paul, in 672 and died in this monastery in 735. For the sake of education he was brought to the monastery already at age seven. The Rule of St. Benedict permitted the entrance of a boy or the 'gift of a boy'. It proved of high spiritual value as the saint exemplified.

At the time Latin was still a living tongue and for him it meant that he spoke it like his mother tongue. He spent his whole life in the monastery: Praying and singing in the Church, studying Sacred Scripture and the Rule, following the discipline and when he was advanced enough to teach and to write. At age thirty he was ordained to the priesthood. He said this about Scripture: "Holy Scripture is above all other books not only by its authority because it is Divine or by its utility because it leads to eternal life, but also by its antiquity and by its literary form." His meditation on God's grace made him realize its inner strength, its dynamic and its power to penetrate a given culture. In this awareness he wrote his work: "Ecclesiastical History of the English People". The joy of salvation reaches us the more we are in agree-ment with God's design of history. Human beings are the way they are in God's plan and we perceive their core, when we look at them from God's point of view. Through prayer he strengthened and gained his moderation, gentleness and breadth of view and he is considered the most learned man of his time.

He didn't force his view on history, but he was so convincing because he described and in spirit participated in the persuasive power of God's Revelation at work in history. At the time of his death he was able to sit in view of the Blessed Sacrament and to let God take hold of him at his departure from this world to the next. He passed away without a death struggle because of his conviction of eternal salvation. Without this conviction the contemplative would easily drift into some form of activism and lack the composure of faith. The activity we find in other Benedictine monks and missionaries is sustained by their contemplation and they could be so decisive through their prayer.

St. Willibrord and St. Boniface
Displayed the Courage of Missionaries

It is in this vein that we appreciate the Benedictine missionaries who came from England to the Continent. St. Willibrord was born a little earlier than the Venerable Bede in 658 also in Northumberland and he died four years after him in 739 in Echternach in Luxemburg. He took his early studies at the Abbey of Ripon near York and entered the order. At age twenty he went to the Abbey Rathmelsgi in Ireland for twelve years. Here he learned about the sacrifice of going abroad for Christ. Frisia, Northern Germany, was still pagan territory and the Frisian people were hostile to this "Roman" influence. Those who were willing to bring the gospel into their midst also had to be willing to take their life into their hands. The missionary could easily become a martyr.

The Frisians were a war-like people and wouldn't give up on their paganism without a fight. We assume that the Benedictines knew this connection between the intimacy with the Crucified Lord and the new life he brings and the courage he may require of giving their lives for him. In 690 he and eleven companions set out for the Mission in Frisia. They had obtained authorization from the Pope and received support from the king of the Franks, Pepin (the Middle) and Willibrord was consecrated bishop and in 695 he founded a monastery in Utrecht and three years after that one in Echternach, Luxemburg. His building of monasteries also emphasizes the combination between contemplation and the spread of the gospel. The monastery could also serve as a safe refuge, unless the enemy opposing was too strong. The leader of the Frisians, Radbod, fought against the missionaries in 716, killed many of them and destroyed most of the Churches. Willibrord survived and Radbod died in 719. Willibrord and the remaining missionaries were able to continue their work and to repair the damages. He frequently retired to the Abbey of Echternach and died there on Nov. 7th, 739. He was immediately honored as a saint and processions (The Dancing Processions) in veneration are still held there to this day.

The second even more influential Benedictine missionary was St. Boniface. He was born about the year 675 or as late as 680 of a noble family in England and was martyred on June 5th 755 in Dokkum, Frisia. Missionary monks visiting his home inspired his religious vocation. After overcoming the opposition of his father he entered a Benedictine Monastery where for seven years he received his basic education. He joined the monks in a monastery close to Winchester and because of his academic excellence he was put in charge of the school and ordained at age thirty.

He had also great success as a preacher. At the age of thirty six or forty one (in the year 716) he pursued his goal as a missionary of his kindred, the Old Saxons in Germany. He set out for Friesland for his mission. He had to return to England for a while because of political disturbances in Frisia. Although he became famous as a missionary of Germany and received the title of Apostle of Germany we have to pause and appreciate his many years in the monastery. During these years his spiritual identity was formed and contemplation was at the root of his work. Missionary activity itself may even have been a way for him to worship God and to draw closer to him. The point was not so much that he knew of some people, who should receive the faith, but that God was paving his own way to sanctity through these people, who became his brothers and sisters in Christ. This mysticism is the code lodged in his heart through which he became spiritually so powerful and effective. After the death of Radbod in 719 he and Willibrord were successful and thousands accepted the faith. Those converts, who believed that God was calling them to the religious life, would henceforth live under the Rule of St. Benedict. In 722 he was consecrated regional bishop and more monks and nuns came to him from England to help him.

He was now in an even better position to built churches, chapels and monasteries. Also the nobility became more interested in the religious life. In 739 Rome named him legate of the Holy See for the Frankish realm and the rule of St. Benedict became the norm for religious. In 747 Carloman, the brother of the ruler, Pepin, resigned his share of the government to Pepin. Carloman became a monk, showing the appeal monasticism had. The see of Cologne became vacant and it would have been normal that Boniface had filled this position, because of his extraordinary accomplishments and service, but the bishops prevented this and he had to settle to become the Archbishop of Mainz and Primate of the realm.

Boniface had adopted a different approach for his mission. The Irish had worked on an individual level, which didn't include the organization of the Church. Boniface went several times to Rome and obtained letters of recommendation from the Pope, which certified him as organizer and bishop and later legate for Bavaria. He provided an effective organization for the Church. At the same time he reconnected the Church of the Frankish Empire with Rome. The local bishops had become rather lax in their obedience to Rome and had developed their own style more or less independent from the Holy See. If this happens for a longer time, then a schism or some fragmentation can easily follow. Modern Bishop Conferences can do something similar.

They develop a policy, which may not be according to the wishes of the Holy Father and they may even try to impose this upon the Holy See. Too much independence leads to alienation from the true Spirit of Catholicity. In his time St. Boniface prevented this. Through his efforts he created the idea of a unified Church in Europe and even the idea of modern Europe is derived from his insight. His understanding was based on his prayerful consideration that God wants unity and cooperation under the spiritual guidance of the Holy Father. When parts of the Church neglect or reject this sense of unity with Rome, then we lose more than we gain. The saint was extraordinary in his sense for this God-given unity of the Church and of the Empire. He was marginalized also by the other German bishops, because they were interested in their own agenda and also because he was a foreigner, from England. In his later years St. Boniface had suffered a lot of disappointment and he withdrew more and stressed his need for contemplation. He was able to go on retreats to the monastery of Fulda, which had been his favorite foundation.

This Abbey had grown out of the need for contemplation. A boy, Sturmi, had been entrusted by his parents to the care of St. Boniface, who brought him up in his abbey, Fritzlar. Later Sturmi was ordained, worked as a missionary, but felt drawn to meditation and Boniface allowed him to live as a hermit for a while. The spot Sturmi had chosen was unsafe because of marauding Saxons and they had to find a place, in which a steady prayer-life was not endangered. This was Fulda and Boniface had appointed Sturmi as its first abbot, who introduced the Benedictine Rule and developed the abbey into a prosperous center of learning, culture and mission with prayer as the core for its existence.

In 751 St. Boniface wrote in a letter to Pope Zachary: "Far removed from all the busy cities of the world in the solitude of a huge forest we have found a spot most suitable for our missionary activity, because despite its isolation the natives can be reached from there. In this place we have built a monastery and settled monks there, who are living according to the rule of our Holy Father Benedict. Through my persistent efforts I have obtained the land from pious and God-fearing men, especially from the former duke of the Franks, Carloman and dedicated it to the honor of our Most Holy Redeemer. I intend it to be of service to the people roundabout as long as I live and am mentally capable."

Besides receiving the sanction from the Pope for his foundation, St. Boniface also secured absolute autonomy for the new abbey by placing it immediately under the Holy See, and removing it from all Episcopal Jurisdiction. This move was in line with the general thrust of Benedictine abbeys, but in this case it has further historical implications. In a different way it was located in "the desert" in agreement with the ascetical tradition of the past and besides this is included a pastoral point of view, namely to be of service to the people roundabout. Besides, this new monastery enjoyed the protection of the Frankish ruler and his subjects in the region.

We can witness how the saint had managed the complexity of new historical circumstances.

He paid attention to the wishes of the papacy, the interest of the Emperor and his representatives, the local conditions of the people living there, the need for independence of the settlement, the control the bishops would like to exercise and his own desire to make the new establishment a place of prayer, learning and culture. It takes extraordinary spiritual gifts for a person to keep all these perspectives. The saint was able to accomplish this and we can admire his genius. Besides their call to prayer the monks had discovered the will of God in this broad historical and cultural mandate and this and other monasteries were of service to the Church, to society and to the Empire. (If besides, they also learned to brew beer and sell it to the natives, the pilgrimages to the monasteries became even more popular. Their presence made the political order more reliable, because the people became more obedient to God and the Emperor through the teaching and the example given by the monks.

In his later years it was a great consolation for the disappointed saint to take refuge in his beloved monastery and to entrust himself even more to God's providence. He was able to let go of administrative opportunities, because he wanted to do God's will and not his own. He didn't participate any more in high politics, focused on the spiritual and even resigned as Archbishop of Mainz in 754. In his heart he consented to one more calling from the Lord. After much prayer and reflection he made one more missionary journey to Frisia and again drew a large number of people to receive Confirmation from him, but a group of hostile opponents closed in on him and killed him along with 52 companions on June 5th, 755. His martyrdom reminded the people of the Empire that a great man had died. He was buried in Fulda.

We can be sure that he totally entrusted himself to the unfathomable love of God, always working in mysterious ways and the contemplative is most intimately involved in this mystery. In his own way St. Boniface had made a tremendous contribution to the future history of the Empire especially of the Franks and later of Europe, in which religion and the state supported and strengthened each other. His contribution was especially favorable for Charlemagne, the great leader of the early Middle Ages. On the historical level Charlemagne was able to bring about the unity St. Boniface had envisioned and to stress the conviction of the people of this era that the state and the religion have to cooperate, if they want to live in the peace intended by our Lord. For people beset by our modern fragmentation it is difficult to even imagine the sense for unity experienced by the contemporaries of St. Boniface and Charlemagne.

Charlemagne
Unified the Christian Realm

Charlemagne was born in 742 and anointed for the kingship in 754 at the age of twelve along with his father, Pepin, and his brother Carloman at St. Denis on the Seine by Pope Stephen III. The Pope had made this journey and administered the anointing, because of the protection the

Holy See needed. Charles accompanied his father on several military campaigns and proved himself through his extraordinary physical strength, his military virtues and his intense nationalism. He actually became a popular hero of the Franks. Charles' father, Pepin, died in 768 and his younger brother, Carloman, died in 771 as well, which left Charles as sole ruler of the realm and Protector of the Holy See, "Patricius Romanus". Subsequently he was able to consolidate Western Christendom under his protection. He was crowned as Emperor in Rome in 800 and died at Aachen on January 28th, 814. He believed that God had called him to this rule and the concerns of religion were important for him. He sought to elevate and perfect the clergy, both monastic and secular. Tithes were strictly enforced for the support of the clergy and the dignity of public worship and Ecclesiastical immunities were recognized and protected. He did much to improve Church music and founded schools of church-song at Metz, Soissons, and St. Gall.

He actually had a strong personal interest in Church music and in particular the Gregorian Chant. Through it he felt like the monks, elevated to the glory of heaven and already on earth participating in the eternal praise of God. Music has always had this impact on the soul of the believer and deserves a special place in the description of the life of the monks and nuns. All ephemeral concerns can be left behind in song and can be entrusted to the Greatness of God, who will ultimately override everything which hinders us from full participation in his glory and power. Charlemagne made an exceptional contribution to cause liturgical music to flourish in his own time throughout his vast domain and even laid the foundations for musical culture still potent today. It is most appropriate therefore to respect his faith and his love of God, which made him a brother to all the contemplatives and made him share their sentiments of drawing close to heaven. His consolidation of the realm was filled with an inner dynamic, which prevailed through the centuries up to the present.

His personal culture bears witness to this also. He spoke Latin well, and loved to listen to the reading of the works of St. Augustine, especially "The City of God". He understood Greek, but was obviously most devoted to his Frankish (Old German) mother tongue. When he died at age seventy two, he had reigned for forty seven years, almost half a century. The stability of the realm reflected the eternal kingdom of heaven. He always had a theologian, for example, Alcuin, as an advisor at his court. He was canonized in 1165 by the anti-pope Paschal III, but his cultus was permitted at Aachen.

The monks had assumed to provide a link between politics and religion and Charlemagne was involved to strengthen this link. For example Benedict of Aniane (745–821), a Goth, the son of the count of Maguelone in Southern France, educated at the court of Charlemagne's father took part in Charles' Italian campaign in 773. After his military service he entered religious life in the monastery of Saint-Seine, to practice contemplation according to the rule of St. Benedict. Later he was enabled to oversee a model-abbey for other monasteries in the empire and to collect several rules, which could be used as guidelines for them. The freedom in regard to several rules also proves that the monks were not forced into a straight-jacket, but could combine various insights to fit different conditions, as long as the spirit of St. Benedict prevailed.

A similar effort had been undertaken by Bishop Chrodegang of Metz, who called priests to monastic life along with their ministry in the parishes, especially his Cathedral.

Monasticism served the spiritual and historical stability and unity of the country. The Frankish Empire was very much built on these two pillars of Church and State and for the people of that time it wasn't a question of any pre-dominance of one over the other, but of being firm in the conviction that God had joined them together and we as mere human beings shouldn't separate what God had joined. From this point of view our modern separation of Church and State means that we have fallen away from God's purpose for human history and we cannot even fathom the price we pay for this separation. Even the monastery in the remote country site was a center of religious life and a center of the civil community. Worship brought people together and provided the opportunity to discuss questions involving the society, which in turn was well structured and secured because of the people's adherents to the requirements of faith. This included the education of children.

Already in 789 Charlemagne had stipulated the establishment of schools in all monasteries. For many generations to come boys were being trained in them and absorbed the Christian meaning of life. Later nuns were responsible for the education of girls, which became a wonderful source of piety and devotion. Education was connected with scientific research. The monks were installed as teachers and protectors of tradition and many were employed to write manuscripts and to develop and maintain the libraries. These tasks given to the monasteries increased the prestige and the impact of Christianity tremendously. The king or the Emperor was able to make certain demands of the monks, which helped him in his cultural and political goals.

Charlemagne was very clever, when he began to establish monasteries in not yet civilized territories and entrusted them with tasks of colonization. What had been considered a withdrawal into the desert was changed and through the work of the monks the monastery and its environs became a flourishing garden. These new foundations were established throughout the Empire and they received the title of "royal monasteries". They were also used as strongholds for the organization of the realm. Charlemagne assumed the authority to choose men of his own liking as abbots in them. They in turn used their position to also strengthen the political establishment. Since both, empire and monastery came from God they were happy to live by the cooperation between the two.

Rabanus Maurus
Leader, Teacher

One of the most prominent monks dating back to the reign of Charlemagne was Rabanus Maurus. He was born about 780 in Mainz on the river Rhine and given the name Rabanus by his parents. In Middle-Age German the word Raban means crow, a black bird. We might very well assume that he was born with black hair and soon developed a darker tan which would not be unusual for children in the Rhine valley with ancestry dating back to the Romans occupying the territory in Antiquity. Over eleven years later, when he was the beloved student of the theologian Alkuin (who had been at the court of Charlemagne) did he receive the name Maurus, which means African, in remembrance of St. Benedict's beloved student with the same name.

The name Maurus led a sculptor of the twelfth century to depict Rabanus Maurus as a black bishop. It seems that the sculptor didn't see any problem with this, but historically it is most unlikely. In any case, Rabanus Maurus was the child of a noble family in Mainz and grew up with the necessary early instruction in the faith. When he was eight years old his parents brought him to the Monastery of Fulda so that he would grow up henceforth as a student in their school. As a gift for his entry they donated a house to the monastery. This substantial donation also explains that the parents intended him as a gift to God, which he would form in accordance with his divine plan for him.

The Benedictine Rule allowed such an early entrance of a boy. The parents wrote and signed a petition for their son and later as a grown-up novice he would ratify their intention in a solemn vow. He described such a procedure later in his book entitled: *The gift of a boy.* Fulda was at that time one of the most important educational institutions and recognized by the Emperor Charlemagne himself. The Emperor wished to have monks, who were pious in their heart, well educated, morally upright and blameless in their behavior. They should also be trained to be good speakers. Rabanus was very much endowed and proved to be qualified to match these ideals and expectations. He made such rapid progress that only three years after his entry, at age eleven, he had matured enough to become a special student of the Theologian Alkuin in Tours. Alkuin as mentioned had been at the court of Charlemagne and also had been the head of the Cathedral School of York; Alkuin soon discovered Rabanus' talent and favored his education. Given the student's complexion and his name he enjoyed his nickname: *The little crow.*

As a teenager from age fifteen to eighteen, i.e. from 795–798, Rabanus had already achieved some recognition for his ability in debate and found mention in a poem of Theodulf of Orleans, who poked fun at young students showing off their play with words. Rabanus returned to Fulda in 801 for the ordination to the Diaconate, for which occasion his parents made a further generous donation to the monastery. He returned to his teacher, Alkuin in the monastery school in Tours and in due course received his liberal arts degree. Alkuin passed away in 804 and Rabanus came back to Fulda. At age 24 he was sufficiently equipped to be headmaster of the school for the younger students. It was most unfortunate that in the years 807 and 810 an epidemic hit the school and a number of the younger students died from it and others left. He even received some blame for this misfortune and his abbot grew angry with him. The abbot confiscated some of his books, arguing that he wasn't permitted to own private property. The abbot put his building projects above the needs of the community and the monks, including Rabanus suffered from it. Rabanus dealt with this stress in his own way by writing a book: *In Honor of the Holy Cross.* He suffered under the willfulness of his abbot and had to find a theological solution for this impasse, which would also benefit his readers.

Many years later when he was an abbot a monk came to him with the complaint that he didn't have anyone with whom he could discuss theological questions. Rabanus referred to his earlier experience and told him: "When I was in a similar situation in which you find yourself right now, I waited for God's inspiration and wrote the book in praise of the Holy Cross. You may want to do the same. Be diligent in reading and write something useful." His recommendation and his reaction to his own stressful situation also show his secret code of the monk. Instead of lashing out, he was patient in his endurance and trusted that God would give an answer at his choosing, in agreement with the Cross of our Lord and Savior, Jesus Christ. Rabanus had to exercise his endurance for about seven years when the Emperor, the son of Charlemagne, Louis the Pius, dismissed the abbot after listening to complaints from the monks of the Abbey. The successor of the abbot was a man of reconciliation and promoted Rabanus, so that he also taught the older students and developed a comprehensive curriculum for the education of the clergy.

His mentioned recommendation to the monk to read, to wait for God's inspiration and then to write something useful, he himself took very much to heart. The monks trusted him on account of his immense knowledge and his ability to hand this on to others. The new abbot, Eigil, who held this office from 818–822 encouraged Rabanus in his educational efforts, knowing that this would increase the prestige of the school. When Rabanus first taught the novices also older monks were eager to join his classes and to learn from him. Other monasteries sent monks to him to complete their training. These became devoted disciples and remained in contact with him also after they left Fulda and returned to their houses. Their continued correspondence with him displays not only their appreciation, but also his style of teaching in the form of dialogue, which they were interested to continue later on.

His writings during this period originated from his interaction with his students. They complained to him for example that they couldn't find a thorough commentary on the gospel of St. Matthew as they had them about the other Evangelists. Rabanus took their suggestion seriously and wrote a commentary about it which they then could use for their instruction and meditation. The date of Easter had been an uncertainty and Rabanus set to work to develop a scientific guideline to settle this question. He chose the style of dialogue for his work, which also shows his interest to talk with others about the things he wanted to solve. These years of teaching and interacting with students were very happy and fruitful ones for him.

Abbot Eigil died on June 15th, 822 and later in that year Rabanus was chosen to succeed him and he held this position of abbot for twenty years, until 842. We can still be amazed that at age forty two he had lived a monastic life for already thirty four years. He had been a monk at heart since his childhood and was able to continue to project this focus of prayer and contemplation as leader of his community for the following twenty years. It is equally important to stress that it is essential for the monk to be in the presence of God through praise and worship and to consider his own life as a preparation for eternity. Getting along with his brothers is very much desirable, since it contributes to this essential aspect of his existence. If this code for the essentials is being neglected or lost sight of, then we get easily side-tracked into something of a mere business nature.

Worship, prayer, spiritual formation, the feast days of the Church and the celebration of the Sacraments are always most important for the monks, but the abbot also had to have an eye for the administration, which in the ninth century included the political situation. The abbot is interested to be responsible for the institution he is guiding, but this includes that his inner disposition gains an even wider application and doesn't diminish in the process. At the time when he became abbot there were over six hundred monks connected with the abbey and 134 were living there. The abbey was an enterprise with substantial properties in the wider area, about 2,800 farms and close to 40,000 acres of land, partially rented out to farmers depending on the monastery. Besides this they owned 28 vineyards. Rabanus also felt responsible for the people connected with the monastery and the salvation of their souls.

Farmers using monastery land had to pay a certain users' fee. They lived in villages and Rabanus saw to it that these villages had a church and a priest who provided the sacramental services for them. He built close to thirty churches in various villages during his time as abbot. Quite often people were in dire need and he had to help them for their survival. He also asked the Emperor to reduce the taxes imposed on the monastery, so that they could buy enough clothing for the monks. Besides these responsibilities he retained a great interest in learning and the leadership of his school. Students from other parts of the Empire liked to come and study there. He also supported the writing of manuscripts and the acquisition of many books for the library of the school.

As Abbot of an important monastery of the Empire he had quite a few dealings with the Emperor himself, who was Louis the Pius. A couple of times the sons of Louis rebelled against him and at one time even managed to depose him and declare that he was incapable to govern. Throughout Rabanus remained loyal to Louis even though he could have gained advantages through dealings with his sons, but his loyalty was more important for him. Louis expressed his gratitude by calling him faithful. Rabanus recommended to Louis to seek peace with his sons, although they had opposed him. The way he was used to foster peace in his monastery and with the many people being in contact with it, so he also was able to foster peace in the Empire. As abbot of this prominent monastery he left a legacy behind and his devoted disciple Hatto took over.

Rabanus Maurus was a man of peace and reconciliation, but his disposition was being put hard to the test. He had to pay a heavy price for his loyalty and his commitment to the truth. The political situation of the Empire was unstable. The Emperor Louis the Pius had two sons from his first marriage and one from his second. He wanted to treat all three alike and the two older ones resented this. Louis the Pius died in 840 and he had designated his oldest son, Lothar I to succeed him. The two younger ones were opposed to this choice and beat him in the battle of Fontenoy in 841 and Lothar was forced to compromise. Rabanus Maurus remained loyal to Lothar, although his monastery was no longer located in Lothar's territory. Rabanus even followed Lothar to Reims for a while and he abdicated as abbot, because the monks of the monastery were politically divided.

Some were on the side of Lothar, although he was no longer the ruler, and others were on the side of the new ruler, Louis, the German, in whose territory the monastery was now located. Documents from this period were dated either under the rule of Lothar or under the rule of Louis. Rabanus used Anno Domini, for example 841 (DCCCXLI). Theologically he may want to show that Jesus Christ is above political divisions. However, there is sufficient reason to believe that some monks opposed him vehemently, which would be the reason for him to get away for a while.

Some historians believe that there was an attempt on his life. It could be possible that some monks tried to poison him, which then would change the reason to get away for a while to an actual escape. The modern psychologist, C.G. Jung (1875–1961) gave his own explanation for the possible attempt on Rabanus' life. He believed that Rabanus was spiritually so high above most of his contemporaries that some didn't understand him and resented him to be among the living. C.G. Jung's explanation is highly respectful of Rabanus and fitting for the psychological setting of the conflict. It doesn't seem possible to determine whether there was an actual attempt on Rabanus' life and we may have to wait for Dan Brown to unravel this mystery. After his extended visit with the Emperor Lothar in Reims Rabanus retired for five years (842–847) to a location close to the monastery, where he could pray and study in private. At first he complained about serious health problems, which could give some reason to think that these were induced.

These historical and personal problems caused him great anxiety as he described it in a letter to Bishop Humbert of Wuerzburg. He also entrusted his feelings to the Emperor and told him that he hardly recognized himself in the midst of this turmoil. He underscored the description of his plight with several quotations from the Bible. We may also recognize the secret code of the monk being at work at this juncture. He was able to withdraw into solitude and to let the eternal truth of the gospel prevail. In his faith and love of God he was able to decipher the code of his circumstances. He didn't feel it necessary to settle accounts with those who didn't like him, but he was able to live on a relationship with God alone. He became a hermit, along with his studies and his correspondence. We may further believe that God imposed this situation on him, and that he felt this imposition deeply, so that he could speak of a truly common danger (*verum etiam communis periculi*) and his very heavy anxiety (*anxietate pregravatus sum*). We can truly admire his sensitivity, the unfathomable depth of his spirit and his honesty.

Amidst his outer and inner turmoil he retained an inner calm in which he could continue on. His tested contemplation paid off, even though the test could have lasted till the end. His health returned and he was able to devote himself to his studies. His former student and friend, Servatus Lupus, wrote to him: "I have heard that you have given up the burden of your office and are concentrating on things divine and that you have left these sweat-filled (sudoris plenam) worries to your friend Hatto". Even the Emperor wrote to him in similar terms: "We are happy to hear about your new residence, far away from all discontent." We assume that Rabanus agreed with these sentiments, although his response-letters no longer exist.

The love of God made it possible for him to experience the light at the end of the tunnel. He wrote books for the Emperor, for his friends, for the Archbishop of Mainz and even for Louis, the German, who had usurped the power of Lothar. This showed his congenial spirit. He didn't hold a grudge. The well-known song: Come Holy Spirit (Veni Creator Spiritus) is ascribed to him and invites us to participate in the grandeur of his spirit leading us to the height of the Kingdom of heaven. In 847 he was called away from his solitude to become the Archbishop of Mainz and up to the time of his death in 856 he had to apply his spirituality in this arena of history. Most of his life he had been a monk and was able to prove his connection with the Lord also in these remaining nine years as Archbishop.

Moslem Impact

Expansion through Extraordinary Military Power

In our observations of Monasticism we have to include the sudden explosion and expansion of the Moslem religion. After the death of Mohammed (570–632) it appeared that this religion would collapse, but his first successor Caliph Abu Bekr united the divided tribes and the second Caliph Omar (634–644) initiated a phenomenal campaign of conquest: Damascus in 635, Jerusalem in 637, Persia in 640–644 while his commander Amru had conquered Egypt in 639–641, which was soon followed by the rest of North Africa and the Southern part of Spain. The Byzantine Empire was not able to withstand them and was happy to defend Constantinople, which also prevented the Moslems from attacking Europe directly. In 732 they suffered a decisive defeat through Charles Martell (714–741), leader of the Franks. The fact that the papacy had turned to the Frankish Empire for its protection was a matter of survival. The conquests of the Moslems continued towards the East: Afghanistan, Pakistan, India and so on. Once nations have been incorporated they tend to stay with this religion. They also continued their attacks on Italy in the following century and destroyed Monte Cassino in 883/884 at a time when the Frankish Empire had lost some of its strength. Some monks were killed and others fled, but they were able to return some time later. The shock was similar to September 11, 2001. In the countries the Moslems had taken Catholicism and monasticism came to an end and many people died for their faith. The people in the Middle Ages strongly believed in their right to defend their Christian territory, because God had brought this Christianity about.

The monks and nuns had to mourn the victims of violence and war and pray to God for the protection of the Christian realm. The threat of our very spiritual identity always contains the danger of moral depravity, but calls from God's point of view to an even closer union with him and his divine will. Especially the tenth century showed this depravity when for example the seventeen year old playboy, John XII (955–964), was elected Pope by the Roman nobility.

However, monks and nuns took the threat to our identity to heart. They felt that the bond with God had been neglected. The life-blood of the contemplatives originates in heaven, although God's grace adjusts itself to all kind of human experiences. The job at hand may have to be done, but it shouldn't sever the contact of the monk with the heavenly realities prevailing over him. In his heart the monk has to know that he belongs to these heavenly realities, and that the earthly sphere is only of an ephemeral nature. These mysterious realities will assert themselves and the renewal of monasticism comes about when they do. They use sensitive, saintly and single-minded human beings to bring such a renewal about.

St. Dunstan, St. Ethelwold, and St. Oswald
Renewal of the Church as Monks and Bishops

Although England wasn't threatened as much by the Moslems it brought about a wonderful renewal of monasticism. St. Dunstan, the son of a West-Saxon noble, was born at the beginning of the tenth century and died in Canterbury on May 19th, 988. He was a prominent Archbishop, but his life revolved around the monastic. In his youth he was committed to be educated by Irish monks and scholars, who often came to the abbey of Glastonbury. He acquired great learning, was a good artist and enjoyed playing the harp.

He received minor orders and was able to serve in the Church. His uncle was the Archbishop of Canterbury, who sent him to the court of the King, probably Wulfhelm. Great learning and skills can easily arouse envy and suspicion in those who don't have them. They have to express their envy and suspicion in an effective way, which will put the person in a bad light. In his case those who envied and suspected him accused him of studying pagan literature, using incantations and practicing magic. The king accepted the accusations and Dunstan had to leave the court. His enemies even attacked him and threw him into a cesspool. With the help of God he managed to get out and escape to Winchester.

We can imagine the experience to have been similar to the drowning-experience of St. John of the Cross. God's supernatural presence is felt by the one at the point of losing his life. In Winchester the bishop wanted him to become a monk. At first he hesitated, because he didn't know, whether he was called to a celibate life. Later he changed his mind and first became a hermit at Glastonbury, praying, studying, working and playing the harp in praise of God. He inherited a fortune and put it to good use for the revival of monasticism. He had become a person of influence and a new king, Edmund called him to his court in 940. Jealousy wasn't wanting and he had to leave again, but later the king was reconciled to him and made him abbot of Glastonbury. He rebuilt the abbey and guided the monks in the Benedictine tradition. He founded a school for boys, which became the most famous of its time in England.

In 946 King Edmund was assassinated, Edred became his successor and St. Dunstan was entrusted with much of the government of the realm. He unified the country also by reconciling the Danish half of the nation, spread regular observance in the abbeys, improved morals among the clergy and the laity and overcame paganism. In 955 Edred died and Edwig, the older son, came to the throne. He was dissolute and willful and didn't want to be corrected by St. Dunstan with the result that Dunstan had to flee for his life. He went to an abbey in Flanders, where he learnt even more about Benedictine observance. In 957 a revolt drove Edwig out of the country and his brother, Edgar, became king and called St. Dunstan back.

The saint could continue with his reforms of Church and State and peace reigned for sixteen years. But in 973 King Edgar gave way to the Reactionaries and they attacked the monks and took their possessions. In 978 King Edward was assassinated. The saint had to crown his successor Ethelred, warning him about the bad times ahead. The saint's influence was ended and he went into seclusion, spending most of the last ten years of his life in prayer. We have to respect his sense for the code of the monks: God's grace will prevail, even when we at times don't feel or perceive it. His power is mysterious and we may only have to cling to him in worship.

His education by monks and scholars, his years as a hermit, his sacrifices for the abbeys, his devotion to the rule and his seclusion at the end of his life make this point that heaven was not only his goal, but also the incentive for his earthly life. The glamorous positions he held in administration didn't distract him from this glory of the world beyond the grave. In the midst of a powerful earthly position he risked and endured exile rather than compromise the gospel. What was unseen was more important for him than what was seen and he had the strength and the sanctity to read appearances through this code, which is different from our mere perception.

St. Ethelwold was about equal in age with St. Dunstan and the two were ordained together and in 955 he became abbot in Abingdon in Berkshire. The Danes had made havoc of the abbeys and few monks were left. St. Ethelwold had to restore monasticism and studies, procured a master for Church music and through his efforts the abbey once again became a nursery for good monks. He continued his work when he became Bishop of Winchester in 963. Through the historical down-turn the canons regular had succumbed to a secular life-style and St. Ethelwold had to replace them with monks, but he gave those canons, who took the habit and submitted to the discipline, a second chance. He acted in the same way with the abbey and nunnery at Chertsey and the monastery in Cambridgeshire. The Abbey of Peterborough had been destroyed by the Danes in 870. This one also was rebuilt and Aldulf, chancellor of the King, became a monk and was chose its first abbot. St. Ethelwold was considered "the father of monks" on account of his humility and his great charity of heart. He is credited to have translated the Rule of St. Benedict into English. The love in his heart would also make the point that devotion and compunction are more a matter of our emotions than an ideal in our mind. The mind will follow, if the code in the heart is right.

The third prominent person in this reform was St. Oswald of Danish descent, a nephew of the Archbishop of Canterbury and ordained a priest of Winchester. He went to Fleury in France and became a Benedictine monk. He returned to England and lived for some years with his uncle, the Archbishop of York. St. Dunstan learnt about Oswald's great qualities and prevailed upon King Edgar to make him bishop of Worcester.

St. Dunstan consecrated Oswald in Worcester in 962. St. Oswald was very much in favor of the monastic reform and of the clergy, but he adopted a more lenient process in his own city. Instead of removing the somewhat lax clergy from their position, he built a second church next to theirs and installed Benedictine monks there. They drew most of the people to their church and seeing this, the lax priests decided to also embrace the monastic rule. (If you can't beat'em, join'em.) St. Oswald loved to celebrate the liturgy with his monks and during Lent he washed the feet of twelve poor people every day and afterwards fed them at his table. On one such occasion when he had washed their feet he passed away on February 29th, 992. (It was probably a leap year.)

Being in close touch with God's grace through their contemplation these three Monk-Bishops brought about a renewed spiritual rule of the "black monks" on the Island. In prayer and worship the truth of God's design dawns in the human soul. When this awareness occurs, human beings still have to entrust their efforts to God's greater glory, which always surpasses our imagination. As mere mortals we have a code of salvation and we do well, if we don't insist too much on our understanding of this code, but admit, that the greater portion is in God's hands. Contemplative monks are the first who are happy to admit this. That is why many of them could become saints. Branches of modern Psychology are reducing human reactions to mere "rational notions" and thereby no longer gain or give access to the secret so important for religion. The contemplatives of the Middle Ages were free from this restriction and were able to open the way to the greater freedom of the Spirit. They enjoyed a freedom, which we no longer have.

Otto the Great

Respected the Church as an Institution of God

In a historical perspective Otto the Great (936–973) is the leader of the tenth century, who renewed the stability and the security of the Empire. Invasions from the East, Slavs and Hungarians, created great anxiety and Otto achieved a decisive victory in 955 and could bring about renewal and peace. Like Charlemagne he perceived his position as given to him by God and he was responsible to Him in his efforts. In 962 he simply deposed the unworthy Pope John XII and Leo VIII was elected in his place. The papacy was taken away from the fighting factions of the Roman nobility and regained its universal importance. Otto believed in the dignity of the papacy and its institution by Jesus Christ. Without recognition of this dignity all levels of the Church will suffer from some form of debasement and the Emperor was instrumental in rejuvenating the sense for the Holy in the Church and consequently also in the monasteries. He chose Bishops as dukes and co-workers, because he believed in the unity of the secular and the spiritual. The state became a part in the enterprise of salvation. Monasteries, which had lost some of their influence and mission to secular clergy and the cities, regained their prestige through the production of Christian art and higher culture. In this strength of the political establishment monasticism could thrive and flourish. A time of peace was granted to those contemplatives who lived under his protection.

Even hermitism found a large number of followers in the tenth century. Theologically this can be a good sign for us. The hermit focuses on God alone, but he also lifts the concerns of all the people in the world up to God in prayer. He is a sign that our salvation is still in progress and that we can live in such a way as to prepare our home in heaven. The hermit draws our attention, because there is something elusive about him and this something may answer our deeper spiritual needs.

St. Nilus, St. Romuald, and St. John Gualbert
Founded a Settlement of Hermits

St. Nilus of Rossano was born about 910 of a Greek family in Calabria and baptized Nicholas. In his younger years he was lukewarm and careless. When he was thirty his wife and daughter died and he suffered a serious illness. These blows brought about his conversion and he completely turned to God. He joined monks of the Byzantine Rite and took the name Nilus. For some time he lived as a hermit and other hermits became associated with him. The Moslems made some raids in Southern Italy and the monks had to flee for their lives. They couldn't suddenly become soldiers and defend themselves. But their flight shouldn't be understood that Christians only have to flee and play dead when an enemy opposes them. They followed their call and left their defense in God's hands. And yet their prayer can also lead to a real defense if God so wills it. In the mentality of the Middle Ages military intervention could become an answer to prayer. The hermits reflected this mentality. At first they were welcomed as guests of the Benedictines of Monte Cassino and later they founded their own settlement of hermits, a laura. The fame of this settlement had also been brought to the attention of the Emperor, Otto III (980–1002), who had begun to rule at age 14 in 994. Otto believed in the sacred dignity of his office, had inclinations towards asceticism and admired and supported those who devoted their lives to prayer. In 996 he had put a German on the chair of Peter, Gregory V, with the interest to stabilize the Church and his Empire. He visited the settlement of the hermits and was truly impressed by their prayer and poverty and made the comment: "These men who live in tents as strangers on earth are truly citizens of Heaven". We understand that the support of the ruler for the religious gives evidence of the prestige they enjoyed. Outwardly they were poor, but they were not spiritually marginalized like the religious in a modern secularized society. We have to respect this difference between the ages.

St. Nilus also found direction for his future through his closeness to heaven and a possible private revelation of the Blessed Virgin Mary led him to start the monastery of Grottaferrata, in which he kept the Byzantine observance and liturgies. This foundation combines hermitism and monasticism. Both aspects are needed for genuine devotion to take hold of our souls. Hermitism is small in comparison to monasticism, but it stresses the single-minded love of God and therefore will always be taken seriously as an incentive and example of the work of God's grace in the Church.

Singular observance of God's grace was also the trademark of St. Romuald in the same century, who developed a real mission about the eremitical life. He was born about 950 as the son of the Duke of Ravenna. In his youth he was passion's slave and enjoyed life on a worldly plane, but even then he experienced sentiments and a longing for a higher call. A decisive experience turned him around. He was about twenty in 970 when his father had a dispute with a relative over some property and challenged him to a duel. His father killed the relative. Romuald was shocked and unable to bear the tragedy in his family. Something had to stop this violence and these outbreaks of temper. He had to flee and took refuge in a monastery. He stayed there for three years, settled down in prayer and let God take hold of him. He observed the community, was displeased with some of the monks, who took life easy and believed that he should be stricter and more focused.

It wasn't difficult for him to find a hermit and to place himself under his charge. Hermitism has to be studied and imitation is the most basic way of learning, especially in religion. Romuald obtained the vocation of being a hermit and others were impressed and willing to follow his direction. He even introduced the Doge of Venice, Pietro Orseolo I to leave his office and to become a religious.

Romuald increased the attraction of this life-style and was successful in many foundations throughout Italy and even as far as the Pyrenees. In Italy a man named Maldolus gave him land for a settlement, which is called Camp Maldoli and St. Romuald's order is named: Camaldolese Order. There he died alone in his cell on June 19th, 1027. His hermits live in a cell with a chapel, in which they say Mass, and the cell is surrounded by a walled garden. The monastery next to the hermitage provides some protection and the necessary contact with the world outside.

The fact that a hermit oversees both institutions also shows that the saint preferred the eremitical life over the monastic. The community should serve the hermits, so that they can devote themselves better to their solitude in greater freedom. Cardinal Peter Damian (1007–1072) wrote Romuald's biography. This also shows the interest of the Church at large in hermitism. The cardinal was aware that the eremitical life is intended to make our call to heaven obvious and plausible. If this ideal isn't upheld, then the life of the Church becomes easily mundane and flat, instead of uplifting and spiritual. The solitary life of the hermit is also a challenge for the monastery and the Church to be concerned about their Christian intention. In his special code the hermit shows the ever greater God to us. The eremitical life had a positive influence upon the life in community, because it stressed even stronger the common practice of prayer and contemplation.

The call to contemplation of St. John Gualbert (990–1073) was even more dramatic than the one of St. Romuald. His older and only brother had been murdered and according to custom it was considered his duty to take revenge. It is hard to imagine the stress he endured. Wouldn't this "custom" only increase crime and violence? And yet he carried a sword and on one occasion he came upon the murderer and could have taken his revenge. The murderer pleaded for mercy and threw himself on the ground before John. It is probably more than a legendary embellishment that John saw the form of the cross as the man lay there before him with outstretched arms. Since Jesus Christ identified himself with the least of sinners, who turn to him for mercy, so it appears that John experienced this man before him. What if this man is changed in the eyes of God? It is no longer his enemy in front of him, but Jesus Christ. Should he kill Jesus Christ? Such is the mysticism of the saints and the secret of the hermits in seclusion. John let the man live. Instead of killing someone he went into a church and prayed in front of the Crucifix and he believed that his decision was confirmed by the Lord and that the forgiveness he had shown had obtained his vocation.

He had found his specific point of view for contemplation. The recommendations of the gospel of poverty, celibacy and obedience are vehicles for the contemplative to be unhindered in the presence of the Lord. He interpreted the Benedictine rule for the sake of prayer. The Benedictine rule recommends manual work for the brothers, but John wanted his monks to be even free from this, so that they could spend more time in adoration.

He therefore admitted lay-brothers into his community, who had the call to work, so that the others could pray more. These shouldn't feel that the order was using them; this would be unchristian. It was just that one vocation goes along with the other and they complement each other. For the group with these two aspects of working and living together he created a monastery. The overall foundation is well balanced. He had a special liking for Moses, who was the strict law-giver, going alone to the top of Mount Sinai and who was at the same time one with his people, "the meekest man on the face of the earth".

His interest in Moses may also guide us to appreciate why John wanted to admit lay-brothers into the community. The shepherd of Mount Horeb had to do a humble job before God called him and the lay-brother of the community may also be very close to God in his heart. It seems that St. John Gualbert didn't have to solicit men to join his order because many came on their own. Quite often lay-people feel the need for a deeper spiritual life before the clergy and the bishops do. They have lived in the tensions of the world and compare this with the peace Jesus promises his followers and because of this experience they are even more willing to give themselves to gospel-values. At the time of St. John there was a movement towards hermitism and people engaged in lively discussion about it. Often priests and bishops were not so much interested, because they didn't want something that wasn't in their control, especially when they were rather lax.

Hermits make it obvious how personal and serious the call from God is. Others may take it from there and give religious life again a broader application.

Cluny
Some Independence for Monks

This was the case with Cluny. William the Pious, Duke of Aquitaine, founded this abbey about 908/910. Once again a layman had the right idea about the religious. There had been a substantial decline of monasticism in the ninth century.

The reason was that the monasteries suffered from lack of protection, lack of freedom and had become dependent upon secular powers (political leaders) and the higher clergy, bishops and cardinals. We can compare this to the church in our modern world: Lawyers, counselors and the media are forcing the Church into a straight-jacket of secularism and get the spiritual intention of the gospel under their control. The anxiety about scandals has forced us to abandon the freedom of God's reign and to submit to standards, which have little or nothing to do with the joy of the Holy Spirit. William of Aquitaine had recognized that contemplatives need to exercise their faith independently from secular powers and interests forcing themselves upon them. Often these powers only exploited the monasteries and William of Aquitaine prevented this happening to Cluny from the start. He secured the freedom of the abbey from within and from without. The community elected the abbot and vowed obedience to him.

The abbey was exempt from the jurisdiction of the local ordinary, i.e. the local bishop. These stipulations were recorded in the document for the foundation and he had obtained these privileges in writing from the Holy See. Stricter asceticism and greater care of their liturgy became the focus of their attention. Taxes from his entire domain were allocated to support the monks and their substantial building programs. The abbey was fortunate to have leaders who fostered growth and enthusiasm for about 250 years: The abbots Berno, Odo, Aymard, Majolus, Odilo, Hugh and Peter the Venerable.

Cluny became the strongest religious power of the Church, given the task of sufficient distance from the world and to avoid the danger of a secular mentality. And yet they didn't take refuge in mysticism separated from society (which is more often the case in Eastern monasticism), but felt spiritually responsible for all their brothers and sisters in Christ. The monks became the great intercessors for all believers through their singular worship of God. They were not pessimistic about society and its history, but supportive through their prayer and maintained important contacts with those in power. Otto the Great personally knew and respected the abbot Majolus; the abbot Odilo was a friend of the Emperor Henry II and the abbot Hugh became the sponsor for the baptism of the later Henry IV and was able to negotiate between him and the Pope when Henry was the Emperor. Cluny became the religious heart of Europe and grew into an association which included almost 2,000 monasteries by the twelfth century throughout Burgundy, France, Italy, Spain, England and Germany.

The monks were involved in scientific research and the writing of manuscripts. Many of these were lost when the abbey was sacked by the Huguenots in 1562. The abbey church was the greatest Church in Christendom with 555 feet in length; it was almost totally destroyed in 1790.

Other associations followed the example of Cluny: Gorze, Brogne, Hirsau, Siegburg and Einsiedeln. The expansion and the impact of these monastery associations on the history of Europe were phenomenal and we cannot understand the development of Western civilization without recognizing the importance of monasticism. Either by way of prayer, learning or through personal connections (members of a family living in an abbey or working for one) the monasteries exercised their influence and built up the faith of the people. Through them religion gained a more prominent place in public. The religious awareness greatly increased and deepened through these religious institutions and the incentives continued to grow.

Very impressively Cluny had regained the freedom of the Church and of the Spirit within the monastery and this freedom gave new room to breathe the joy of heaven so essential for all believers. The Church at large had to regain this same freedom and affirm that it is an institution of Jesus Christ, who calls us to a new life in him and who will not be coerced into earthly restrictions and limitations. The struggle for this freedom was entrusted to a monk connected with Cluny, the later Pope Gregory VII.

Pope Gregory VII

"I have loved justice and hated iniquity that is why I die in exile."

Pope Gregory VII was born in 1020 in Tuscany with the name Hildebrand and at an early age he was entrusted for his education to the Benedictine Abbey of Santa Maria on the Aventine Hill in Rome. This means that he entered the abbey as a child and was brought up in the atmosphere of the Monastery and early in his life he made his profession as a monk in Rome. This school was penetrated by the strict observance of Cluny and Hildebrand made this his own. His mind and heart were monastic and he had to view the Church in this light. This code of monasticism is part of the identity of the Church and believers only alienate themselves from this identity if they are unaware of this code. He became the chaplain of Pope Gregory VI and accompanied him to Cologne, when he was driven into exile. As often before it was an exile, which makes a person realize even more the home we have in heaven.

After the death of Gregory VI, Hildebrand withdrew to Cluny and lived there as a monk for more than a year when Pope Leo IX called him back to

Rome in 1050. He then showed his extraordinary skill as an administrator, retrieved much Church property, which had been alienated by the greedy and dishonest Roman nobility and the Normans, augmented the revenues of the Holy See and stabilized the administration. He held this position and evaded being elected Pope a couple of times, until his election was unavoidable in 1073. His inner strength and the acuteness of his mind were at their height. He had to be ordained to the priesthood first after his election, since he had only been a deacon.

He took the name Gregory VII. He was the man for this historical hour. The Christian world was in a deplorable state, suffering from a general debasement. Society and the Church suffered from widespread corruption, scandals and abuses and a decay of clerical morality. Pope Gregory responded with the Gregorian Reform, especially strict norms for the clergy, against the married priesthood, simony and lay-investiture (political leaders installing bishops and abbots). His injunctions called forth a most violent storm of opposition throughout Italy, Germany, and France. However, he did not relax his efforts.

He sent legates to all parts of the Church, who were empowered to depose anyone who wouldn't follow his instructions. He believed that as the soul governs the body, so the Church has to govern the state; and he believed that the Pope is the head of Christendom. Furthermore he was convinced that the Christian Faith can only be preserved if the flood of immorality is stemmed at all costs. In 1075 he excommunicated "any person, even if he were emperor or king, who should confer an investiture in connection with any ecclesiastical office". The German Emperor, Henry IV, declared the Pope deposed and Gregory VII excommunicated him. The Emperor had to ask for forgiveness and crossed the Alps and met the Pope in the Castle of Canossa on January 28, 1077. The Pope granted him forgiveness, but four years later he had to excommunicate him again, when Henry IV supported a counter-Pope. The Duke of Normandy came to Gregory's aid, but his troops did so much damage to Rome, that Gregory VII had to flee. At first he escaped to the Abbey of Monte Cassino and then to the Castle of Salerno, where he died on May 25th, 1085. His last words were, "I have loved justice and hated iniquity that is why I die in exile". Although God had called him away from the monastery to renew the Church at large through his reform, he remained a monk at heart and read the code of his existence in the light of his devotion to God. His exile became his final monastery, awaiting like every other contemplative the reward of heaven for his earthly faith journey.

The renewal he had brought paved the way for the success of the great saints of the following centuries. In the grace of God the lives of the saints are mysteriously connected and the saints are sometimes privileged to decipher this connection, which affirms the validity of their individual missions. They can go back in their mind and discover the very root of their own vocation. The Church became strong again because of the increase of interior devotion of all the contemplatives, who through renewed protection could lead lives of greatest holiness. In eras when this interior devotion is being neglected and when the Church operates on a merely administrative level the Church becomes weak and its impact on society goes flat. Lack of moral integrity may only indicate the neglect of interior devotion. The Gregorian Reform made the monastery again very attractive. Great numbers of religiously motivated men and women became monks and nuns.

St. Bruno
Founded the Grand Chartreuse

As hermitism gained prominence, a new founder in France was St. Bruno, although he was not born in that country. He was a native of Cologne, Germany, born about the year 1030 and it seems that there he received his first schooling, but while he was still a boy (a pueris) he went to Reims in France to complete his studies. Afterwards he went back to his hometown to be ordained at about the age of twenty five or in 1055.

The following year, Bishop Gervais recalled him to Reims to help him run the diocesan school and a year after that he was made head of this school. He held this position until the year 1075. One of his more illustrious students was Eudes of Chatillon, who later became Pope Urban II. In 1075 Bruno was named chancellor of the diocese of Reims by Bishop Gervais, but the bishop died soon afterwards and was succeeded by a bad character, Bishop Manasses, who lacked piety and had a bad temper. St. Bruno and two other priests felt obligated to file a complaint about their bishop at the Council of Autun in 1077 and they obtained the suspension of the unworthy prelate. As could be expected, Bishop Manasses responded with violence. He razed the houses of his accusers, confiscated their goods, sold their benefices, and appealed to the pope. St. Bruno went to Rome to defend the justice of his cause.

Rome confirmed his findings and together with a revolt of the people against their bishop, Manasses had to withdraw. The clergy wanted to have Bruno as their bishop, but he had other plans or another calling. The trauma he had experienced certainly contributed to his intention to withdraw from the world, but his first objective was to live out his singular love of God in solitude and prayer. In 1080 he headed with six companions for the area of Grenoble, a spot in the Alpine region and there ascended to an isolated place higher in the mountains, now known as Chartreuse.

The area is almost always covered with snow and the growing season is very short. They built a little monastery, so that they could live in poverty, prayer and study. Eight years after that his illustrious student had become Pope Urban II, who called him to his side as his advisor. He couldn't refuse and with a few companions he went to Rome. Shortly afterwards the Pope had to flee from the invading forces of the Emperor and St. Bruno had to join him on his escape to the South. He then petitioned the Pope to let him live a contemplative life and received his permission.

In the diocese of Squillace in Calabria he began a second monastery in the same way he had done in Chartreuse with the emphasis on the eremitical life along with the community. The Great Count of Sicily, Roger, supported his efforts (building an abbey) and St. Bruno was privileged to baptize the son of this Count in 1097, who became the future king of Sicily. Following the invitation of the Pope to leave his eremitical settlement, the Grand Chartreuse, was a severe test of his obedience, but the opportunity to found another after the trial had passed was a consolation for him and his brothers.

In his spirituality it is essential that solitude and penance go hand in hand with the joyful awareness of the grace of the Lord. The joy of soul always attends the sacrifices, which are made in a pure spirit. The solitude of the monks is not morbid introspection, but their life is already heaven-blessed and therefore already an earthly reflection of the future glory of the saints. The further his life progresses the more firmly does the contemplative consider himself to be accepted by the Father in heaven. The normal sadness of departure has been entrusted to the Greater one and the monk unravels this secret in his heart. The saint could also cope with the death of his closest friends in this light of greater glory. His former student, Pope Urban II, died in 1099, his first companion, who had become the prior of the Grand Chartreuse passed away the following year and his close friend in Calabria, Count Roger, died in 1101.

St. Bruno was aware that his own end was close at hand. At the end of September of that year he gathered his monks around his bed, made a public confession and entrusted his soul to God on Sunday, October 6th, 1101. Over two hundred monasteries followed his mixed rule, i.e. hermitism and monasticism, and spread across Europe. His first foundation, the Grand Chartreuse, has weathered the storms of the centuries and is still an inspiration in our time. The recent movie about it: *Into Great Silence* shows the life of the monks and makes it obvious that the devotion to eternal life remains constant and that there are still human beings who let it penetrate them in the here and now. The fifth prior of the Grand Chartreuse, Guigues du Chastel (1083–1137) wrote a Constitution and he rebuilt the Chartreuse after an avalanche had destroyed it in 1132.

There existed a great interest in the eremitical life in the eleventh and twelfth century; the theology behind it is, that the world is a place of exile, separated from heaven and the hermit wants to endure the exile in the intimate belief that through prayer and worship God comes closer to him. This belief also sustains the monks living in community, if the contemplatives give sufficient time to prayer. In order to do this some people renewed the Benedictine Order.

St. Robert, Abbot Alberic, and St. Stephen Harding

A Rough Life in the Forest

One of the first who engaged in this endeavor was St. Robert of Molesme. He was born about the year 1029 and experienced the call to the religious life very early. He entered the order at age fifteen and made great progress in his faith and his studies. After his novitiate the community elected him as their prior, although he was the youngest. Shortly after he had to direct a daughter house, in which the monks had become rather lax; but they were unwilling to take any correction and he moved on to guide a group of hermits in the forest of Collan. The location was harmful to their health and Robert moved with them to the forest of Molesme in 1075. These moves also show that the monks were the cultivators of uninhabited territory. Through their hard work the rugged terrain or desert was turned into a place where people could stay and make a living.

People in the eleventh century were interested in what the religious were doing and they held those who led austere lives in poverty in high esteem. The poor monks of Molesme became famous and even St. Bruno came in 1082 to Robert and asked for instructions about hermitism from him. The respect they earned led to big donations from the people and wealth alienated them from the Spirit of the Gospel, so that they began to take life easy and relaxed in their spiritual efforts. St. Robert wanted to bring them back to their origins, but he was opposed, so that he obtained permission from the Holy See in 1098 to start a branch of the order of his own.

With twenty close followers he went further into the forest, to Citeaux, to pray and work, clear the ground, cultivate it along with the cultivation of their souls. Their holiness grew apace and those left behind in Molesme realized the mistake they had made in not trusting Robert and to let him go. They asked the Pope to send Robert back to them. Robert obeyed the order of the Pope to go back to Molesme and Robert suffered under this demand for obedience and made a sacrifice for sanctification out of it, but he wrote to his brothers in Citeaux: "I am here in body because obedience demands it, but my soul is with you." Through all of it he proved his constancy and passed away in Molesme on April 17th, 1111.

Those who stayed on in Citeaux accepted this far away place, south of Dijon, and saw in it an opportunity to draw closer to God through the hardships they endured. The pure spirit of monasticism was at work in them and their second Abbot Alberic could be equally successful, although he held the office only for a few years, until 1109, when he too went to his eternal reward.

The third founder of Citeaux was the Englishman, St. Stephen Harding, who outlived the other two by over twenty years. He had received his early education in the abbey of Sherborne, but there he didn't become a monk, but he was preparing for his future call. In order to clarify his vocation he went with a friend on a pilgrimage to Rome. In those days the journey was made on foot, unless occasionally a cart pulled by oxen gave them some rest. Each day the two recited all the 150 psalms together and prayer formed a close bond between them. On their return they came to Molesme and they had to wonder whether this contained a message from God for them. Stephen believed so and went further to Citeaux, but his friend went back to England. Citeaux was the least cultivated, gloomiest and darkest place in the heart of the forest. Fortunately the Duke of Burgundy, Odo, sent some workmen to help them build their settlement.

It took a lot of hard work to change it into land which would produce something to eat. Often the brothers had to starve. After Alberic, St. Stephen took over as abbot. He believed in making even greater sacrifices in piety and didn't want the nobles to hold court at Citeaux and even was opposed to use any costly things like chalices, vestments and so on for their services. This discouraged visitors and young people to join them and finally starvation stared them in the face. His monks remained loyal to him. To make things worse a contagious, deadly disease began to spread and one monk after the other died. When again a brother was at the point of death, St. Stephen asked him to bring him a word from beyond the grave, telling him whether he was on the right track, or whether he should change his method. This brother did appear to him after his death and told him that God was very pleased with him and that he should continue on.

Sometimes they had to go begging from door to door for alms in order to survive, but their poverty, patience and persistence paid off when St. Bernard came with thirty relatives and friends in 1112 to Citeaux. St. Stephen was happy about this unexpected success and he was able to start a dozen more monasteries. He wrote a "Charter of Charity", which brought about a new organization with one center of government and regular visitations for all the monasteries belonging to this new branch, called the Cistercians. St. Stephen Harding died in 1134.

St. Anselm of Canterbury
Visionary

*A*long with the impressive rise of the Cistercians the traditional Benedictines continued to do well and brought forth probably the most accomplished monk by way of mysticism of the eleventh and the beginning of the twelfth century. St. Anselm of Canterbury was raised sky high above all the controversies between different orders and institutions. Because of his singular view he gives people the impression that we are called to a higher awareness of God's ever greater reign over us. God provided him with a place of birth (he was born in 1033), which by its very elevation makes us aware that we are called to a higher life in Him. The town Aosta is located in a higher region of the Alps, in Burgundy not too far from the Mount St. Bernard. Here St. Anselm was born and here he learned the first lessons of his faith from his very devoted and faith filled mother. Her love of God inflamed the boy's heart and besides this love he was endowed with an extraordinary mental capacity and eagerness for learning. The very mountains where he lived assured him that God must be on a summit and he endeavored to go up there himself. Besides this his mother had taught him that God dwells on high. One night in a vision he experienced this desire to go up high to the peak of the mountain and run to the court of God, the great King. He found the King with only his cupbearer.

He went close to the King and sat at his feet. The King commanded his cupbearer to give the boy some moist white bread and he tasted the joy of a great feast. Still the following morning he knew how real this vision had been and he openly talked about it. The impression remained vivid in his soul, so that many years later his biographer, Eadmer, was able to record it. It would be too easy to dismiss his vision to have been nothing more than a dream. We do better to recognize it as a private revelation comparable to the one seen by the visionaries of Fatima in 1915, when an angel gave them Holy Communion. As these visionaries so also the saint was penetrated by a sense of worship. Heaven is close to those receiving the grace of contemplation.

It was natural for him to ask for admission in a monastery as early as possible and he tried this even before he was fifteen years old. The abbot refused him. He prayed that God would give him an illness, but the abbot still refused to let him in. The way into the monastery was not as smooth as he wanted it to be and he became somewhat distracted and began to have fun like kids his age. However, his mother kept things under control. When his mother died he lost his orientation for a while and the harsh treatment he received from his father made everything only worse.

With a friend he left home and they took life easy for three years, but applied themselves to some learning in a school in Burgundy. This alienation could have led him to go downhill and to look only for fun in his future. Later he regretted these few pleasure-seeking years, but the wisdom in his heart was more pronounced and he had to try a new course of action. He went to the abbey of Bec in Normandy, whose abbot was the good teacher Lafranc, known for his accomplished theology. Lafranc accepted him as a student and was impressed by his abilities and took him under his wings. He became Lafranc's best student and soon was permitted to teach along with him. After some years (in 1060) he was permitted to be clothed in the habit at age 27. Three years after that his master was appointed Abbot of Caen and St. Anselm was made Prior, an office he held for fifteen years. He was then elected abbot and was able to head his community for another fifteen years, until 1093. Besides enjoying a few carefree years in his youth he had spent most of his life in a monastery and with heart and soul focused on the presence of God, beginning with his intense devotion and experience as a boy. While still Prior he wrote his Monologium giving proof of the existence and the nature of God.

Through the centuries this book has been contested and only accepted as fully valid by a few accomplished scholars, who viewed their own life from similar sentiments as those of St. Anselm. His proof of the existence of God is actually quite reasonable: Our own existence as mere mortals is ephemeral and gives us only a limited notion what existence is. Even for this limited notion we need the awareness of someone, whose existence is neither ephemeral nor questionable and this is what we call God. Before we get to ourselves, we are already in need of God, who alone has brought us to this point. In and through God do we understand ourselves. It was equally natural for the saint to contemplate God's truth, his beauty and his goodness as he did in his Proslogium.

The vision he had as a boy supported him in these impressions. As a boy and later as a monk he stood in the awe inspiring presence of Almighty God, who along with his majesty cared for him like a loving Father. St. Anselm's privilege as a writer was that he was able to give his description with unparalleled clarity and precision in terms of penetrating logic. Many people who disregard him may not match his logic either.

As a monk and as an abbot he was man enough to incorporate his carefree youth into his idea of God's ever greater love and freedom. A neighboring abbot was complaining about his lack of success in training the students of his school. The saint showed his sense of freedom as follows, "if you planted a tree in your garden, and bound it on all sides so that it couldn't spread out its branches, what kind of tree would it prove to be when in after years you gave it room to spread? Wouldn't it be useless with its boughs all twisted and tangled? But that is how you treat your boys, cramping them with fears and blows, debarring them also from the enjoyment of any freedom."

The saint knew that God created human beings with this sense of joy and freedom and that he wants them to come to him with gratitude for his gifts. Through his thinking and prayers Anselm showed his secret code of monasticism, which ultimately set him free to be what he was in God's presence without any hindrance or limitations of an earthly nature. The closer he drew to God, the more liberated he became and the code lodged in his heart had shown the way to his greater inner freedom and this joy of the

Holy Spirit within him. St. Anselm of Canterbury was a monk penetrated by this glory of heaven for which there is no substitute.

For the final sixteen years of his life he became Archbishop of Canterbury and the priests and people there welcomed him with great enthusiasm and sang the Te Deum when he accepted this position against his will and was consecrated in December 1093. They saw the glory of heaven on the face of this holy man. King William Rufus had kept the see vacant for several years for the sake of revenues. Money was more important to him than religion. As Archbishop of this important see Anselm proved to be most effective in dealing with powerful opposition against the security and freedom of the Church. He was alert and committed to defend the freedom of religion and the dignity of worship against threatening opposition.

He had to travel to Rome to defend himself against King William and on this trip he wrote the most famous treatise ever written about the Incarnation: Why did God become Man? Being most aware of the political circumstances of the Christians only deepened his sense, that God should guide our actions towards the glory we find in him. After some struggles for his ministry he was able to live the last couple of years in peace. He could entrust his soul to God, whom he had worshiped and of whom he knew would receive him lovingly. He left an extraordinary legacy behind for the sciences of philosophy and theology, for the Episcopal office and especially for monasticism, which was at the core of his spiritual life. The height in which his spirit operated was not meant to obtain a broad application as we find in some popular saints, but showed God's eternal truth prevailing over time.

In some sense St. Anselm can leave room for a separation between the monastery and the world, but not by way of being polemical against the world, but rather as an invitation to draw closer to God through contemplation and prayer, whether this takes place in some worldly occupation or in the monastery. For him the Benedictine monastery was suited best. He died in 1109. He had been privileged that he could search for God as a scholar and after his academic career applied his teachings as a bishop.

In our understanding of the monks and nuns we do well, if we admit some private revelation through which a person makes this most intimate contact with eternal glory and because of it begins a new life. This decisive transition is so remarkable, so that others greatly benefit from it and are able to entrust their lives to the person called and with his help to God, who has granted the privilege.

St. Norbert, St. Hugh de Fosses, and St. Bernard
Working Miracles for God's Kingdom

Such a transition we observe in St. Norbert of Xanten (born 1080) in Germany, in the lower Rhine Valley and he died in Magdeburg in 1134. As a young man he became a member of the court of the Prince-Bishop of Cologne and later he was named almoner of the Emperor of Germany, being responsible for the charitable organization of the Empire. He had been ordained deacon and was offered the position of Bishop of Cambray, but he didn't accept, because he was more interested in a life of leisure. Only a miracle could save him. He was riding on a horse, when lightning hit the ground in front of him, which frightened the animal. The horse threw him off and he lay on the ground like dead for nearly an hour. This humbled him and changed his life.

We believe that he became aware not only of his alienation from God, but also of the glory he offers those who come to him with renewed faith and trust. He became a penitent, gave up his former life and concentrated on prayer, meditation and fasting. He founded the Abbey of Fuerstenberg and endowed it with his own estate. He was denounced to the papal legate as a hypocrite and accused of preaching without a license.

In answer to these allegations he gave away everything he had, walked barefoot to see the Pope, Gelasius II, who was in Southern France in exile. The Pope gave him permission to preach everywhere he liked. And yet he was very much drawn to focus on God and prayer, consulted a hermit and gained much confidence for his compunction of heart. He founded an abbey called Premontre and disciples gathered around him; an order began to grow. This attraction of followers also assured him that he should expand his influence for the salvation of souls, when the opportunity arose. Also lay-people wanted to join and he let them become members of a "Third Order", besides women who became nuns of his order. Besides spending much time in contemplation he also preached. He himself had drifted away from the Church in his younger years and therefore he knew how easily this can happen, but he also knew how to bring people back to their faith. He was quite successful with people in the Netherlands, who had suffered this alienation from the Church or who let it happen.

His prayer and preaching led to a rapid growth of the Order, showing God's blessings. In Wuerzburg he miraculously healed a woman who was blind. The people there were so amazed that they wanted him to become their bishop, but he secretly got away from this. He was known to the Papal Legate through his contact with the Pope and also to the Emperor Lothair and both brought him to the point to accept the vacant see of Madgeburg, which is not far from Berlin.

We appreciate in this process also the mentality of the Middle Ages: The religious and the secular authorities were concerned for the spiritual well being of the citizens, because the unity of society was derived from the faith-connection with God. His "higher position" didn't make the saint ostentatious, but he wanted to remain a humble monk and when he arrived at the Episcopal residence in Madgeburg the porter thought that he was a beggar and asked him to go to the other beggars in the city. But the people in his presence shouted: "He is our bishop." Once installed, he wanted to enforce stricter discipline for clergy and laity. A number of people responded with protests in the streets and even wanted to kill him. A few times he made a narrow escape from attempts on his life. He couldn't change his course of action.

Clergy who didn't want to be obedient he replaced by members of his Order, but others were willing to cooperate with him. Local citizens had alienated much ecclesiastical property. The saint acted severely, because they had stolen not only from the Church, but in his eyes they had stolen from God. For him this situation was very disturbing and discouraging, because it indicated a widespread corruption and he decided to leave the city altogether. At this juncture the people became more aware of his close connections with the Emperor and the Pope and they didn't want to risk displeasing them. They begged him to come back and promised to be more submissive in the future. And true enough he was more successful with his reforms from then onward. They also understood that he couldn't compromise the gospel.

One more challenge of his earthly life awaited him. After the death of Pope Honorius II a schism divided the Church. One section of cardinals had elected Cardinal Gregory Papareschi, who took the name Innocent II, while the rest of the cardinals had chosen Cardinal Pierleone, who was the favorite in Rome and who called himself Anacletus II. Innocent II had to flee from the city and take refuge in France. St. Norbert, like St. Bernard, was convinced that Innocent II was the right heir of the chair of St. Peter and favored his cause. He spoke in his favor at a council in Reims and won the support of the German Emperor, Lothair and also of the German bishops. St. Bernard had obtained the same support in France. Also England and Spain had acknowledged Innocent II.

However, it was only with the help of armed forces that the Pope could reenter Rome. Through the influence of St. Norbert the German Emperor consented to lead an army into Italy. In March 1133 the Emperor and the Pope entered the Holy City accompanied by St. Norbert and St. Bernard and Innocent could assume his position as the successor of St. Peter. St. Norbert's health began to fail, but he returned to Germany and remained with the Emperor for some time as his advisor. In March 1134 he returned to Madgeburg, but he was so weak that he had to be carried on a stretcher and he died there after Pentecost on June 6th. He was canonized in 1582.

St. Norbert stands out through his connections with the Emperor and the Holy See, but this historical importance is more like a by-product of his existence. The humiliation he had suffered at the time of his conversion was at the same time a call to accept God's grace, which is the essential for the monk. God's grace is inexhaustible and the saint is privileged to be given a glimpse of this richness. His life is an interpretation of this grace and when believers take this to heart then they in turn acquire an awareness of what lies at the core of those close to God. The believer would short-change himself if he looked upon the saint in mere historical terms.

He had a great impact for the renewal of the clergy, who were more closely connected with the bishop and were enriched through their life in community under generally accepted guidelines. His order expanded especially towards the East of the River Elbe, where the members were of great benefit for the mission of the colonization of this territory. Eastern and Northern Europe became spheres of influence for them.

In France, St. Hugh de Fosses (1093–1164) continued the work of St. Norbert, but he and his followers concentrated more on contemplation, which often is more enduring, because it doesn't suffer so much from the ups and downs of history. And yet the monk has to be willing to be involved, when God requires this.

St. Bernard of Clairvaux had to adjust to God's will and be closely in touch with the "Price of our Salvation". He was born in 1090 at Fontaines, a castle near Dijon, the son of a noble of Burgundy. He had five brothers, Bd. Guy, Bd. Gerard, Andrew, Bartholomew and Bd. Nivard and a sister, Humbeline. Already as a child he loved to be alone, which was a form of meditation.

One Christmas eve he had a vision of the infant Jesus and from that time he cherished a great tenderness for this mystery of love and mercy. As in the cases of St. Anselm and St. Norbert we have to acknowledge such a private revelation which makes the faith most intimate for the one being blessed by it. Such a privileged moment doesn't interfere with a person's natural disposition, but goes along with it. Bernard's mother died when he was only seventeen years old and he became greatly depressed, but his lively sister helped him to overcome his brooding and inability to function. Besides these mood-swings he was attractive, witty, affable and sweet. He began to think to get away from the world and to become a monk, but his friends tried to talk him out of it.

However, he turned tables on them and convinced most of them as well as four brothers and an uncle to come along with him. It seemed that Nivard was still too young, so they left him at home and Guy said to him: "Adieu, my little Nivard! You will have all the estates and lands to yourself." The boy answered: "What! You then take Heaven, and leave me only the earth. This isn't fair." St. Bernard arrived as mentioned at the monastery of Citeaux with thirty companions in 1112 and St. Stephen Harding welcomed them with open arms. We have to recognize the simple and sincere intention of these men.

They wanted to hide themselves in God through prayer and asceticism even to the point of death. Nothing was to separate them from the eternal love of God. This code was firm and undeniable in their heart and they knew that there is no substitute for it. After three years, in 1115, St. Stephen Harding asked St. Bernard and twelve companions to found another house in the "Valley of Wormwood" surrounded by a forest (later called Clairvaux). It was uncultivated and the land was poor. They had to eat coarse bread and boiled beech leaves for vegetables, but the reputation of the house and the holiness of St. Bernard spread quickly and soon the number of brothers increased to one hundred and thirty. In 1121 he worked the miracle of restoring speech to a man so that he could confess his sins before he died and other sick people were cured. The church of Foigny was infested with flies and St. Bernard excommunicated them and they all died.

The malediction of the flies of Foigny became a proverb in France. When people had flies in their house, then someone would say: "Why don't you act like St. Bernard? Excommunicate the flies and they will die!" Of course, if they didn't have the ability to work miracles, then nothing would happen, but the remark was enjoyable.

For St. Bernard it was possible to let God work for him and this was due to the saint's humility and faith. God changed Bernard's plans. Instead of being hidden in meditation he had to become more and more concerned about the needs of the Church and the world at that time. He wrote about humility and the new Order. He was accused of being too strict and he answered with his "Apology" in which he defended his approach to the monastic life and made it clear that the invectives against the Order didn't have any foundation.

He wrote Pope Eugenius his longest and most important treatise: "For your consideration" (De consederatione), recommending him to spend time in daily contemplation and self-examination, which give life to all other virtues. He reminds his Holiness that in the many tasks of his high office he is in danger to fall into forgetfulness of God, which in turn leads to hardness of heart. Similar insights he had to enjoin on the Archbishop, writing about "The Office of the Bishops" (De Officiis Episcoporum) and he also wrote about "Grace and Free Will". His words were not always welcomed.

When he assisted at the Council of Troyes in 1128 and the bishop of Verdun was deposed, he was denounced in Rome and Cardinal Harmeric, on behalf of the Pope, wrote Bernard a sharp letter of criticism, saying: "It is not fitting that noisy and troublesome frogs should come out of their marshes to trouble the Holy See and the Cardinals". St. Bernard explained that he had been dragged to this council and had fulfilled his duty and he added: "Now, illustrious Harmeric, if you so wished, who would have been more capable of freeing me from the necessity of assisting at the council than yourself? Forbid those noisy, troublesome frogs to come out of their holes, to leave their marshes, then your friend will no longer be exposed to the accusation of pride and presumption." This letter made a great impression and St. Bernard was justified.

When, as mentioned, in 1130 two popes had been elected the saint like St. Norbert was on the side of the true one, Innocent II, who had to flee to France to take refuge from his opponent. St. Bernard and St. Norbert were happy when they accompanied him back to Rome, supported by the Emperor.

St. Bernard had become "the Oracle of Christendom" through whom the people learnt God's decision in this case about the true Pope. The Emperor, Dukes and the Pope were in constant contact with the saint, because they sought his advice. He was willing to help them with his insights and yet he didn't neglect his fervent love of God through political affairs. Essentially he was always a monk, a saint and a mystic who wanted to lead people to a deeper inwardness through which they were in closer union with Christ. His gentleness and sensitivity can be perceived in the way in which he for example interpreted the "Song of Songs", revealing his emotions to the reader. Faith goes beyond mere reason and is opposed to mere rationalism, which has always been a dangerous offshoot of Christianity and St. Bernard was firm in his witness to the depth of belief.

He had to give his opinion to the Pope about the writer Peter Abelard and stated: "Peter Abelard is trying to make void the merit of Christian faith, when he deems himself able by human reason to comprehend God entirely...the man is great in his own eyes".

After this statement and the verdict of the Holy Father, Peter Abelard was obliged to retire in the Abbey of Cluny, where he died in 1142.

The Albigensian heresy was making great advances in Southern France, Languedoc, and the papal legate asked St. Bernard in 1145 to go there and preach to the people. The saint obeyed, although he was ill and weak. Through his preaching and many miracles the people came back into the fold of the Church, at least temporarily.

Already before that time in 1144 the Turks, i.e. Muslims, had captured Edessa and threatened Jerusalem and Antioch. The Christians believed in their God-given right to protect the Holy Sites and in his alarm the Pope asked St. Bernard to preach a Crusade. He did so and his preaching was accompanied by many miracles in France and Germany in 1146 and 1147. He roused the Emperors and their troops, but the crusaders were led by no other motive than the prospect of plunder.

His preaching couldn't protect the crusade against misconduct, lack of faith and lack of discipline and the overconfidence of the German troops. Greed, intrigue and betrayal of the Christian nobles had taken hold of the crusaders and the crusade turned out to be a great failure and disaster. The saint had to shoulder this burden as well. He sent an apology to the Pope and expressed his conviction that the sins of the crusaders had led to this failure. He had put his heart and soul into this work in this historical hour and the failure lodged in the heart of those, who should have first joined him in prayer and devotion to God.

This they didn't do and had to bear the consequences of their infidelity. And yet, despite the integrity of his own heart, his reliance on God's grace and his confidence in God's ever greater mercy the saint bore this disaster as a heavy cross on his soul. The burden of the entire twelfth century was placed on St. Bernard's shoulders, and he didn't carry it without suffering. Even amidst his suffering he could remain loyal to Christ, who supported him in an intimate and mysterious way. The secret code of the monk became the code, which Jesus Christ had written upon the tablet of his heart and the saint was able to desire to be with Christ and to long for death. God accepted all this when he took him to himself on August 20th, 1153 at the age of sixty three. He had founded an additional 68 monasteries and the order had grown to 350 at the time of his death. In 1153 there were 700 monks at Clairvaux. By the year 1200 there were 530 monasteries belonging to this order and by 1500 they had grown to 700 for men and 900 for women. A branch for women had come about already in 1200.

Cluny, from which the Cistercians had branched off, also thrived. St. Bernard had respected their abbot, Peter the Venerable (1122–1156), who already in 1139 traveled to Spain and found two translators, who knew Arabic, and translated the Koran for him. The Church was involved in this struggle against the Moslems and they hired Knights to help. The ideal of this struggle is to bring Moslems to conversion to Christianity, but this isn't easy. Without genuine efforts of a mission we only get into a life and death struggle between the World Religions and our modern mentality to dodge the struggle may very well lead to greater defeats than the Christian world in the Middle Ages suffered. We may want to rediscover that the monks were closer to the truth than we, who want to solve all questions with a little politics. Something more is needed and people in the Middle Ages, especially the contemplatives were aware of this something more.

Otto von Freising

His Own way of Presenting History

This was the case with Otto von Freising. He was born about 1111 and died in 1158 at Morimond, Champagne in France. While still a child he was made provost of the Monastery Klosterneuburg, close to Vienna. He studied in Paris and entered the Cistercian Order. In 1137 he was chosen as bishop of Freising, close to Munich. As a Prince of the German Empire he possessed great influence and brought about many improvements for his diocese. He appreciated the mutual benefit of religion and society and he wished to prove that spiritual well-being in this world depends on the harmonious cooperation between Church and State. Supreme power is only in the hands of God and human beings have to be responsible to Him, otherwise their power will disintegrate and decline. As a historian he was also interested to show the world as a stage of conflict between Christianity and paganism or heresy.

Christians must live side by side with pagans and heretics and pray and work that God at his chosen time will turn their hearts to the truth and love of the gospel. He applied his insights to the history of mankind and to the history of the Church and thus became possibly the first, but certainly one of the most important representatives of the medieval philosophy of history. In his work, called "Gesta" he explained that peace came about when the conflict between the Pope and the Emperor had ceased. He felt the misery of the world, but also trusted in God's victory over everything discouraging for our future. As a Cistercian Otto had been called away from the monastery to become a bishop, but in his heart he remained a monk and at his end he died in the monastery he had entered in his youth. As a participant and contemporary of this fast expansion of the Order he coined the phrase: "The world became Cistercian" in the twelfth century. He experienced this growth of the order and discovered the historical circumstances which fostered this growth.

It was followed by decline. The Cistercians had been involved with an extreme use of energy in the historical affairs and exhausted their spiritual resources. For the time being this was God's call for them and their achievements speak for themselves. Contrary to their intention of leading an eremitical life they had become absorbed in external affairs. They had accepted the challenge and given proof of the extraordinary success of monasticism. Never before in history had the monastic movement involved as many people and gave young men an opportunity to become monks or young women to become nuns. As such the movement also gives evidence of the religious enthusiasm of that century and the renewal it brought to the Church. Families of the nobility and common people alike were happy to give a child to God, so that his life on earth may already give birth to the praise of God, which is the destination of all believers in the eternal kingdom of heaven.

Thousands of young men and women entered the monasteries with hearts filled with faith and love of God. The code of salvation had become their most intimate bond with the Lord and the eternal life he offers to believers. It had become obvious to them that heaven is a place of glory and unending praise of God. There is something extremely uplifting in this awareness and these devoted souls knew that there is no substitute for this praise in heaven. They answered the question for themselves: "Then, why not join in?" In their prayer and their song they did so, recognizing that here on earth our song is still lacking the perfection of the eternal and yet it already finds its inspiration and faith-filled participation from this final goal.

They had deciphered the code for eternal life for themselves and they could be swept away in this resounding chorus. Along with the many external changes taking place there was also a tremendous increase in Church music. Five monks can already form a group, singing the psalms, but when there are five hundred in a big stone-built church then their song echoes so powerfully that it absorbs the individuals and they participate in a reality, which far exceeds them. The monks were led to a beauty and unity, which they could truly experience as a gift from above. Sacred music was transforming them and brought them closer to the Throne of the Godhead.

They were affirmed in their faith that unending praise was their goal and they could cope very well with the journey they had to make until they would be admitted to heaven. The mysterious code gave them courage, which superseded all earthly trials. Instead of weakening them in their ephemeral tasks it only gave them greater strength to hold their ground where they own efforts were demanded. Their union was a union of the spiritual and of the spirit. The psalms, songs and passages from the New Testament, which they sang together, were the primary source for their unity and love for each other.

The historian and bishop, Otto von Freising, was, along with the people of the Middle Ages, somewhat pessimistic in regard to the earth and yet the extraordinary praise of God echoing forth from the churches and chapels outweighs the somber note of their realism and denotes a spiritual joy, which cannot be constructed with mere earthly calculations.

It is essential for modern observers of this sacred tradition to know the joy of the Spirit which guided the monks, so that we also can renew this joy in our own search for God.

The Crusades had an impact on Monasticism, but more through their side effects. The very contemplative Pope, Urban II, had called for them in 1095 and intended that they reclaim the Holy Land for Christian pilgrims. His intention was noble and concerned with devotion. He couldn't anticipate the brutality, which had been set in motion. At first Christian hordes plundered and killed Jews in German cities on their way, but they were massacred by the Turks. The organized troops entered Jerusalem in 1099 and slew the inhabitants, men, women and children alike. And yet from then onwards Christians could visit the Holy Sites.

Almost a century later on July 4th, 1187 Saladin's army destroyed the Christian army on Lake Tiberias and retook Jerusalem, but the confrontation between Christian and Moslem forces continued and the Crusade took on a life of its own by being directed against Constantinople in the beginning of the 13th century. This was no longer in touch with the original intention. The Crusades had become an instrument in the hands of European princes, who pursued their own interests through it and eventually they became a never-ending story of conquest, commerce and genuine prayer of those going on a pilgrimage for the love of God.

Despite all this, three Religious Orders were created. The Orders of Knights, who besides the vows of poverty, chastity and obedience promised to assist pilgrims, who became ill or exhausted on their journey or needed help, when they arrived in the Holy Land. This assistance included protection against infidels: The Johanniters were founded in 1099 (they wore a black coat with a white cross), the Templars, founded in 1118 (they wore a white coat with a red cross) and the German Order, founded in 1189/1190 (they wore a white coat with a black cross). In the midst of uncertainty and danger these orders focused on the basic requirements of our faith and the ever present need to exercise Christian charity. They can also convince us that contemplation and prayer will eventually show God's grace renewed.

We may compare the Crusades to the Dallas Charter for the Protection of Children of the Conference of the Bishops of the United States. The intention was to protect children from abuse. This is noble. And yet in many cases it led to an anti-clerical Crusade, in which lawyers, counselors and the media have taken control of Church affairs. The intention of the bishops became an instrument in their hands pursuing their own interests.

Despite its limited success we have to fear that the major down-turn of morality through abortion, divorces and a general promiscuity receives even less attention and the Crusade against the priests is only dealing with a symptom instead of with a problem on a broader scale.

And yet, despite all of this, we hope that many people find their way to more consistent contemplation, which cannot be touched by anything on the surface.

During these centuries of the Crusades many pilgrims and the mentioned Orders found their way to this contemplation and we believe that this is what God is looking for. Besides this interior experience of God's grace the Crusades also strengthened the community spirit and broadened the horizon of the Christians. They received enlightenment through the Byzantine, Oriental and Islamic cultures, which in turn enriched Philosophy and Theology, especially Scholasticism. They also increased their love of God through the things they endured and prepared the way for the Mendicant Orders.

The charisma of the contemplative is his participation in eternity alongside his participation in the Cross, which is the transition to eternal glory. Eternity doesn't come to an end and those closely in touch with it have been granted an experience of this. Their bequest to friends or to companions in an Order is connected with this charisma. As long and as much as their friends or followers are penetrated by the aura of this charisma, friendships or religious orders will be firmly established. Otherwise these will cease to exist. This was not the case with the older Orders in the twelfth century. They continued to thrive and absorbed the incentives which came from the East and increased the wealth of their theology. The monasteries of the older religious Orders remained appealing and attracted young men joining to become monks or young women joining to become nuns.

And yet developments took place which required a different response from the Church. The Crusades became an incentive to be in closer touch with how Jesus had lived and what he had taught. Those who returned from the pilgrimage to the Holy Land wished to be more like the Lord and consequently people were hungry for the Word of God as it is found in the gospel. Simplifying their life in this way could easily bring them to oppose the wealthy Church of Feudalism.

The laity took greater initiative and some disagreed that the hierarchy owned a lot of property. A Reformer in the Netherlands, Tanchelm, fought against the hierarchy and even denied Christ's presence in the Eucharist. The wealthy businessman Peter Waldes discovered the ideal of poverty in 1173 while reading Mt. 10,5ff and gave away all his possessions and preached repentance. He believed that Jesus had called him to do this.

The Pope responded by excommunicating and persecuting him and his followers. They went underground and became more hostile to the Church. The Beguines in Belgium, pious women began their lives of devotion in 1170 and emphasized reading the New Testament, cared for the sick, did manual labor and educated girls in their faith.

Pope Innocent III

Papacy at its Zenith of Power and Prestige

A similar movement began in Milan and Pope Innocent III was able to incorporate them into the Church. The Albigenses in Southern France were directly opposed to the Church and its teaching, which led to a war against them in 1209–1229 after the papal Legate had been killed in 1208. Entire cities were devastated and depopulated and the Inquisition was instituted. The heretic was viewed as a revolutionary during the Middle Ages and this led to such a harsh treatment.

The scenario in the twelfth century indicated that confrontation didn't solve the problems and a better response was needed. Pope Innocent III (1198–1216) made serious endeavors of integration. He was only thirty seven when he was elected and during his reign the Church reached the zenith of its power. He was an accomplished theologian and especially one of the greatest jurists of his time. His dealings in the historical circumstances of Christendom were very effective in regard to the increase of stability in Europe and the prestige of the Papacy. Along with his keen awareness of politics he was not blind to the vices of luxury and power, which had infected many of the clergy and part of the laity. He was further aware that such vices breed discontent and resentment especially among the poor, who seriously feel the neglect they suffer. He also knew about the 'movement' of poverty for the gospel and as mentioned his efforts were partly successful to integrate them into the Church. This also shows his Christian conviction and his responsibility towards the gospel. He was able to exercise remarkable power, but this was at the disposal of God's revelation. His earthly situation didn't divert him from the truth as given to us by God. God has given a function to power and Innocent III recognized and granted this function instead of making an idol of it.

His greatness therefore has to be perceived not so much in his lofty position, but in his spiritual freedom and his dignity.

St. Dominic, St. Francis of Assisi, and St. Clare
Virtue of Humility

The first saint and founder of an Order he had to deal with in this freedom was St. Dominic. St. Dominic was born about the year 1170 in Calaroga, in Old Castile and he died on August 6, 1221. Little is known about his father, Felix, but his mother Joanna of Aza was a saint of her own right and was beatified in 1929. She had two older sons and a daughter and some years later she asked God for another child. In a vision of St. Dominic of Silos she received the message that she would have another child, who would be a shining light in the Church. Because of this vision she named him Dominic and in art he often portrayed with a star on his forehead, as for example in the Dominican Church in Zwolle in the Netherlands.

Once again we have to acknowledge a private revelation in connection with a new development in the Church. Dominic received his first and deepest impressions of the faith through his mother and her fervent prayer. From age seven onwards he was educated by an uncle, a parish priest, who prepared him for the school in Palencia. Still a student he was made a canon of the cathedral of Osma, where he also was ordained. The Chapter of this Cathedral followed the Rule of St. Augustine. For about seven years St. Dominic spent most of his time in contemplation and he was known for the gift of tears. Copiously weeping for his own and others sinfulness was part of his prayer. Through tears God allows a person to wash away sins and his life becomes even more radiant in holiness.

If we look for a secret code of the monk, we can find it in a very personalized form in these years of meditation of St. Dominic. His later accomplishments have to be seen as connected with this preparation. In 1201 he was chosen as Prior of the Chapter, but otherwise he was able to continue his ardent life of prayer for another three years. This brings the total number of years in contemplation up to ten. Quite unexpectedly God changed the course of his destiny. In 1204 Alfonso IX, King of Castile, needed to negotiate a marriage in Denmark for his son, and he designated the bishop of Osma as ambassador. Dominic accompanied the bishop. On their way they passed through Languedoc in Southern France and stayed in the house of a man who professed the Albigensian heresy. With penetrating wisdom, great compassion, and we assume with copious tears, St. Dominic argued with this man through the night and in the morning the man was converted and rejoined the Church.

The Albigensians stressed purity and human perfection to such a degree that they no longer admitted the need of the Sacraments or the Incarnation of our Savior. St. Dominic knew and brought the man to this faith, in which we cannot do without them, if we want to be saved. God alone is our savior. In our faith and in our good works we cooperate with his grace, but faith and good works are no substitute for him or his grace. For the saint the conversion of this man was a grace filled occurrence or a miracle, which gave him the impetus for his future. He had experienced the man as a brother in Christ, someone for whom Christ died and he wanted this brotherhood of salvation, so that God's love could prevail.

He and the bishop fulfilled their mission in Denmark, but unfortunately the princess they brought to Castile died. The two went to Pope Innocent III and presented him with a plan to do missionary work in Russia. The Pope changed their mind and asked them to begin their mission in France, where as they knew so well the Albigensians were threatening the Church. The Pope knew that the Church is strong because of the faith of its members, not because of any outward power. They accepted this offer and first went to Citeaux, the Cistercian Abbey, which was conducting missions against the Albigensians.

However, the Cistercians were ineffective in their efforts because they did their job with too much argumentation and pomp. St. Dominic and his bishop developed another plan. Instead of threats and being overbearing, they used love, persuasion, and peaceful discussion. They were able to respect the heretics and helped them to overcome their resistance to God's greater mercy. The method was even more successful for women and girls, who were converted and found their way to houses of prayer. On a second visit with Pope Innocent III the saint obtained approval of a nunnery in Prouille. Unfortunately the saint was unable to prevent a civil war between Catholics and Albigensians and the harshness of the Inquisition.

The Inquisition had been instituted before his time as a preacher and it is unfair to identify him with it. To an inquisitor accompanied by soldiers he said, "The enemies of the faith cannot be overcome like that. Arm yourself with prayer, rather than the sword. Wear humility rather than fine clothes." However, St. Dominic became a friend of Simon de Montfort, who led a military campaign against the Albigensians and crushed them.

Simon de Montfort died in battle against them in 1218. The saint was on the side of mercy, especially for women and children. His sword was the word of God and faith in his heart. He desired many to join him in his work and to let it grow on a larger scale and for centuries to come and for this reason he established his Religious Order, the Dominicans, known as the Order of Preachers (OP).

For his rule he took passages from St. Augustine and added his own constitutions. By way of the Code of the Monks we acknowledge that contemplation was indispensable for him. The friar has to discover where God is leading him and he can do so only in personal prayer, thereby finding the will of God for him. Seen from the outside, the Order of Preachers may appear as a setting for active ministry, but from the inside, from the intention of its founder and the members it is based on contemplation. Without this basis we have only a business and no Religious Order. In this light it is essential to recognize the spiritual code and not to get side tracked into the appearance. St. Dominic saw in the person who had strayed from the truth first the brother and he appealed to him as a brother and not as an opponent. He inspired the victory of faith as he said, "A man who governs his passions is master of the world. We must either rule them or be ruled by them." He wanted to establish a unity given by God and this unity was given as a fruit of his meditation. Under the auspices of this god given unity people can come together as members of an Order.

St. Dominic wanted to present his rule to Innocent III, but on July 16th, 1216 the Pope died and this delayed his trip to Rome. Soon afterwards Honorius III was elected and St. Dominic obtained approval of his Order in October of that year. The saint had gained great popularity because of his heroic sanctity, apostolic zeal, and profound learning. Pope Honorius supported the spread of the Order through a Bull addressed to all archbishops, bishops, abbots, and priests. The inspiration given to the saint was recognized by many. Through his efforts St. Dominic responded first to the religious needs of an entire region, Languedoc, then he had to include France, Italy and many other countries. He therefore developed a new form of Order, which is able to spread across borders of dioceses and countries. This was something new by way of organization and proved most fruitful for the worldwide mission of the Church. The new development was not intended to create a separation from the historical roots of monasticism; on the contrary it should be seen as a historical update. St. Dominic was a monk and through the grace of God, a new kind of preacher.

To be based on the teaching of the apostles is part of the identity of the Church, part of monasticism and also the new order had to be based on the same. The new order was interested to point out the continuity of tradition.

This was also important in regard to the Heresies they were dealing with. As always the heretical circles claimed to posses the true interpretation of the gospel and therefore justified their criticism of the Church. The new order was in a position to substantiate this claim as well and could engage in a serious dialogue with heretics. The Dominicans were interested to show their seriousness in the way they imitated the life of the apostles and to convince the heretics. In their poverty they followed the poor apostles and the poor Jesus Christ.

They had left everything, walked from place to place and proclaimed the gospel in imitation of the recommendation of Jesus in Matthew 10:9 f: "Provide yourselves with neither gold or silver nor copper in your belts; no traveling bag, no change of shirt, no sandals, no walking staff. The workman, after all, is worth his keep." The heretics could now see with their own eyes how serious these new preachers were. St. Dominic was committed to a good education of his priests, so that they were in a position to explain the faith well and be flexible in their conversations.

The new order also favored the cause of women. Already in 1217 the first convent for Dominican nuns was established. There was a women's movement and the order was able to receive it well. The ideal of poverty as followed by the Dominicans was also adopted by two more religious orders: The Augustinian Hermits and the Carmelites, who came from the Holy Land to Europe in 1228. Like St. Norbert so also St. Dominic gave access to lay people to belong to the Order. They are invited to become members of "The Third Order of St. Dominic, or Brothers and Sisters of the penance of St. Dominic." Besides being appealing to all believers it also increased the sphere of influence of the Order. People from all walks of life could consider themselves belonging to the Order, to receive more companionship, friendship, and support for their witness to Christ. The years of prayer and meditation had given St. Dominic the acute awareness of the closeness of God through the humanity of Jesus Christ. When Jesus says in the Gospel, "I was hungry and you gave me food," then he accepts every human being and establishes a bond as God-given. When St. Dominic met the heretics in Languedoc, then he had this experience of Jesus saying through the heretic, "I was thirsting for the truth and you gave me the truth." This is Christian mysticism, which can take on ever new forms. If we separate St. Dominic or the Dominicans from this mysticism, then we get a busybody, who may accomplish many things, but our judgment doesn't go to the depth of his soul. It is important that we recognize his mysticism. In his code he deciphers his call and can give birth to a new approach of preaching the truth. The saint was so familiar with the truth that he knew most of the New Testament by heart, but he didn't use it as a stiff indoctrination, but as life-giving good news which applies itself to those he addressed.

St. Dominic died in 1221 and his death didn't diminish the work of his Order. He had given birth to his approach and his followers could continue to translate it into the institution of the Dominican Order. Their success was phenomenal because of the continued inspiration they had received from the founder. God was directing their efforts and as long they stay in touch with this original revelation they will continue to be fruitful independently from any outward achievements.

Almost at the same time as St. Dominic another Religious Order was brought forth in Italy. The environment of the Catholic Church was similar to the one encountered by St. Dominic, but the inspiration came about differently through St. Francis of Assisi.

St. Francis was born as Giovanni Bernardone in 1181 or 1182 in Assisi and he died there on October 3rd, 1226. His father Pietro was a wealthy cloth merchant, who had business dealings with France and because of his fondness for this country he called his little boy Francis, or little Frenchman. His mother, Pica, came from a devoted family. Francis had several siblings. He received some basic education from the priest of his parish, St. George, and later from the Troubadours in literature. He was also influenced by the Romanticism of Knighthood, popular at the time and he liked poetry and music, being able to compose songs. He always had quite a bit of money and enjoyed spending it on pleasure and even showing off with it. By nature he was careful not be sinful and from the goodness of his heart he was generous to the poor. St. Francis was not arrogant or proud because of his good fortune, but loved a good time, even showing off his pretty clothing.

Throughout his youth he was handsome and filled with enthusiasm and naturally his friends loved him very much, because he brought so much joy into their lives. He was outgoing and made people happy and they loved to be with him, especially when there was a party going on.

He was even accepted as a leader by his gang, when they tried their strength in arms or games of Knighthood. These proofs of courage could quickly become serious, because rivalries between cities were frequent and young people could easily become involved in them. There was a military confrontation between Perugia and Assisi at the beginning of the thirteenth century when Francis was about twenty years old.

Of course, he had to join the force of his city and learn his lesson. They were defeated and he was made a prisoner of war. It didn't bother him too much and he was released after a year, but some time afterwards he became sick and this blow after the first one tested his patience. He proved to have a lot of spiritual strength and he became more serious. He decided to become a soldier in Southern Italy and got the necessary equipment.

As he was on his way he met a beggar and he exchanged his good clothes with the man's shabby ones. Following this meeting he had a dream in which he saw a palace filled with arms, which were all marked with the sign of the cross and during another illness he heard a voice saying to him: "Francis, serve the master rather than the man!" Once again we ascertain a private revelation giving him some insights for his future. He began to pray and discovered that in the spiritual warfare, on which God puts us, we have to begin with mortification and victory over ourselves.

Francis went to extremes in this regard. One day he met a poor leper, who would be repulsive to everyone, but he gave him a gift, embraced and kissed him. This shows the penetrating awareness of the saint. The sick beggar wasn't just a poor creature for him, but the presence of Jesus Christ as his words explain: "I was sick and you comforted me." This identity indicates the change taking place in the saint. Through his love for the sick he wanted to be closer to Jesus Christ. There shouldn't be anything between him and God. By the same token he also experienced that Jesus accepted him as a means of salvation, when he heard his words from the crucifix, "Francis, go and repair my house, which you see is falling apart." He was about twenty seven years old at the time, in 1207. At first he believed that God wanted him to restore a church-building.

He sold some of his father's merchandise and a horse and wanted to give the money to a priest of St. Damian's. His father was angry at what he had done and carried him home. He beat him, put fetters on his feet and locked him up. His mother released him, but his dad hit him over the head again and demanded that he either sober up or renounce his share of his inheritance. The case was brought before the bishop. Francis gave up his inheritance and took off all his clothes and in his nakedness he gave them back to his father, saying, "The clothes I wear are also his. I'll give them back" and in true spiritual joy he continued, "Up to now I have called you father on earth, but now I say, 'Our Father, who art in Heaven'." The bishop covered Francis with his cloak. It is the office of the bishop to cover and protect not to detect and criticize. Pietro Bernadone had become Francis' ex-father. He left this hearing fuming with rage and at the same time filled with exceeding sorrow. This event is one of the most dramatic in Christian history. Francis accepted the frock of a worker, on which he drew a cross, put it on and tied it with a rope, his first habit.

He was very happy in his poverty, which he loved above everything else, and he praised God for it. Here also it is crucial to recognize the mysticism of the saint. His poverty and abandonment made him more like Jesus crucified and he understood that God had called him to his side and made him a disciple. He couldn't imagine anything better than this friendship and was glad to become a beggar along with Jesus. It is Christian mysticism at its height and he knew very well that it can evolve into contemplation or into action and one shouldn't be excluded from the other. If believers, even if they are Franciscans, do not recognize this mysticism or this extraordinary code of the monk, Francis, then they do not follow the saint either. People observed that Francis loved poverty and they had to add that this was the surest way for him to be in the presence of the Lord. That is why he was delighted to become a beggar. Even if such a rugged existence would shorten his life span, he would be delighted, because then he would go to heaven.

The stories in which he was in heaven already during his earthly life are no mere figure of speech, but reports of his experiences. But he had to continue on; in a monastery he asked for a job and they let him wash dishes for a while. He gladly accepted this work. The money he made he used to help lepers or to restore churches in the neighborhood. In the spirit of poverty the gospel became predominant for him. In this spirit God made him a prophet and a worker of miracles. When he repaired the church of St. Damian he said to the people, "Here will one day be a monastery of nuns by whose fame our Lord will be glorified over the whole Church." In Spoleto he healed a man whose face was disfigured from cancer. From an outcast he became a man whom people would seek out.

The power of the gospel shone forth from St. Francis and men desired to become his companions because through him they were in the presence of God. The first of these was a wealthy tradesman of Assisi, Bernard da Quintavalle. He said about the saint, "This man is truly a servant of God." The second was a well known canon of the Cathedral, Peter of Catteneo. Francis gave them the habit on April 16th, 1209. The third was brother Giles. After some time the group had grown to a dozen. As a rule St. Francis chose words from the gospels, almost selected at random by either hearing a gospel at Mass or by opening the Bible and let God choose phrases for them, a secret code. He didn't want to determine the rule himself, but let it come from God's treasure of wisdom as set forth in his Revelation. These counsels of perfection he brought to Rome the following year, 1210 and asked for their approval from Pope Innocent III.

After his famous dream of seeing St. Francis propping up the Lateran Basilica the Pope gave his general commission to the Order to preach repentance. The abbot of Monte Subasio was most supportive of this new community, let them use a chapel and build huts. In his spirit of poverty, St. Francis didn't want to accept property, but only use what was necessary. Even his own body he used as a property for the glory of God. In his severe temptations against purity he chastised his body, because he wanted it to obey the gospel mandates. It wasn't morbid self-preoccupation, but the presence of the liberating power of the spirit. Those who had joined him were very happy in the spirit they found in this new community. Their poverty was no hindrance for their unity, but bound them more closely together, since they experienced God's immediate provisions for them. Their preaching and their example were most effective.

Word got around that nobody had to feel any reluctance to become a member of the order, because there were no barriers. If Francis was a friend of beggars and lepers, then everybody could come to him. Only unbelief and sinfulness would create barriers and the brothers were strong enough through God's inspiration to overcome them. Those who came only had to cooperate with God's grace. Their very name also indicates that they were interested to let God's grace prevail over them. Fratres minores or minor brothers could mean those belonging to the lower classes of society, but it seems to be more comparable to the gospel as in the parable of the Last Judgment, Mt 25:40 where Jesus says: "I assure you as often as you did it for one of my least brothers, you did it for me."

If the title of minor brothers were bound to social conditions, then it would no longer apply, when these conditions change; but if the title is of a theological nature, then it is timeless. We have to take the title in a theological sense, because St. Francis was first of all a religious man. In line with the gospel, for example, Mt 25:40, the name denotes that the Franciscan is a brother of Jesus Christ, who himself became poor for our sake. This position is likewise an invitation to others to also want to be on the side of Jesus, even if this includes some sacrifices. Along with the sacrifices is given the awareness of the glory, which only Jesus Christ can bestow.

St. Francis was called by the Lord to this existence in which he read his own life and that of others in the light of the gospel. Those who encountered him became intimately aware of the grace of God in him, even the animals, which were drawn to him, in whose heart the power, which had created them, was so strong. They too had to respect this power as when he scolded the swallows, who had been twittering during his sermon, whom he addressed as follows, "My sisters, the swallows, it is now my turn to speak. You have been talking enough all this time." He also told the birds perched around him to praise their Creator. A rabbit would not leave him at Lake Trasimene and the wolf obeyed him. These examples point to the mysterious power within him and the secret code, in which he came to know himself and the world around him.

The spring of 1212 brought him more followers. The noble girl, St. Clare of Assisi and some of her friends wished to join the order. In line with his prophecy she came to him, because she too wished to fulfill God's will for herself and for the Order of the saint. St. Francis was delighted and understood her vocation very well. He accepted her, cut off her hair and gave her the habit. Along with his own vocation she was the contemplative sitting like the sister of Lazarus, Mary, at the Lord's feet, listening to him and imploring his favor for all the requests she knew. When St. Francis called himself the minor brother of Jesus, then she was to be the minor sister, along with the women belonging to her community. This vocation also is theological and not a nice gesture to be a prayerful support of the Franciscans. She also insisted on extreme poverty for the nuns against the wishes of the Pope. He finally granted her wish after learning God's will.

The Poor Clares, as the Order was later called, stress the secret of God's code even more, because they live in seclusion, away from any public observation. God calls us to a kingdom, which is not of this world, and the contemplative stress its invisible nature. St. Francis never separated the contemplative from the active life and the Poor Clares fit his interest in contemplation as do the hermitages, for which he also wrote regulations for those living in them. In some way St. Clare asserted herself when she asked to join, but it was on account of her belief in God's call.

It was not a question of the role of women in the Church, but the awareness of a divine call. In this awareness she and her followers accepted their prayerful position through St. Francis from God, following the recommendations of the Gospel. The role of women in the Gospel is prominent and yet clearly distinct from the men, who are called by Jesus. People in the thirteenth century didn't think of changing this basic set-up as elaborated in the New Testament. If we believe in God's Revelation, then we do best to accept the structure given in Sacred Scripture, instead of comparing it to any exigencies of our time. Our world has to adjust to God's plan and not try to make him fit our insights or needs. St. Clare and her followers witness to this and the call to obedience, which leaves room for God's greater design of salvation.

The mystery remaining is better suited to our nature than ready-made and restricting formats. There may even be justification if the correspondence between St. Francis and St. Clare was later destroyed, because something that sounds romantic may only be an indication of a God-given unity and the romantic would restrict the freedom of the Spirit.

Shortly after settling St. Clare and her sisters in the cloister, in the fall of 1212 St. Francis had the burning desire to convert the Moslems. The expedition to Syria failed because of a shipwreck and the following spring he devoted himself to evangelize Central Italy. A year later he tried again to reach the Moslems in Morocco, but he became ill in Spain and had to return, probably in the winter of 1214–1215. He was present at the death of Pope Innocent III in July 1216 and shortly afterwards Christ appeared to him and granted any favor he might ask. He asked for a plenary indulgence for all people who visited the chapel of Porziuncola after they confessed their sins. The first general chapter of the Order in 1217 made administrative recommendations for the missions.

St. Francis visited Rome again in 1217–1218 where he met St. Dominic. The following year he devoted to missionary tours in Italy, which were a continual triumph. Clergy and people came in processions to meet him, when he came to their towns, and they welcomed him with songs of rejoicing. The extraordinary enthusiasm made it clear that Francis had become a conqueror of souls. In Camara, a town close to Assisi, the entire congregation begged him to be admitted to his order. We have to appreciate this unifying power of God's Spirit at work in the saint. Similarly to St. Dominic he began his Third Order called Brothers and Sisters of Penance.

The glory of the Lord shines through this Penance and makes it a joyful experience. In 1219 he set out again to evangelize the Moslems in the Near East and fearlessly passed over to their camp, was taken prisoner and led before the Sultan. He was received kindly, but was not able to convert them. And yet his interest to do so is the core of our encounter with Islam. His approach was better than the barbaric battles of the Crusades and demanded even more courage. If this greater courage of the missionary is missing, then we will have wars. Our modern world is not better off in this regard than the thirteenth century and we may have to learn to take St. Francis to heart and realize how much up-to-date he is. The modern martyr, Charles de Foucauld, who was killed by Moslems, expressed his longing that God would again give to the world a man like St. Francis of Assisi.

We only deceive ourselves if we believe that scientific advances relieve us of the basic requirements of the spirit. These remain the same, despite all the accomplishments of technology.

After his visit with the Sultan he went to Palestine and commissioned the Franciscans to guard the Holy Places. Francis had to rush back to Italy, because his two Vicar Generals had imposed more severe fasts on the monks than the rule required. He arrived in Venice in July 1220. Close to 5,000 brothers and about 500 applicants came together for the Chapter. In 1223 he was in the town of Grecchio in the valley of Rieti and presented his most popular custom, the manger scene for Christmas. It reflects his feeling for God's gentle love for all mankind. In prayer and quietness he obtained graces from God, which he was careful to conceal from men. Towards the feast of the Assumption, August 15th, in 1224 he went with Brother Leo to Mount Alvernia for strict contemplation.

Here he received the stigmata, the wounds of Jesus in his hands, feet, and his side on September 17th. For him the stigmata were a source of consolation. When he was ill and someone wanted to read something to him for comfort, he said, "Nothing gives me so much consolation as to think of the life and passion of our Lord. Were I to live to the end of the world I should stand in need of no other book." The two years, which remained of his life, were years of intense suffering and yet also of greater happiness in God.

He paid a last visit to the convent of St. Clare and despite his great pain he composed the "Canticle of Brother Sun", which he set to a tune and taught his brothers to sing. He went back to Assisi and when his death drew near he welcomed "Sister Death". St. Francis of Assisi was penetrated by a mysticism, which revealed ever greater and more profound secrets in a very simple fashion. The whole world became for him a great ladder, on which he could climb higher and higher and arrive at the glory of Heaven. His familiarity with the Eternal Son of God was most captivating and has never ceased to draw people to the Christian faith.

Shortly before his death the Lady Jacoba of Settesoli wanted to pay him a farewell visit along with her two sons and her servants. Usually women were not allowed to enter the friary, but St. Francis made an exception for her and to circumvent the rule he called her "Brother Jacoba" and let her enter. He kept his sense of humor and his joy to the very end. He died on Saturday, October 3, 1226. There was no limit to the love in his heart; everybody could come to him, the poor, the sick and the fallen. His love was all-embracing, because he was such a unique reflection of the love of the All-powerful and eternal Godhead. His influence has continued to grow through the centuries. It is important to notice the faith filled reaction of his contemporaries as well.

He evoked something that was latently present in them. They were accessible to conversion and to a deeper faith. Through the saint they recognized a dignity and a sense of joy, which may have been dormant, but which could burst forth in jubilance. The saint renewed this sense of being children of a beloved Father in Heaven, whose joy and glory are inexhaustible. Worship and prayer bring human beings into contact with him. Without this response of the people and the Church at large, his enthusiasm for God would have been more contained within his contemplation, which remains a most important aspect of the Franciscan Spirit.

We thank Divine Providence that Clare of Assisi understood and followed the intuition of the Franciscan spirit so very well. She was convinced that God has designed his graces to flow through the prayers of those who are devoted to him. This is the reason for hers and her sisters' seclusion. She guided her monastery for almost forty years from 1215–1253, although she was rather ill for the last twenty seven. In spite of her ill health her faith was strong and prevailed. In 1244 the forces of Frederick II (1194–1250) were trying to conquer the city of Assisi. Frederick II was a highly complex person and he wanted to unify Italy, he protected the Jews and Moslems alike, but for Assisi his advance was just a danger the citizens were facing. As a cloistered nun St. Clare didn't negotiate with him, but she had a greater power at her disposal. She prayed for the protection of the city and held a ciborium with the Blessed Sacrament in sight of the enemy.

The forces fled and she and the people were rewarded for her prayer. In art St. Clare is portrayed as holding a ciborium. The Church recognized her sanctity already during her lifetime. Pope Innocent IV visited her twice. She was declared a saint in 1255 only two years after her death. We appreciate her code of monasticism in her sense for poverty accompanied by her trust in God's providence, her humility accompanied by her courage, and her mortification and illness accompanied by her sense for God's eternal love in Jesus Christ.

We are also grateful for the wisdom and broadness of mind, in which Pope Innocent III approved the Franciscan movement and its rule. There was something new and different about this movement and there was a process involved, in which this newness could be integrated. Some traditional features proved the continuity of the religious life. Like the Dominicans the Franciscan Order is very flexible and the brothers could be sent everywhere for missionary activity and they soon obtained teaching positions in leading Universities like Paris, Oxford, Cologne, and others. Besides being very much involved in pastoral ministry, they also stressed their intellectual pursuits. The monasteries of the Poor Clares branched out to many parts of the world. In the quickly growing societies the Mendicant Orders were able to make many people feel at home in the Church. Without these Orders many might have fallen away or never been in close touch with the revealed truth and the sacraments of the Church.

Through personal, valuable and meaningful contacts do people come to the faith and the Mendicants were able to make these contacts. The reason for this was not so much the work they did, but that the founders had discovered anew this truth that Jesus Christ is present in each and every human life on this earth. In eras when this truth isn't clear or even rejected the Church will have little or no impact on the ups and downs of history. People, who are only nominally Christian or Catholic are just swept away by the twists and turns of society. The Mendicants could involve the growing masses of people without depersonalizing them or treating them as sheer numbers.

This growth also extended to the intellectual sphere as members of these orders became remarkable scholars. St. Dominic had brought so many people to the faith because he connected them with the gospel and showed them how much God desired them to be part of his kingdom. Once they had made this intimate contact they were happy in their love of God. The intellectuals of the thirteenth century continued: If we search out God's greatness in his creation and the endowment of the human spirit, then we increase our love for God and for those who participate in our search.

St. Albert, St. Bonaventure, and St. Thomas Aquinas

Application of Faith to Intellect

Thus research strengthens our faith in God. This approach is an extension but also a renewed application of contemplation. One of the early ones who found his vocation on this course of action was St. Albert the Great. Born as the son of the Count of Bollstaedt, in Lauingen on the Danube in 1206 he was brought up in this Catholic home. In his youth he went to Padua, where an uncle lived and he pursued his studies at the University there. He was greatly attracted by the preaching of the Dominican, Jordan of Saxony, and asked to be received in the Order. He was accepted in 1222. His father disagreed with his choice and planned to retrieve him by force, but he was moved to another priory, probably Cologne. Along with his ordination he became a teacher of Theology in 1228.

His special gift as a Universal Doctor was the combination of natural science and theology. He spent most of his life in different Universities. Research strengthened his prayer and contemplation and these in turn invigorated his interest in scientific discoveries.

He realized that the human mind is an instrument of God's design of nature and he exemplified this insight through his comments of the writings of the Philosopher Aristotle. His intuition also made it possible for him to discover the abilities of his greatest student, St. Thomas Aquinas, and to favor his career. When he was fifty four he was appointed Bishop of Regensburg, but he resigned this office after only two years, because he wanted to continue as a scholar and as a teacher. In him we can recognize the code of the monk at work. Through nature, history and especially the history of salvation God has set us in motion towards him.

Rank and social status were secondary to him in comparison to the spiritual and intellectual. He was aware how much we are drawn to God, if only we let him draw us. This presence of the Lord was the primary motivating power in him and he had greatly appreciated this same power in his beloved disciple St. Thomas. When St. Thomas died in 1274 it was a great shock for him. Three years later he had to defend his disciple's writings in Paris, where they were seriously attacked as being unorthodox by Stephen Tempier, the bishop of Paris and other theologians. The bishop didn't even agree with a saint in heaven and obtained a local condemnation of certain points of his writings. This condemnation was lifted about one hundred years later.

In 1278 Albert suffered a sudden loss of memory, possibly a stroke and lingered on for two more years until his death in Cologne on November 15th, 1280. He had set the tone for enhancing our prayerful disposition through our intellectual curiosity. His preference of being a monk as compared to a bishop speaks on his behalf and on behalf of prayer and research, bringing our hearts and minds closer to God and his heavenly reign over us than the political maneuverings ever present to the Episcopal office. He had made this sobering distinction when he left his office as bishop behind after also having suffered sufficient disappointments.

The close friend of St. Thomas was the Franciscan St. Bonaventure. He was born in 1221 close to Viterbo in Italy, some four years before St. Thomas Aquinas. A legend about his childhood tells that he received his name from St. Francis after he had been cured by him from a serious illness. The legend makes the point that Bonaventure during the first five years of his childhood was a contemporary of St. Francis of Assisi, had experience of him and enjoyed everything about him, especially his closeness to the common people and his deep sympathy for everything human. Bonaventure kept his love for the simplicity of St. Francis and the Order and he wrote the most extensive biography of him.

Through this he also shows that he valued the popular devotion of all Catholics and his own intellectual career didn't alienate him from the simplicity and general understanding of the Gospel. Intellectual pursuits can easily estrange a person from the simple joy of God's kingdom as recommended in God's Revelation, but St. Bonaventure kept his childlike trust in God despite his steep career as a teacher of Theology. "The Poverty of Christ" one of his books calls us to this simple trust in God's goodness even if we feel poverty as Christ felt it in his life. As he was growing up it was natural for him to consider becoming a Franciscan, owing his life and his spiritual identity to the saint. Consequently he entered the Order very early in life, at age seventeen in 1238.

After his novitiate and early studies he went in 1242 to Paris to continue his education under the Englishman, Alexander of Hales, who unfortunately died three years later in 1245. Bonaventure began teaching with great success in 1248 and continued until 1255, when the Mendicants at the University were under serious attack. St. Bonaventure's theology reflects his heartfelt love of God and stresses the mystical side of our faith.

He received the title of Doctor Seraphicus, enlightening his students like a Seraphim. His insights have their orientation in St. Augustine and Plato and stress the importance of our will towards God. We find God in our love for him, through which "Our mind can make its journey" to Him (another title of his works). His teachings were accepted by the Franciscan Order and set the standard for many generations of scholars.

However, he didn't find easy acceptance from the University of Paris, who felt threatened by these newcomers of the Mendicant Orders and even discontinued their teaching for a couple of years from 1255 to 1257. St Bonaventure wrote (as mentioned) his defense: "The Poverty of Christ". The new orders didn't really promote something new, but wanted to imitate the poverty of Christ, in which believers find the most adequate approach to God and become more like him.

In this likeness they are also filled with the joy of the Spirit, which is the trademark of believers and certainly was the trademark of St. Francis. St. Bonaventure expressed it as follows: "A spiritual joy is the greatest sign of the divine grace dwelling in a soul". The soul is aware of only being on the journey towards God, which set his heart only more firmly on him, or as he put it: "God Himself, all the glorious spirits, and the whole family of the eternal King wait for us and desire that we should be with them; and shall we not long above all things to be admitted into their happy company?" He believed that the human heart was created in order to soar towards heaven and his writings served as an incentive for this.

Besides teaching he became General of his Order 1257, a position he held until his death in 1274. He always had an eye for practical ministry in the Church and the concerns of all believers. He also did his best to overcome the tensions in the order between those who advocated a strict interpretation of the Rule of St. Francis and those who were more relaxed, called Relaxti.

In 1265 he successfully refused to be named Archbishop of York, but in 1273 he had to accept the position of Cardinal-Bishop of Albano. At the time the envoy of the Pope arrived he was washing dishes and after he had cleaned his greasy hands he accepted the Cardinal's hat. He held this position for about a year until July 14th, 1274 when he died at the Council of Lyons. His writings continue to prove the connection between contemplation and our lives as believers. Our lives are meaningful when they are filled with the eternal truths and the promises made to us in the Scriptures.

Without this connection with what God has promised we become disoriented and sad. Even through his demanding theology the saint wants to increase the simple joy of the believing heart. To renew and encourage this simple joy for the rapidly growing masses of people in the many cities of Europe made the Mendicants, Dominicans and Franciscans, so successful. Their attraction derived from this common belief that God doesn't leave anybody out of his love and protection. People who so easily would be marginalized, neglected and abandoned were accepted and felt their value as creatures of the Eternal and Ever-living God. The Mendicants didn't create this bond, but they had discovered that this bond was a gift from above and they too could rejoice with everybody that God had called them together.

Ultimately all of creation comes together in a mysterious unity known to God alone. This was the Spirit of these new orders and virtually no one could stop it, because they were movements under the direction of the Holy Spirit.

This also applies to Bonaventure's close friend and illustrious Master of Theology, St. Thomas Aquinas. He was born about 1225 in the castle Rocca Secca, close to Aquino and only a few miles from the abbey of Monte Cassino, the cradle of Western Monasticism. When he was only five years old he was brought to this monastery as an oblate as the rule of St. Benedict permitted. A close relative of the Aquino family was the abbot. Naturally endowed with the spirit of contemplation he also possessed great intellectual curiosity and abilities. He thrived in the environment of the Benedictine Order for almost nine years, the most formative years of his life. His later prayerful poems, prayers and chants are also rooted in these meditative years of his childhood. We have to be very grateful to the Benedictines for recognizing and fostering his talents and for recommending him to further studies outside the monastery.

Upon the advice of the abbot the family sent him to the University of Naples in 1239, where he studied for five years. Most likely the abbey and his family wanted him to return to Monte Cassino after his studies, but plans changed. In Naples he became strongly attracted to the still young Order of Preachers. In view of the resistance of his family to such a step he was advised to wait, which he did until he was nineteen. In 1244 he was clothed in the habit of this new order. His mother was especially furious. He had entered an order of begging brothers and after having been sidetracked a couple of times she sent her older sons with troops to arrest him and place him in confinement. He was imprisoned by his family for nearly two years, until 1245. They even tried to break his vocation through seduction, but he didn't give in and was only strengthened in his resolve to remain chaste. Instead, he studied the Sentences of Peter Lombard and parts of the Bible by heart and wrote about Aristotle, his most favorite philosopher from Antiquity.

His family relented somewhat and let him return to the Order. He came to Cologne in 1245 and as pointed out studied under St. Albert the Great and went with him to Paris in the same year. They returned to Cologne in 1248 and he taught under Albert as a Bachelor. After his ordination he was sent to Paris as a teacher in 1251. During these years he planned his chief work, Summa theologica:

God and his perfection, his goodness, his being eternal and everywhere present, his unity and simplicity, his life and will, his love and justice, his providence and power, his creation especially of human beings as a composite of spirit and body, our feelings and our will, our imagination and our choices, our relationship to angels and demons, our happiness and the circumstances of our actions, our delights and the distinction between good and evil, the effects of love and hatred, our longing and satisfaction, our pain and sadness, our anger and anxiety, virtues and sins, venial and mortal sins, God's law and human laws, grace the new law and our merits, faith and redemption, unbelief and apostasy, peace and compassion, jealousy and discord, war and sedition, wisdom and ignorance, cleverness and good counsel, just judgment and reparation, dignity and respect, injustice, murder and theft, slander and false accusation, closeness to God, devotion and prayer, worship and sacrifice, adoration and superstition, obedience and gratitude, kindness and generosity, patience and courage, fasting and chastity, lust, addiction and healing, contemplation and meditation.

These and similar topics of the Summa give evidence that the saint was familiar with all human emotions and reactions and knew how to view them in God's great plan of salvation. He expounded these themes on about one thousand five hundred pages.

In comparison to his friend Bonaventure he treated his topics in a different light. Bonaventure experienced ideas as ideals which we fully perceive and enjoy when we are in heaven. St. Thomas Aquinas following his master St. Albert the Great perceived that the ideas God has of his creation can be found by our discernment and right judgment. These ideas are invisible, but we create them in our mind. This approach is actually more practical and the Greek master Aristotle was a good educator in this regard.

In his youth, Aristotle, the son of a physician, thought of discovering the soul of a dog and he killed the poor animal. This incident happened about 370 BC i.e. 2,380 years ago. This means the animal wouldn't be alive anymore, even if Aristotle hadn't killed him. The discovery Aristotle made, was that he couldn't find the soul of the dog, but it exists anyway, because this idea is what gives the dog life. The soul exists, although it is invisible. In our Christian understanding these invisible realities are even more important, because it is from heaven that God's creation has made its start. We need these heavenly ideas for our understanding of God's creation and even more so for our appreciation of his salvation. For this reason St. Thomas had such a great respect for everything created, very similar to St. Francis of Assisi's love for the animals. And yet, we are bound to God's revelation, in order to have the proper respect for his creation and salvation. The bond of love running through creation and salvation are lodged in the bosom of God. Without him our appreciation of these is insufficient and the bonds of love he makes possible have to come from him.

We may for example apply this to marriage and friendship, so much under attack today. If a married couple is convinced that God has brought them together, then their union has a validity, which far surpasses their physical or sexual contact. The same can be true for genuine friendship as the one described above between St. Basil and St. Gregory of Nazianzen. In the case of the two monks there is no sexual expression and yet their friendship is nonetheless a fully developed bond of human love. In our modern world such human friendship usually receives only a label of cynicism, which makes the issue, for example in homosexuality, only more virulent.

This very modern cynicism cannot claim St. Thomas Aquinas as supporter; neither can people who are prejudiced against homosexuals claim him as their supporter. St. Thomas Aquinas knew what spiritual bonds are and we have to learn from him; otherwise we only develop something of a physical nature to describe spiritual bonds and like Aristotle we only have a dead dog instead of a live animal, whose soul is still active and well.

A serious and long lasting misunderstanding or lack of understanding of St. Thomas Aquinas came about through the Renaissance. True, St. Thomas used Aristotle as his philosophical witness, but he used him in a Christian perspective. Renaissance simply put Antiquity first side by side with Christianity and later even above Christianity and is partly responsible for renewed paganism in our modern world. So far this error hasn't been corrected and we don't have to be surprised when we witness new forms of paganism. St. Thomas Aquinas didn't make such a mistake and we have to be very careful and diligent in our study of his writings. His was a penetrating understanding of God's plans and he applied this very diligently to the world as he experienced it. This is also one reason why he joined a Mendicant Order, because he knew God's work in them.

Through prayer and research he had been made aware that God was there first to love him and draw close to him. This was true not only for him, but for everyone created in the image and likeness of God.

For the saint this involves the topic of the relationship between Christians and other world religions and in particular the Moslems, which has become again so important in our modern world. During his life there had been a considerable amount of cooperation between the two and Christians had benefited greatly from importing scientific and religious discoveries from them. This should also be true for us today, considering their deep devotion to God, the strength of their families and their ability to give especially men a role, which is closer to the Bible than our modern model in our Western Democracies. St. Thomas Aquinas was aware that the Emperor Frederick II (1194–1250) had grown up in Sicily where Norman, Greek and Moham-medan civilizations lived side by side, often strengthening and encouraging one another.

This Emperor had been quite successful in fostering this cooperation. He suffered being excommunicated by Pope Gregory IX in 1227 for not being eager to undertake a crusade to incorporate the Holy Land. Later he fulfilled the Pope's wishes to some extend, crowning himself King of Jerusalem. His strength had weakened the Pope, who in 1245 left Rome secretly and went to Lyon to summon a council. The situation was not very happy as a contemporary writer described it: "Injustice reigned supreme. The people were without leaders and Rome was troubled. Clerical dignity was lost sight of and the laity was split into various factions. Some were loyal to the Church others adhered to Frederick and became enemies of God's religion." After the death of the Emperor the situations for the Christians became more dangerous, because the Moslems put greater pressure on them. The thought had to occur to everybody: If things are already so difficult in most parts of the Church, how much more difficult are they in areas, where the Moslems expand their territory, for example in Spain. Towards the end of this decade of 1250 St. Thomas prepared a response to this complicated situation and later wrote his Masterpiece: Summa contra Gentiles, about Christians and Non-Christians. The overall situation also makes it obvious that the saint didn't write as an untroubled Professor, who can develop a theme according to his leisure. St. Thomas Aquinas felt responsible to give a response to a complex issue. On the one side the Christians owed much to their contact with this other world religion, but at the same time they couldn't agree with their basic theology.

It was typical for the saint that he didn't answer in any way agitated, but in the most objective fashion about the Religion instituted by Jesus Christ and what this means in our encounter with another world religion. Especially the University of Paris was the favorite place where this intellectual encounter between the two world religions could come about. An earlier Pope had said about Paris that it was the oven where the bread of Christianity was baked and we might continue about St. Thomas Aquinas, that for him it was cool in the furnace. Despite the pressing concern he kept the dignity of an apostle to proclaim God's truth calmly as a gift for the world and as an invitation for others to accept.

This Summa therefore explains simply how God is in Himself, how he created and relates to his creatures, who originate in him, how his creation is directed towards him as its goal, how God has revealed himself and how we experience his love in the Sacraments of the Church he has instituted. This very objectivity makes him a timeless witness of the truth, who remains so convincing because he elaborates the truth with complete composure. We still can take him as a model witness because he describes the real bond which God has brought about with and for us. He first reflects on who God is, on what he has done and when we are firm in this reflection, then the opportunities of faith and the obligations derived from it follow naturally and are free from the usual oppressive indoctrination.

It is evident for him that the Gospel comes first and he doesn't water it down for the sake of some dialogue or compromise and he submits to the way in which it has come down to us. He views it as a decisive sign of the truth of the gospel beyond the miracles recorded there that it has come down to us through the preaching of simple and uneducated men, who brought it about that Christians accept its difficult message, expect such an extraordinary fulfillment after their earthly life and endure hardships willingly because of it. The basic requirement of Christians is to accept the message of Sacred Scripture as it is without any additions from our side. When this requirement has been met then we follow the demands of reason very well. He affirms the traditional cardinal virtues of wisdom, justice, courage and moderation. These are included in the New Testament and connected with the natural disposition of our emotions and their goals.

They do not have to be imposed on a will in us, which would be opposed to them. God's grace elevates and brings our nature to perfection. Our wisdom enables us to keep our eternal salvation in view, whatever we might otherwise be doing. Through wisdom we struggle in our daily lives in such a way that the light of contemplation is kept burning and isn't extinguished on account of activities. Many experiences are merely accidental and indifferent to contemplation and we don't have to let them interfere with the depth of our soul and its destination. It is also from this depth of our soul and our reason that we can be successful to avoid giving in to these ever present dangers of lust or cruelty.

The saint felt his vocation to apply his prayerful insights to the actual situation of all human beings in history and we can still apply them very well. It is also for this reason that he became a member of the Dominican Order. By the same token he didn't leave the Benedictine Order behind as something of the past, but took this background along and used it well. After 1252 he was supposed to prepare for his doctorate, but there was a delay because of a conflict between the University and the Friars.

It had begun as a confrontation between the university and the city of Paris. The city guards had killed one student and wounded three others. Further, the city refused to meet any demands of the university and stipulated that in the future only those students would be admitted to the doctorate, who agreed to subscribe to their requests. The friars, Dominicans and Franciscans, didn't agree and therefore they were not admitted. The Pope intervened for them in 1256 four years after the conflict had begun. St. Thomas and St. Bonaventure were promoted to the degree of Doctor on October 23, 1257. From then onwards his life was set; praying, preaching, teaching, writing and traveling: Rome, Anagni, Bologna, Orvieto, Viterbo, Perugia, Cologne, Paris, London, and so on. Even in this outward fashion he had to resemble St. Dominic, being like him inspired by his contemplation. His works and activities flowed from his closeness with the Lord. He was seen in ecstasies and levitations and many were convinced of his sanctity during his lifetime. His hymns: *Pange lingua, Lauda Sion, Adoro te devote* and others also witness to his piety. Pope Gregory X invited him as consultant to the Council of Lyons in 1274 and despite his failing health he made plans to attend, but he lost his strength and he had to end his journey in the Cistercian Abbey of Fossa Nuova. The monks gladly offered him their hospitality and urged him to dictate a short commentary on the Song of Songs. He died on March 7th, 1274, scarcely fifty years of age. Many miracles attested to his sanctity. His writings are enormous and he has been declared a Doctor of the Church. He belongs not only to the history of his Order, but of the Church and of all Mankind.

He encouraged the familiarity with all of nature, trusting that God's grace brings nature to perfection. It was probably in accordance with the grace of God that he died in the Monastery called, "Fossa Nova" or "New Channel". This would then be a symbol that St. Thomas Aquinas was a new channel of God's grace, meeting our weak human nature and leading it upwards to his divine life. Such was and still is the impact of the Mendicants.

St. Thomas Aquinas had given a framework for dealing with the Moslem Religion in his Summa Contra Gentiles, which was not easy to implement on a practical level. John of Matha had founded an Order towards the end of the twelfth century, which had received its blessing from Pope Innocent III in 1198, whose members wanted to retrieve Christians imprisoned by Moslems in Northern Africa and Spain. Often it was possible to pay a ransom and the people could return to their homes; sometimes the Members of the Order had to be willing to release prisoners by taking their place. Monks would undertake this risky exchange as witness for Christ also in the hope that they would be able to do some missionary work among the Moslems.

They could also take this step as the acceptance of martyrdom, if Christ willed it. This would be a peak-experience in the heart of the contemplative: If this decision to give my life in ransom for someone captured by the Moslems leads to an imprisonment until the end of my life or to my execution, does Christ want and accept this sacrifice and does it in consequence bring me to my eternal happiness in heaven? St. Francis had shown this kind of courage and the members of this order were also willing to go to this extreme. We truly admire their courage and derive the insight from it that an Order is a way of life coming from God and being directed towards him. There is a truly existential moment involved in any spiritual commitment.

Servites and the Carmelites
Returning to the Opportunity to be Alone with God

The cause of stricter contemplation is also stressed by the Servites, founded by seven young men in the city of Florence, who withdrew from the world around them so that they could devote themselves exclusively to prayer. The Order began in 1233, initiated by Bonfilius Monaldi and six friends. This was upon an apparition of the Blessed Virgin Mary. The seven founders were lay-men in the way that many hermitages and orders grew and prospered. The simplest trust in eternal life is essential for contemplation. Through these founders the order has clearly defined historical roots.

This is different for the Carmelite Order, which became and still is one of the most renowned contemplative Orders. An early notation from the second part of the thirteenth century states that the holy fathers of this order lived and prayed on this mountain from the days of the prophet Elijah and that their successors after Jesus Christ built a chapel there in honor of our Lady and received the title "Friars of the Blessed Mary of Mount Carmel" and the first general chapter took place in 1287. To trace their origin back to the prophet Elijah is theologically chosen very well, even if there are some historical problems. Elijah and his disciples are viewed as models of perfection well suited for monks and nuns.

The prophet is aware that people are estranged from God because of their sin, which blocks their contact with God and makes love impossible. This alienation from God has the consequence of some misfortune as for example in 1 Kings 17:1, 'Now Elijah the Tishbite, of Tishbe in Gilead, said to Ahab, "As the Lord the God of Israel lives, before whom I stand, there shall be neither dew nor rain these years, except by my word."' Lack of rain and lack of food are the consequence for the people's sinfulness. Sinners have forgotten that man has been created to be the image of God. And yet, the estrangement from God still leaves hope, which the prophet raises through the words, "except by my word".

The prophet can pray for the people and God can change their destiny; this is hope and the prophet and later the monk are put into this position of prayer. However, this position doesn't give the prophet or the monk any immediate recognition or acceptance. On the contrary, he has to flee for his life and accept a place of solitude and contemplation. He was powerful before men, but before God he is without power. In obedience the prophet and later the monk or nun will often be lonely and abandoned. He has to accept this humiliation, but still trusting that God's plan will succeed and bring him glory. The Carmelites follow this path and exemplify that the theology of the Old Covenant is also part of the New, although it is accepted within our Christian perspective.

The dangers in the Christian era are equally great and the monks and nuns have to be prepared to walk in the footsteps of the martyrs. Some Carmelites on Mount Carmel were killed by the Moslems in the fourteenth century, but others were able to return and built a new monastery there.

St. Louis, King of France, also visited Mount Carmel in 1254 and a few hermits could come to Paris and start a hermitage in Charenton, near Paris. In 1291 the Monastery on Mount Carmel was again taken by the Moslems and the monks put to death. By that time the pressure put on the Christians in the Holy Land had become so great that they had to leave and settle in Christian territory in Europe.

There they were well respected and the Order grew very much. They began monasteries in the larger cities and lived in community instead of being hermits. Especially when they were close to the Universities did young people feel a vocation, and their numbers increased. In the middle of the thirteenth century they were already established in Cambridge, Oxford, London, York, Bologna, Naples and other cities. Given some modifications their theology was very successful and people in the cities enjoyed coming to their services and listen to their homilies, often given by renowned preachers. This combination of intellectual endeavors and contemplation worked very well for them and for those close to them. They were and still are more given to contemplation, but as an Order they resemble the Mendicants.

For some Orders engaged in many social, educational, health and research concerns there is always the great danger that contemplation, prayer and the focus on God is neglected or even pushed into the background. These secondary goals so easily capture our attention, because they can be seen, measured and they show our success on the human level. This is not the case with "mere" prayer, which may not be able to show any results, except when God chooses to reward it. His reward can be internal, taking place in the depth of the human soul, and be kept as a secret between the two partners, God and man. Like Elijah, the contemplatives may always have to be willing to take the risk of such inwardness and leave everything else in God's hands. Many monks and nuns have proven their conviction exactly in their courage to take this risk. We have to admire them for this and also acknowledge that this gives evidence of the grace of God being at work in them. The sufferings they were able to endure often joyfully also give evidence of this grace of God. In many instances not even bishops and the clergy in the cities liked them very much or even opposed them.

Bishops and clergy were usually pursuing pastoral goals and objectives and may have developed little understanding for genuine contemplation. The presence of Carmelites got in their way and yet we appreciate these contemplatives all the more, because it was from this spirit that the Church received and still receives its inner strength. It is also from this spirit that people could cope with historical changes and blows of fate. The contemplative entrusts himself to the Lord, even when the storms of history rock the boat and threaten to sink it. For him the joy of eternal life is present and breaking through even when everything seems to fall apart. The hope and security given by the contemplative may at times be the most decisive service rendered for the Church and the World. It is also in this attitude that the traditional Benedictines continued to be strong and able to renew their inner and outer resources. We can depend that God will always keep genuine meditation in some parts of the Church intact.

By the fourteenth century monks and nuns had made tremendous contributions to the Church and to the various societies and their endeavors. They had deepened and increased the love of God and promoted the participation in the spiritual and temporal goods, which God provides for human beings. The growth of populations had been challenging, but also brought improvements and readjustments, so that many could lead better lives and be confident, that they were fulfilling God's plan in their regard. Christianity had created a unity, which was accessible to everybody in some way. The different religious orders had brought revivals and made many feel welcome, who already had fallen away from the Church and become heretical.

Black Death

A Challenge for Centuries

One challenge of the fourteenth century was the Black Death. Sailors had brought this disease in October 1347 from the Orient to Messina. People in Sicily tried to flee from it, but instead it spread even faster. Already in the same year, 1347, there died 530,000 people from this disease in Sicily alone. In the following year it had spread to Spain, France, England, Germany, the Netherlands and other parts of Europe. Considering that the Center of Europe had about 100 million people at that time one fourth or 25 million lost their lives. A census of Pope Clement VI extended its base of calculation to include a total of 160 million and of these 43 million died from the Black Death. The disease continued its devastation through the centuries and came to a halt in Europe only by 1820. In India it still claimed 1 million two hundred thousand lives in 1907.

Besides the loss of human lives the disease had an impact on the religion. People realized how little our lives are in our own power and that we owe everything to God. Many people gave in to despair but those devoted to God became even stronger in their faith, encouraging everybody to look up to God, to invoke his mercy and his saving help. Often prayers were answered and people could point out, where a pilgrimage, a chapel or a sacred image had miraculously stopped the advance of the Black Death.

People who had been away from the Church took this threat to their lives as an opportunity to return to their faith and priests and religious were able to prepare those for death and the life of eternity, who were at the point of dying. Some of the saintly people were so powerful in their prayer that patients, who had contracted the illness, were instantly cured. They then knew that God was involved and continued to live in gratitude and piety, following the ethical demands of the gospel.

St. Catherine of Sienna

One of the Greatest Women in Christendom

One of the most remarkable saints and Dominican Tertiaries, Catherine of Siena, was born in 1347, the year the Black Death began to spread across Europe. She died in Rome in 1380 at the age of thirty three. In her case it was also a private revelation which started her vocation. At the age of six she was walking along with her older brother, Stefano, when she was drawn to look up and she saw Jesus, St. Peter, St. Paul and St. John. Stefano called her several times and took her hand until she heard what he was saying and she said to him, "If you had seen what I saw you wouldn't have done that." This simple narrative of the two children can convince us of this truth. From then onwards she felt drawn to eternal life, made a vow of virginity at age seven and wanted to spend as much time in prayer as possible. Her family made this very difficult for her, but she accepted suffering and rejection for the sake of Christ and grew in inwardness. When she was sixteen she had gained enough independence and situated herself as a hermit in the family home. For our topic we observe that hermitism is often the base of a religious vocation. Like St. Anthony, St. Benedict, St. Patrick and others she also had to endure most degrading temptations of the flesh. These isolated her in her imagination, but made her rely all the more on

God's presence. In 1366 Our Savior appeared to her again and she received a ring of spiritual espousal from him, visible only to her and not to others.

In 1370 she experienced a mystical death accompanied by a vision of Heaven, Hell and Purgatory. Persecutions, isolation and abandonment were intended by God to prepare her for a great mission. She began to take care of the sick in hospitals and in the streets and loved to take those who were most repulsive, even when they were ungrateful for her care. People began to notice her sanctity and were drawn to become her followers: Blessed Raymund of Capua, the English William Flete and others. They felt accepted and understood in her presence and called her "Mamma".

Unlike the saint the politics in the Church were not sustained by faith and grace, but had become a rather mundane business. Pope Gregory XI was in exile in Avignon and served the King of France instead of the spiritual needs of the Church; like modern bishops, who serve the lawyers, the media and the stock market. The city of Florence for example deeply resented the Pope's attitude and the Pope responded by sending his legate with a well equipped army against the city of Florence. This made things only worse and the citizens had to suffer greatly from the treatment they received from the Holy Father. Everybody knew that something wasn't right.

Florence wasn't the only place suffering from social, religious and political troubles. Catherine sent several letters to the Pope, which were not well received, because they were considered to have been written in "an intolerable dictatorial style". We are assured that Catherine looked at these things from God's perspective and felt obligated to be strict and severe. Since this didn't work she had to go to Avignon herself and meet the Pope. She had a threefold message for him: To go back to Rome, to reform the clergy and to start a Crusade to reclaim the Holy Places for the access of pilgrims. This last item was as difficult as it had been for St. Bernard and yet she hoped that the many frictions and factions within Christendom had to be overcome and this could happen, if there was a common cause.

We can believe that sometimes God favors the lesser of two unavoidable evils, which makes it clear that the position of the saint isn't easy. Surprisingly the Pope was very much impressed by her and later she had the true Christian freedom to call him "my sweet babbo". In spite of all severity the Christian message is one of joy and spiritual delight. The Pope did return to Rome in 1377, but wasn't able to do much, because of the chaos prevailing there.

He died the following year and the following Conclave was forced through threats from the public, who had sent armed soldiers to enforce their demands, to elect a Roman as Pope. The Conclave elected the Archbishop of Bari, who called himself Urban VI. The French Cardinals and one Spaniard declared the election invalid and they elected their own, Clement VII. Now we had two Popes. This led to the most tragic constitutional crisis the Church ever experienced and this crisis lasted for forty years. Christianity was breaking apart, because both had successors and the fight became only more vehement and brutal. St. Catherine was on the side of Urban VI, but there are serious doubts about this pontiff's personality. He acted willfully, brutally and fanatically.

Each Pope banned the followers of his opponent, so that all of Christianity was banned. Theologically the situation was intolerable, but the Church had to endure it. Catherine remained faithful to Urban VI. She wrote her masterpiece known as "the Dialogue of St. Catherine". In it the Eternal Father talks with the human soul. This work affirms our insight that contemplation comes first, before any involvement of the Christian on the historical level. Man must remain in the cell of self-knowledge if he wants to come to God. His journey through life is only meant to prepare him for his unique encounter with the Lord, which is more than words can describe. Catherine even had the experience that the Church crushed her, but she could accept this, because of the eternal life giving her an unheard of opportunity, despite everything announced by the Church. Also in the person of Urban VI she might just have accepted a lesser evil. Her intentions to do God's will were nonetheless beyond reproach and she has been called the greatest woman in Christendom.

Along with her extraordinary involvement on the political and historical scene she affirms the intense need for meditation; without it our actions will always be superficial. The saint remains so convincing because of the depth of the spirit she opened up and made accessible for many through the centuries. She also makes it obvious that prayer has to precede any work, if our journey should have the right direction. Remarkably her life was hidden in God and yet revealed so much of the joy of heaven and the participation in her love continued and the bonds of friendship with God intensified.

In retrospect we have to be grateful to God for having given the World St. Catherine of Siena, who was able to encourage believers when they were faced with the greatest struggles and experienced storms that mere mortals cannot weather. Time and again we have to reckon with this possibility of encountering insurmountable obstacles along with the God-given mandate to keep on going anyway. To give up the struggle would be defeat, but we know that the Christian message is one of final victory in Christ.

The soul searching required at these times can enhance our dignity and our belief that God prepares us for higher goals.

A spiritual movement in the Netherlands developing at the same time as the dramatic life St. Catherine of Siena was rather successful in this regard. This reform movement also made its beginning among lay-people. They felt deeply the need for a more developed interior life and looked for practices to bring this about: Prayer, meditations, pilgrimages, reading Sacred Scripture and devotional books. Eventually this movement reached many people and the contemplatives in various convents could very well connect with this and make it their own. Their own spirituality was being enriched.

Modern Devotion, Geert de Groote, and Thomas a Kempis

Scripture in a Personal Manner

This movement of piety had started through Geert de Groote from Holland. He was born in Deventer in 1340 and died on August 20th, 1384. Although he was born seven years before St. Catherine of Siena his spiritual career began almost at the same time as hers, since he was a late bloomer and she certainly was an early starter. He first went to a Chapter school, then for higher studies to Aachen and from there to Paris. He studied medicine, theology and canon law and returned home at age eighteen and at age 22 he was appointed as teacher at the Deventer chapter school. He enjoyed the esteem of his country men, who sent him on a mission to Pope Urban V. For a while he taught philosophy and theology in Cologne.

Through contacts with a fellow student of the Sorbonne in Paris, Aeger of Calcar, prior of the Chartreuse near Arnheim he had a conversion experience and he began the practice of the devout life and for three years he withdrew into the mentioned monastery for the sole purpose of recollection and prayer. This in turn developed within him apostolic zeal and he began to preach. He attracted many people to prayer and giving their life over to God. His endeavors needed a very practical application and he founded the "Brethren of the Common Life" at Zwolle.

He had to undergo severe trials and some people were so strongly opposed to him that they achieved that his preaching license was withdrawn from him. He appealed to Rome and the Holy Father gave him a positive response. Unfortunately his reinstatement arrived only after he had passed away. He died on August 20th in 1384 at the age of 44. At the time he was helping people suffering from the Black Death and he contracted this disease as well.

He believed that he had to take this risk for the sake of charity. His mysticism was very practical and he came spiritually closer to eternal life when he helped those in need. His conversion and his years in prayer as a contemplative brought him to this strength of faith so that he could be so effective in his preaching of reform. Meditation of Sacred Scripture, regular prayer, and the study of the mystical writings, especially of the German Mysticism of the time, made it clear to him, how important inwardness of the spiritual life is, and that it has to be combined with love of neighbor. He practiced and preached self-control and charity. His biography was written by Thomas a Kempis, who also wrote the "Imitation of Christ", one of the most influential devotional books in the history of the Catholic Church.

Thomas a Kempis was closely connected with Geert de Groote, since he was still trained by Groote's successor. Thomas a Kempis was born about 1380 and died July 25th, 1471, at the age of ninety one. When he was thirteen (in 1393) he went to the school of the "Brothers of the Common Life" in Deventer, where he was educated for seven years. Deventer was the center of the new devotion, which from there spread to the Low Countries. The members follow the biblical mandates of poverty, chastity, and obedience and combine love of God and love of neighbor. All this is done in simplicity, humility and devotion. Already upon the recommendation of Geert de Groote they had established a congregation in Windesheim, near Zwolle.

Thomas applied to be accepted in Windesheim in 1399 at the age of nineteen. He was welcomed and clothed as a novice in 1406 and ordained to the priesthood in 1413. He belonged to this community throughout his life, was sub-prior and for most of these years he lived in Windesheim. Despite their lives of dignity and integrity some people had expressed their suspicion about them and had obtained an interdict from Pope Martin V. As a consequence of this interdict the community had to live in exile for three years, from 1429–1432, when the question was settled in their favor. In his "Imitation of Christ" Thomas a Kempis lets the Gospel form our heart and our soul, so that we become suitable inhabitants of Eternal Life. In integrity and inwardness he deals with such topics as: Inordinate Affection, Avoiding too much Familiarity, Acquiring Peace, Resisting Temptation, Compunction of Heart, Patience, Familiar Friendship of Jesus, Love of the Cross, the Secret Judgments of God, the Suffering of Injuries, Rest in God, the Excellence of a Free Mind, Recovering Grace, Renunciation of all Covetousness, the Delight of God, How to govern ourselves, Longing for Eternal Life, on Bearing being desolate, Our Hope in God and our Longing to be united with Christ and so on.

Thomas a Kempis was an epitome of monasticism and the Secret Code of the Monk is expressed most appropriately in his "Imitation of Christ". The transition to eternal glory is taking place in this preparation of the soul and the believer can make this code his own by conscientious application. He is not aloof, but he has grasped that we are empowered through God to let the ephemeral be only the stepping stone towards the eternal. Seen in this light, his code and message are timeless and exclude no one, who is willing to undergo his training. Thomas a Kempis was a priest, but the movement he represented and fostered so well was first a lay movement.

Once it had been well established and when their intention had been compared to other religious communities it was obvious that this was a new religious order, whose members were first of all attracted to the eternal. Thomas a Kempis was just penetrated by the presence of the Divine and when he had talked with people only for a short time he often excused himself, saying, "I must go. Somebody wants to talk with me in my cell." People caught on quickly that this someone was God and that he didn't want to let too much time elapse between the conversations with Him. There is something genuinely peaceful about his "Imitation of Christ".

The reader can step aside from any preoccupation and rely on God's never ending love. He doesn't have to try feverishly to match the eternal, but let it sink in and to his surprise it is there for him. Reading something spiritual enhances this experience or as Thomas described it, "I have looked everywhere for rest and haven't found it except in little nooks with little books". The reading of his "Imitation of Christ" is easy and prepares our own transition of participating in the Life of Grace very well.

The reader can let God's grace take over and at a juncture chosen by the Lord Eternity takes over and the earthly journey is conducted from this different plane. This transition has proven so powerful through the centuries and brought about the extraordinary success of this book. Thomas a Kempis didn't set himself up as a teacher of a new doctrine and his book goes along very well with many other meditations and prayers. He didn't compete with anyone and for this reason his book has been acceptable for many religious in other Orders. Quietly and peacefully his influence could grow for lay-people and religious alike and he could become a great source of strength and consolation whenever there were greater demands made on people to help them to focus on what is essential. Being in touch with eternal life is all the more needed when religion is so much politicized and loses the necessary aura of the holy. As Thomas a Kempis for example expressed it, "If we are not careful, we can easily be deceived and attracted by the vanity of the world. Often I regret the things I have said and wished that I had not spent so much time in worldly company." God makes it possible for individuals to stress this touch with the eternal, even when they have to do so against overwhelming opposition.

Monasticism may even have to call all the people in the Church to renew this commitment to the eternal through a healthy distance from the affairs of the world, through inwardness and penance, so that they are accessible to the liberating power of God's Spirit.

Savonarola
A Martyr for Integrity

𝔗his call to renewal was very powerful, but also very tragic in the life of Girolamo Savonarola (1452–1498), a Dominican, who died in the city of Florence. At age 22 in 1474 he heard a sermon on repentance from an Augustinian, which became a turning point in his life. He was very talented and had studied especially philosophy and medicine. His grasp on the dangers of the spiritual life was very penetrating and given his personality he was interested to correct errors. Instead of channeling our energies on the divine the Renaissance era had unleashed our love of anything we can enjoy, even if these joys last only for a moment. Instead of submitting our basic human emotions to God's plan of salvation the Renaissance idolized these emotions and from a Christian understanding simply renewed the ancient paganism.

Branches of modern psychology do almost the same thing. Savonarola discovered this transition from Christianity to paganism within a society, which by and large believed itself to be in good standing with God. People didn't really switch over to the ancient paganism, but they had created a mixture of letting their enjoyments take control of their lives and to let our belief in God become a mental notion.

This mixture had led to wide-spread depravity and Savonarola couldn't agree with it. He observed what he called in his poem "The Decline of the Church" and he believed in the renewal of the Church. His early efforts were along the lines of the "Imitation of Christ" of Thomas a Kempis, although there is no connection between the two. He practiced greater austerities and more fervent prayer. He was called by his superiors to teach the novices and he followed the insights of St. Thomas Aquinas.

This saint takes our emotions very seriously, but had the skill of integrating them into God's plan of salvation and he wasn't vehement or irascible in chastising vices. Savonarola's personality was different from that of St. Thomas Aquinas, but he was equally justified in his views. If he had remained in a state of contemplation, then his life would have been different. But the Dominican Order feels obligated to be involved in society, so as to bring about improvements there. Savonarola began to preach in Florence and Brescia and he applied the Book of the Apocalypse to the historical circumstances, announcing that God was unleashing his punishment, if the people wouldn't reform their lives. From 1490 onwards he was very successful in Florence as a preacher of San Marco and also as a reformer of the Dominican Monastery. The number of brothers rose from 50 to 238 under his leadership and the citizens flocked to his sermons. Besides attacking the vices of the people he also dealt with those of the Roman Curia. Pope Innocent VIII (1484–1492) celebrated publicly the wedding of his illegitimate son from the time before he became a priest and made the thirteen year old brother of the bride a cardinal. Pope Alexander VI (1492–1503) had four illegitimate children from an adulterous union with Vanozza de Cataneis.

These instances only indicate that there was a lot to be chastised by the pious monk in Florence and he had to pay a heavy price for it. Through his preaching he ended the tyranny of the immoral Pietro de Medici, whom the citizens drove out of town. He favored the French king, Charles VIII, to conquer the city and he began to establish a theocratic democracy. Unfortunately this led to regulating morality through spying and denunciation, which means indoctrination of conduct instead of soliciting the cooperation of the people and this in turn led to opposition to him.

Pope Alexander VI called him to Rome to defend himself, but he refused to go there on account of his ill health and because of the dangers for him.

The Pope forbade him to preach but Savonarola ignored this prohibition and resumed his sermons in San Marco. In 1498 he was excommunicated, but he remained defiant, celebrated Mass, distributed Holy Communion and resumed his preaching. He was arrested along with two members of his community, put on trial and the three were condemned to death "on account of the enormous crimes of which they had been convicted". They were hanged on May 25th 1398 and their bodies burned. He was filled with dedication to the truth and the awareness that human beings have to exercise responsibility before God and yet he also wondered whether he had acted rightly. He died as a witness to the truth and as one who entrusted his destiny to Almighty God. He knew that his life belonged to God and he had lived out of this personal knowledge.

If we compare Savonarola with the Modern Devotion as exemplified by Thomas a Kempis we may want to prefer the greater introversion of the latter, because it leaves more room and time to those who should improve their lives. The interior suffering of the latter could even be greater because it isn't visible. By the same token we have to admire the courage of Savonarola and do well to consider him a martyr. The Dominican Order is trying to initiate his canonization process and they are justified to do this. Savonarola was not a heretic, he was faithful to the Revealed Truth and he distinguished between the positions instituted by God in the Church and the often feeble mortals filling these positions. He remained true to God until his bitter end and we believe that God rewarded him.

It is difficult for modern people to imagine the impact of the schism (two Popes for the one Church) on all believers, religious and lay-people alike. And yet the people of the fifteenth century had to endure this uncertainty despite their deep religious motivations, which always rely on God's unifying power.

King Siegmund, Councils of Constance and Basel, and the Fall of Constantinople

We can still consider it a blessing that the German King Siegmund (1410–1437) had such a strong interest to bring the schism to an end. He managed to convoke the Council of Constance and give the nations greater influence for the election of the new Pope. This influence is unique for this particular Council. It took a couple of years to arrange for a conclave of the 56 Cardinals in 1417.

A strict conclave even requires that the Cardinals receive less and less food every day, so that they will succeed quickly to obtain the result of one candidate. The Conclave convened on November 8th 1417 and began its election process. On November 11th Cardinal Oddo Colonna needed only two more votes to reach the needed two third majority of the election. People were walking outside in procession praying for God's assistance and a Boys' Choir sang "Veni Creator Spiritus".

Two undecided Cardinals were moved so much, that they also put in their votes in favor of Cardinal Oddo and the forty year schism had come to an end. The newly elected Pope took the name of the saint of the day, Martin. This took a heavy load off the shoulder of many believers, because of the inner peace needed to lead Christian lives. Especially contemplatives, who desire to be in harmony with the One God, want this presence of the One Successor of St. Peter, who guarantees that this Church is built on this one Rock. They cannot comprehend, that this Rock should be split asunder. When and as much as this unity doesn't happen, the Contemplatives have to suffer in their soul for greater unity in the future. Their intense desire may be hidden from public view, but it is real nonetheless. We can still be grateful that this ordeal of the Schism had come to an end.

This Council also issued decrees for the reform of the Church, which focused very much on the hierarchy and the monasteries. Both were in great need to be more closely in touch with God's intention for them. But after their promulgation they were not implemented and were left on the shelves to collect dust. This was a grave mistake, because the Church at large suffered more and more and people began to resent the absence of deeper spiritual motivation among the religious. This grave mistake contributed greatly to the Reformation of the following century.

The Council of Basel (1431–1437) had raised great hopes to help the Byzantine Church, which was increasingly under pressure from the Moslems. For our topic we have to consider especially the extraordinary spiritual wealth of monasticism of the Eastern Church and their conviction how much our earthly situation depends on heaven's blessings. The situation in Constantinople had become desperate and the Greek Emperor came to Basel accompanied by 700 delegates, including the Patriarch of Constantinople.

He was no longer able to withstand the Turks, who were ready to attack.

Only a Crusade could have saved the Empire from ruin. We still can be surprised that the Council accomplished a decree of unity, which expressed even the joy of heaven, "Laetantur coeli" about East and West joining together in faith. Not even the Primacy of Rome was considered a hindrance for this brotherhood of believers. The goodwill shown by the Emperor and his delegates was not favorably received in his realm when he returned and the West didn't give him the needed military assistance, because it didn't want to engage in these efforts so far away from home.

The individual nations in Europe were looking after their own interests. The result was devastating. The Turks took Constantinople on May 29th, 1453 and killed thousands and thousands of Christians and led a huge amount of people into slavery. The West was shocked, but it was too late. We not only regret the loss of lives and of freedom, but also the heavy loss of prayer and contemplation in the many monasteries in the East. The established unity of the Council of Basel was revoked. The spiritual leadership which had had its seat in Constantinople moved to Moscow.

Some things in the religion of the West had become unhealthy. Relics and saints were looked upon like charms and people were easily looking superstitiously for miracles. They were too much inclined to be afraid of witches or the demonic. The administration of the Church had become a system of taxation instead of support for the sacraments. Moral misconduct of religious and laity had become a problem and entire religious communities were affected by it. The Papacy of the Renaissance had declined, because of mere earthly concerns and bad Cardinals elected a bad Pope and he in turn selected Cardinals who were like him.

This was similar in the Cathedral Chapters and the respective bishops. Monasteries and convents had become places, in which the nobility deposited family members, which they didn't want at home. When they didn't have a religious vocation, then they didn't fit in the monastery or convent either. The lower clergy was poor and had to ask for payment for their services, so that they could survive.

Many monasteries and convents struggled on as best they could under these conditions. Quite often the misconduct of individuals was not so much their own fault, but the result of social and ecclesial conditions they had to endure. From this aspect we also have to evaluate our modern tendency to just blame the individual, instead of obtaining a more comprehensive view of the circumstances given to human beings.

PART III

Renaissance and Rationalism

Still the Basic Forces in our Modern Mindset

owever, these negative aspects should not be overestimated. Much in the Church of the fifteenth century was very good. People made large donations to the Church and many impressive Masterpieces of Churches were built and the enthusiasm for their construction was exceptional. The Gothic Cathedrals and Churches from this era are still awe inspiring for us and convince us how much they were a result of the faith of the people of that time. Their paintings and windows witness to their religious conviction and how much they valued the artistic expressions for the sacred mysteries we believe in.

Monks and nuns were involved along with all the faithful in charitable organizations and were instrumental to establish hospitals, nursing homes and homes for the poor, which set the standard for future centuries. What we have today was begun in the late Middle Ages. There is no indication of a general hostility towards the Church or the danger that many people would fall away from this divine institution. People were very actively involved in the Church, attending Mass, devotions and many pilgrimages and especially celebrating the Feasts with great solemnity and joy.

Good preachers drew large crowds of listeners. The Church accomplished much for the religious instruction of the faithful and their desire to be at peace with God also through confession and penance was most sincere. The Church of the fifteenth century was vibrant and committed to God's Revelation and continued efforts of reform could have achieved the desired and needed improvements. The clergy and the religious were willing to improve their own lives and then to be in a better position to assist reforms and to lead the faithful to a better understanding of the gospel and make all to feel more at home with the Lord, but their strength was limited especially when they were faced with the storm of the Reformation.

We cannot agree with the phrase that the Reformation came because of a decline in Church and society. This phrase is too simple and doesn't apply. The Reformation came because the corrections went too far, lacked the moderation of religion and discarded the peace needed for the growth of a loving bond with God. We have to observe that especially contemplation was lost in the shuffle.

Martin Luther

Reform was Needed, but the Reformation Could Have Been Avoided

Martin Luther (1483–1546) made great advances in the direction of genuine contemplation. He certainly had a great struggle imposed on him through a very difficult childhood under the scrutiny of a severe father and a mother, who also could be rather harsh. He was born in Eisleben, Germany in 1483 and died there in 1546. He had to suffer severe brutality in his home and had little joy as a child. This stressful situation at home directed his thoughts to run away from there and to take refuge in a monastery and to become a monk. He did well in his studies of Latin and at age fourteen he had to sing for bread along with the students in Magdeburg. He began to study at the University of Erfurt when he was eighteen and received his bachelor degree in 1502 and his master's on Epiphany of 1505. During this year he experienced his conversion when lightning struck and he made a vow to enter the monastery.

We can compare this event to the accident of St. Norbert of Xanten, when he fell from the horse during a thunderstorm. We assume that the power of the divine accompanied this event and he made himself available for God's plan for him. He entered the Augustinian monastery at Erfurt in July of 1505. To recognize God's presence through occurrences of nature is part of our human condition and only speaks to the genuineness of his faith in God. Biblical studies were flourishing at that time and the rule of the Order emphasized the need of reading Sacred Scripture regularly. His later strong interest in the Bible began during his years in the monastery. As a monk he was at peace and happy and he was able to focus on his studies without any disturbance. He was ordained to the priesthood in 1507 and the following year he was sent to Wittenberg to teach philosophy and to continue to study theology.

In 1511 he made a pilgrimage to Rome in fulfillment of a vow to make a general confession and this visit strengthened his religious convictions. He was made sub-prior the following year and advanced to the doctorate in 1513 and became a member of the faculty for theology as lecturer on the Bible. He received an additional appointment as Vicar for the district of the Order in 1515. He was probably over-conscientious in the fulfillment of his duties and exhausted his energies to the max. When the plague hit Wittenberg in 1516 he was very courageous in helping those in distress. Despite all his hard work and accomplishments he developed scruples about the question whether he had done enough and saw in himself only sinfulness and corruption.

To make things worse, Pope Julius II had published a Bull of Indulgences in Germany to raise funds for the construction of St. Peter's Basilica in Rome. Fr. John Tetzel, a Dominican monk, preached the Indulgences in the Wittenberg area and people who had heard him came to Luther for confession.

John Tetzel was an accomplished preacher and his theology was sound and yet people resented this burden of giving for a Church in Rome. Luther's biblical research and the complaints he heard in the Confessional broke the camel's back and on October 31st, 1517 he nailed his ninety-five Theses on the castle church door in Wittenberg. This door was commonly used for announcements of lectures and business of the University and there is nothing unusual about his placing these theses on them. His planned discussion aimed at correcting the abuses of Indulgences. This was pastorally sound. However, in his case his theses received a little more attention. They were forwarded to Rome and questioned as being heretical.

The one who suffered most in this affair was the Dominican monk John Tetzel. The young Saxon nobleman in minor orders, Karl von Miltitz, was sent to him as nuncio and he treated Tetzel most severely and unfairly. At that time, 1518, Tetzel was already in failing health and Miltitz blamed him to be the originator of the whole affair and threatened him, that the Pope would express his displeasure about him. The charges and the threat he had to endure only hastened his death, which occurred on August 11th, 1519. It was something like a prelude of the Reformation.

The heat was on and the Reformation began. Luther was excommunicated in 1520; his years as a monk were over. And yet, we have to respect Luther's monasticism. His whole life revolved around God and his action. He devoted his existence to deepen his and the people's faith. He was entirely penetrated by the Word of God. There was never any doubt in him that God was the final judge of him and everybody else. Faith, grace and Scripture had become so pre-dominant for him that nothing could stand up against them. Through his masterly translation of the bible he was able to bring God so close to the people that they were in awe of God's presence.

Through him God's power burst forth with elemental force and the conviction only grew that we are in God's hands. He retained a core-conviction of Christianity which remained a major force through the centuries and he restricted this core to the common believer and the common priesthood. This restriction made the common priesthood stronger for a while until the energy it had drained from the simple monasticism had been used up. We do not doubt the inspiration he provided and yet we regret that he discontinued his understanding of true monasticism.

One of the simple questions of the Reformation was: "What can we do in our religion without Rome?" and the following centuries have given the proof that a lot can be done without it and we can give them credit for it; by the same token we are convinced that when believers can do already so much without it, why not do even more along with it?

We also do well to respect Luther's basic view of the prerogative of Faith, Grace and Scripture and we only assert that faith should be wise enough to assert the rights of reason, grace gracious enough to allow the beauty of nature and scripture broad enough to inspire the wealth of tradition. It might even be up to the monks and nuns to live in this greater mystery of salvation so much needed in a world of mere business.

Luther, as we know, got married, had six children and his marriage was happy and yet the inner core of his being remained theological. He was brutal when he believed that he announced God's judgment when for example he wrote "Against the murderous and robbing rabble of peasants". The result of his recommendation was devastating. The rising of the peasant's was suppressed, 1,000 monasteries and castles were leveled to the ground, hundreds of villages destroyed and over 100,000 people killed.

He had to ask himself whether he had relinquished the spiritual power to the temporal, so that religion could become a mere decoration of political power. The monk by comparison lives in this awareness that there is no substitute for religion. Despite his later contempt for monasticism he retained the awareness that some monks are true Christians and he also retained like a monk a one to one relationship with God, especially when he was exhausted and martyred in prayer.

In his own divine freedom God called him home. Shortly before his death he was asked to go to Eisleben, his native place, to settle a dispute between two brothers. After he had fulfilled his duty he died on February 18th, 1546. God let the Reformation happen and yet it would have been better, if it had been a reform instead of a Reformation. A reform for the monks would have been to make their lives more contemplative instead of being involved in too many tasks on a cultural and social level, which often only distract them from their call. The spread of the Reformation also meant the end of monasticism in these areas, which eventually included Northern Europe.

England had a very strong and consistent tradition of monasticism since the 6th century. There were about 800 abbeys in the Kingdom and they were places of contemplation, pilgrimages, liturgies, spiritual and social guidance, learning and research. A monk like the Venerable Bede had discovered that God's grace was flowing through these centers of meditation and that England was healthy because of them. This was still the case at the time of the Reformation there. Inner renewal and focus on contemplation was needed and the religious and the people were able and willing to bring this about. However, this didn't happen.

Henry VIII

Monasteries Closed, Reformation at Hand

Henry VIII (1491–1547) brought monasticism in England to a tragic and brutal end. He had some serious inclinations towards religion and it is possible that his father had meant him for the Church, because he was not the heir to the throne. The heir was his older brother, Arthur. However, Arthur died in 1502 and Henry became the heir and he was also obligated to take the designated bride of Arthur, Catherine of Aragon, when he would succeed his father to the throne. This happened in 1509 when Henry was eighteen years old. He fulfilled his obligation to marry Catherine, although she was five years older than he.

They were married for eighteen years and had seven children, but only one, Mary, survived her childhood. For some years he remained faithful also to the Church and he was opposed to the Reformation. In 1521 he wrote a book "Asserting the seven sacraments", in which he also confirmed his belief in the supremacy of the Pope.

His passion estranged him. He had a son by Elizabeth Blount in 1519 and in 1527 he wanted to marry Anne Boleyne. He had a total of six women, two he divorced, two he had executed, one died in childbirth and one survived him, although the order for her execution had already been issued.

Needless to say, his interest to protect monasticism in his country was rather small. The Pope didn't go along with his policies, but the bishops of his realm didn't do much to support the Pope, except for Bishop John Fisher of Rochester. This also means that the bishops didn't do much to uphold the monasteries. They were at the mercy of the King, who declared himself

Head of the English Church in 1532. His chancellor, Sir Thomas More, could no longer go along with him and he as well as Bishop Fisher were assigned to the Tower and finally to the Block. Both became martyrs in 1535 and are highly venerated by the Church. And yet despite all this he issued six articles of Faith in 1539 in which he upheld Trans-substantiation during Holy Mass, Holy Communion under one species, Masses for the Dead, individual confession, priestly celibacy and the vows of the religious.

Those who violated these articles were threatened to suffer the death penalty. The Archbishop of Canterbury, Thomas Cranmer, was in great straits to conceal his secret marriage and his protestant beliefs. And yet despite his Catholic sentiments the smaller monasteries were confiscated in 1536. This led to a great protest of the people, known as the Pilgrimage of Grace. The reaction of the people also shows that their trust in the monasteries was strong and their commitment to the Catholic tradition firm. However, their protest didn't help and soon the larger monasteries were also confiscated, a total of 800. Many monks and nuns died as martyrs and we honor and respect their courage and constancy. Protestantism gained influence later, but the High Church has maintained its commitment to the Sacraments.

The Catholic Church had to deal with the heavy losses through the Reformation and the shock these brought about. Any dispute or dialogue with the leaders of the Reformation was not promising and the response to this challenge had to come from a renewed commitment to our tradition and the monasticism found therein. The avenues opened by God were independent from the Reformation and brought new vibrancy and perspective to our tradition.

St. Ignatius of Loyola
Mystery of Salvation

The most impressive effort was begun by St. Ignatius of Loyola (1491–1556), who was first of all a mystic, a contemplative and a saint. His reputation for his organizational skills and his keenness as a "Counter-Reformer" are secondary. He grew up without any contact with the Reformation in the Castle of Loyola in the Basque region of Northern Spain. There he received his basic education, especially in the Catholic Faith. In

1517 he became a military officer in the army of the Vice-king of Navarra, and also in the service of Charles V. They had to defend the city of Pamplona against the French in 1521 and he was seriously injured by a canon-ball, which hit his leg.

The doctors had to set it and later break it again and reset it, which he endured without any anesthetics, and it took several months until the leg was healed. Reason enough for him to pass the time through reading and prayer. This brought him to conversion. Things he read for mere entertainment and passing the time left him dry and unfulfilled, but biographies of the saints like St. Francis and St. Dominic increased his inner joy and he became interested to imitate them, so that he also could share their holiness and glory in heaven. This was a matter of personal experience and conversion. Consistent with our tradition he reflected on the eternal life promised by God and the art, in which human beings can obtain this life.

This brought him consolation and peace of mind. Like St. Bernard of Clairvaux he also had a vision of the Blessed Virgin Mary holding the infant Jesus in her arms. He was delighted and committed to lead his life for the greater glory of God. For almost a year he lived in a cave close to Manresa and could visit the Dominican Friars for the sacraments. However, his peace was disturbed by overwhelming anxiety and sadness. He became scrupulous about every little detail and knew that he had to overcome these attacks upon his happiness. He had to search his conscience, knowing right from wrong, asking for forgiveness where this is needed. He began to prepare his most important work, "The Spiritual Exercises" during this year in Manresa. He had made this transition from his career to redirect his life towards God's plan for him.

Despite the obstacles he believed that a greater good would prevail in the end and he could make the necessary steps in this direction. It was not a controversy between our unworthiness as creatures and God's grace in the face of our opposition to him, but a dialogue between his work of salvation and our adjustment to his plan and his ways. Consequently he did things, which are very simple and commonplace, but strikingly beautiful and redeeming for the Christian who wants to be enlightened by Heaven.

He meditated on God's decision to redeem mankind through the birth of Jesus in Bethlehem and his being an infant in the manger; similar to St. Francis of Assisi showing a mother and her baby to the people. This simple scene is suddenly connected with the revelation coming from the eternal Godhead. When he repeated this meditation, then he became more immersed in this mystery. The same he does with the Presentation of our Lord in the Temple, His simple life in Nazareth, His Baptism in the Jordan River, His public ministry and his preaching, His Celebration of the Eucharist with the Apostles, His Agony and Death, His Call to acquire greater and greater love through him and our service in the Church, instituted to be a means of Salvation for all.

The saint didn't have to solve a problem, but only to perceive the ways in which our participation in the Love of God increases. The obstacles he and everybody have to overcome are spiritual and have to be addressed on the level of discerning spirits and opponents to our well-being. Basically his Exercises are very simple and meant to be simple. Everybody who can read is able to read them and to follow their meaning. At the time St. Ignatius started his religious career he was a lay-man and already a thirty year old military officer. He confirms the awareness that God often makes a beginning where we wouldn't expect it and even the saint didn't expect to receive the grace of a personal revelation.

The greatness of God is always beyond our imagination. For him everything was directed towards the improvement of his own soul and for the souls of others. This was his experience and later his interest for his order. At that time he also became acquainted with the Modern Devotion, which had gained a lot of influence among the religious orders like the Dominicans of his time. This devotion is also geared towards the inner life of the human spirit and isn't really interested in anything outwardly striking or impressive. St. Ignatius of Loyola has to be appreciated in this light. Some striking external achievements of the Jesuit Order are often an aberration from the recommendations of the saint and the Jesuits have to be indifferent towards these.

At first he didn't even think of the foundation of an Order, but of settling in Palestine as a hermit and remain in seclusion. His year in Manresa already had made a beginning of being a hermit, but this didn't materialize. He went on a pilgrimage to the Holy Land in 1523 and even entered Jerusalem on a donkey. On his return he began to advance his education, but he had to study along with boys, who ridiculed him. Besides his studies he taught religion to others, but this roused suspicion about him and he was brought before the Inquisition and even incarcerated twice for a short time. He finally went to Paris in 1528 to further his studies in Theology. His first companions joined him there and with six of them he made vows on Montmartre: Poverty, chastity, obedience, a pilgrimage to Jerusalem and the care of souls. His inspiration was that everything should be for the greater glory of God and that Jesus Christ after his death and resurrection wants to draw all to himself and reflect the glory of his Father. The name given to his Order is of a purely theological nature: The Society of Jesus (SJ). Heaven is this Company of Jesus and the Order endeavors to prepare it through their work on earth, but this preparation shouldn't be confused with the heavenly reality.

Ultimately the Jesuit should be indifferent towards everything of an earthly nature. The vows and their life-style made them monks. They offered their service to the Holy Father and promised to be especially obedient to him and to be willing to accept any assignment, which he would give to their members. St. Ignatius and his Order became selective in choosing new members in imitation of Jesus Christ calling his Apostles. This means that the choice they make is based on a theological motivation: to bring people into the fold of the Church. St. Ignatius also decided that the Society would not have a female branch. The reason for this was to be able to maintain a strong spiritual focus free from distractions and also in imitation of Jesus Christ, who called men to be apostles.

The suggestion has been made that a couple of nuns in a spiritual sense beset the saint in the early years of the Society so much, so that he decided against establishing a female branch of his Order. Such a reaction could be understood from a psychological point of view, but it would be unworthy of a saint in the Catholic Church.

He was willing and prepared to make any sacrifice for the greater glory of God and if the sacrifice of endurance had been part of God's plan for him, then he would have joyfully endured it. His clear conviction to not establish a female branch of his Order therefore has to be seen from a purely theological point of view. The fact that Jesus called men as his apostles was normative for him. The saint lived out the gospel in this way. The popular argument: If Jesus had lived at a later time, then he would also have called women to be his apostles, is theologically incorrect.

It is not a time, which determines Jesus Christ, but it is Jesus Christ, who determines every time. He came in the fullness of time. All time and seasons belong to Him. It is possible that Jesus didn't call women to be his Apostles, because they are close to Him anyway, but even such a consideration is of secondary importance. Of first importance is, what he did, and the saint is faithful to what is of first importance. This is how we have to view the saint. His choice of companions didn't give anyone reason for pride and the feeling of superiority, because everything depends on the greater mercy and glory of the Lord and neither the saint nor any of his followers ever claims that he deserves his call from God. Also the Society of Jesus is an Order for service in the Church, of minor brothers of Jesus, as are the Franciscans.

The Order grew so quickly because of the very personal touch to deepen the faith of all the people in the Church. In his mysticism the saint had discovered that God loves all human beings he has created and that they in turn are privileged to rejoice in his creation.

In this vein the modern Jesuit, Karl Rahner, described the "Mysticism of the Joy of the World". Through his Incarnation Jesus Christ deals with everything that is poor and weak in the World and saves those who suffer. The Jesuits could continue the traditions of the Church, the Sacraments, veneration of the Saints, pilgrimages, indulgences, liturgical ceremonies, sacred images, the beauty of Church buildings, like the Baroque and music. Human beings are privileged to cooperate with God's grace. God is so great that he solicits our cooperation with him as the saint explained: "Pray in such a way as if everything depended on God, but act in such a way as if everything depended on you." He understood his teaching as a way to lead people to the love of God.

His early followers engaged in missionary work already before the middle of the sixteenth century. Francis Xavier went to India, Japan and China and was happy to bring the gospel to the poor. He even believed that mere intellectual pursuits in the Universities could be an aberration from the Gospel and wanted intellectuals to consider that Christianity has to be concerned about all the people marginalized in society and the world at large. Also St. Ignatius warned those going to the Council of Trent to first visit the poor and the sick and not to make disputations their first priority.

Jesus came to bring the good news to the poor and not to start a debate about theology. St. Peter Canisius (1521–1597) from Holland felt called to preach in Germany, where people had suffered so much alienation and he was most successful through his Catechism, which brought the simplicity of the gospel home to the people. The mission in Northern Europe and England became very difficult territory where many people died for the faith. In 1556 when St. Ignatius died the Order had already 1,000 members and twenty years later 4,000; in 1600 there were 8,520 Jesuits and by the end of the seventeenth century already 20,000. The large number of saints of the Jesuit Order also make the point that the Order is first of all interested in inner sanctification, which then can lead to outward success, if God wills it. The interest in the inner sanctification of the soul applies to both men and women. Through his clear distinction derived from Scripture the saint was equally concerned about women in the Church; the Jesuit Hugo Rahner described this in his "Ignatius of Loyola: Correspondence with women". The saint's personality is not only above reproach, but also above any thought of a prejudice, because of the universality of Salvation.

For Ignatius it was important that everything is seen from the perspective of God's Revelation, independent from the fluctuations of our emotions. The mysticism he maintained is essential in our awareness of contemplation, which has to be the foundation of our belief and our deeds. This code of the monks in the line of St. Ignatius also brought it about that a number of his followers became acknowledged saints in the Church: St. Peter Canisius (1521–1597), St. Francis Xavier (1506–1552), St. Francis Borgia (1510–1572), St. Aloysius Gonzaga (1568–1591) and St. Robert Bellarmine (1542–1621) to name just a few. They make it obvious that the same mysticism was also at work in them for the greater Glory of God.

St. Angela Merici and Mary Ward

In Agreement with St. Ignatius of Loyola

A similar transition from contemplation and mysticism to active involvement was the foundation of the Ursuline Nuns through St. Angela Merici (1474–1540). She was very close to an older sister and became an orphan when she was ten. The loss of the parents made them even more committed to their prayers, believing in the bond heaven establishes with those who have gone before, especially loved ones. Unfortunately, the older sister also died, even without the Last Rites. Angela took this also to heart and as a Franciscan Tertiary she prayed and made sacrifices for the repose of the soul of her sister. She asked for a sign showing her the sister in eternity. It was granted and she was much comforted that she was in heaven.

On account of her devotion and her private revelation she became concerned about the spiritual well-being of girls in the town. Girls were often neglected in their education also in regard to their faith and she knew the connection between a good formation and stability in life. Her vision and her devotion had made it possible for her to regain her trust and confidence and she wanted the same to happen for others. She applied her insights and we appreciate that her work of education followed her inner conviction. The school in her home flourished and she was invited to start such a foundation also in the neighboring town of Brescia. She also made a pilgrimage to the Holy Land and one to Rome in 1525 to obtain indulgences and was recognized by Pope Clement VII for her dedication and her success. This encouraged her for starting the Ursuline Nuns for the education of girls in 1535. They had to use their homes for their work and later received permission to establish a Religious Order, which grew quickly in Italy, Germany and France. In the eighteenth century they also came to the United States.

In our view we realize that prayer and a private revelation were at the root of this Order. This has to be part of the institution and its education, so that it doesn't drift into a mere outward effort of competition and success. She knew the importance of education, but her deeper conviction came from the goal of our existence. Without this contact with God's grace education will easily be in jeopardy.

In the seventeenth century Mary Ward (1585–1645 of St. Omer, England) approached education similarly to St. Angela Merici. She began her religious career as a cloistered nun, first with the Poor Clares and then of her own, but she didn't believe that this was what God was calling her to accomplish. She had to apply her faith, so that girls and young women could grow spiritually and intellectually.

However, this doesn't mean that she went away from prayer and contemplation to become more active. She was very interested in the writings of St. Ignatius of Loyola and followed his spirituality closely. This means that everything should be directed to the Greater Glory of God and that our situation on the earth isn't separated from the goal he has in mind for us. In order for young women at her time to direct their lives in such a spiritual way they were in need of a better education and conditions, in which they could dedicate themselves to their faith.

It also means that Mary Ward accepted the writings of St. Ignatius without any problems and didn't consider that the saint had any prejudice against women. However, there were suspicions raised about her, especially since the nuns were not cloistered, but the General of the Society of Jesus was very much in her favor. Her order branched out and was very successful in Flanders, Bavaria, Austria and Italy. She applied for approval of the Holy See, but unfortunately her application was not granted and her institutes were suppressed. But they were already working well and the local governments protected them. They could continue despite this stigma of being suppressed.

Along with the set-backs the suppression had caused they continued and even flourished as the "English Ladies" as they were commonly called. Seventy three years later in 1703 the Order was approved by Pope Clement XI. Eventually they had thousands of students and many orphans, whom they cared for and prepared for life through the education they provided.

As for St. Ignatius we also acknowledge this mysticism in Mary Ward. The uneducated girl was for her a sister for whom Christ died and in serving her she knew that she was serving Christ. Angela Merici and Mary Ward are connected with St. Ignatius through their interest to apply their prayer to their work with those in need. This connection is made in response to God's interest in the salvation of all mankind.

By the same token this connection is derived from contemplation pure and simple, which God in turn puts to good use as he wishes. For our research we are interested to discover the renewed impulses for this contemplation. Time and again God calls individuals to focus on singular prayer and this becomes a source of new life in the Church.

St. Teresa of Avila and St. John of the Cross
God Turns Pain to Joy

The Carmelite Order received such an impulse of reform to focus on prayer alone through St. Teresa of Avila (1515–1582). The secret code of the nun was virtually grafted in her soul. Already as a child she wanted to become either a martyr for Jesus, so that she would be with him in heaven as soon as possible, or to be a hermit. She intended to walk over to the Moslems, who lived very close to her home in Spain, thinking that they would immediately put her to death and she would be in heaven. Her uncle prevented this enterprise.

Her second choice as a child was to live as a hermit, so that nothing earthly would be between her and God. However, she needed some time to mature, which she did. She entered the Carmelite Order in 1532, but her first years were not easy. She suffered illness for three years, but God healed her. The miracle was even more important than the physical health, which was its result, because it had brought her in contact with the glory of heaven, which she had desired from her childhood. What she had gone through in her physical situation she also had to endure spiritually, several years of extreme desolation of soul alternating with periods of comfort, enlightenment and happiness. These low-points and the deeper joy she had afterwards even took her fear of death away. Others noticed the genuineness of her experiences and asked her to write about them. She thought that these were just normal thoughts, but they became classical descriptions of our faith journey.

In a clear and almost scientific analysis she knew that the human soul is like an "Interior Castle". From the outer rooms we have to go deeper and deeper inside, so that we reach the treasure of God's grace hidden within. We naturally love the things God has created, but we have to view them in his light and have to discover, that they shouldn't distract us from him. We next look for good conversations and religious practices to focus more on God. We are more self-controlled and have acquired enough wisdom for our meditation. Our prayer becomes more quiet and peaceful, since we surrender more to God. Next we are enabled to receive God's presence as a gift from him, even if we are asleep. Then we experience his love more and more, but this goes along with suffering like illness, discouraging remarks from others and persecutions. Finally, we are united with God like two flames of candles, which are joined together. Her descriptions are very personal, but everybody can apply and use them.

In this process they became a great source of renewal of the Carmelite Order, but also for all believers, who want to gain greater depth in their love of God. In her case this union with God led to miracles like bringing her nephew, who had been crushed by a falling wall, back to life or seeing the martyrdom of some Jesuits one month before the news of this reached Spain. In the new monasteries she founded she emphasized the original more severe rule and the members are called "discalced", wearing sandals instead of shoes. She also wanted to make up for the losses of monasteries through the Reformation.

Monasteries are places of the persevering presence of the Lord and often the Contemplatives are just meant to keep this light burning and St. Teresa of Avila was very talented and gifted to inflame this light in many followers throughout the world.

She had also encouraged St. John of the Cross (1542–1591) to renew the male branch of the Carmelites. John had grown up in a poor, but good family and in his youth he had to make a living as a servant in a hospital, but was also able to pursue his studies in a college run by the Jesuits. In 1562 he became a Carmelite and six years later he started a reform-movement of those more committed to the original rule, which was not as soft as the conveniences, which had crept in with the passage of time. In most severe trials he had to achieve the greatest detachment from anything earthly. These trials he called: "The dark Night of the Soul". God's wisdom is experienced as painful for the soul, because we are so much inferior to it and have to overcome so much, so as to be in contact with it. The impurity in us has to be burned away, so that we reach the light of Christ.

In this process he experienced that at times he was abandoned by God, but afterwards felt God's greater love for him. His witness to his theology was not very well received. His reform efforts were criticized to the point that his superiors imprisoned him and virtually left him in a small room to die. In a vision the Mother of God showed him a way to escape.

This famous escape became part of his mystical theology. Our life is intended to end in union with God. This mystical union or marriage between a soul and God has a far greater intimacy than the conjugal love between husband and wife, because it is the encounter with the eternal and unparalleled love of God. In this love he was able to be absorbed in the "Living Flame of Love". Despite the hardships and sufferings he endured he was of joyful spirit, he liked to sing and write poems, which are masterpieces in World literature. He enjoyed going on long walks and praising God for the beauty of his creation. Everything uplifting on this earth indicates the greater joy we find in heaven.

There is no disdain of the earthly, but it is taken as a token for the greater and permanent reality given in heaven. The moral and ascetical requirements for this "Ascent to Mount Carmel" are fulfilled gladly, because they facilitate the approach to the throne of God. To meet these requirements makes him even more joyful. Having received the invitation from On High he can deal with tragedy, disappointments and losses. He does not ignore the impact of original sin on our nature, but this doesn't weigh him down. He simply admits that our sinfulness often catches us by surprise and we cannot liberate ourselves from its impulses. These impulses are part of who we are and we should accept them like companions on our faith-journey, handing them over to the greater saving power of God.

St. John of the Cross was very much involved in the work of renewal of his Order, because at heart he was a true contemplative. His very existence is like a sign, which points out the future prepared for us by our Lord. He has been declared a Doctor of the Church, which means that he has great value for everyone and is universal. The male branch of the Carmelite Order is also committed to pastoral ministry besides their call to contemplation and we discern that the need for meditation is of first importance for them.

We can admire the Carmelite Nuns who have remained a strictly contemplative order. It seems that God is smiling on them. They have become the largest Order strictly devoted to prayer in the Catholic Church today. Their inner strength gives evidence that the Church needs this secret channel of God's grace being at work on His terms and not ours. True contemplation liberates the Church from its insistence on self and opens our view for the gospel. This is most urgently needed in our modern world of self-preoccupation.

The Discoveries and the Religious Orders
Expanding Awareness of God's Greatness

The discoveries also led to new beginnings for the Religious Orders. The Portuguese reached the Cape of Good Hope in 1486, Christopher Columbus discovered America in 1492, Vasco da Gama found a way to India in 1498, the Portuguese reached China in 1516 and circled the world for the first time in 1519–1522 and they came to Japan in 1542. The conquest of Middle and South America was conducted in the form of a military invasion, but the conquistadores were accompanied by missionaries, Franciscans, Dominicans and Jesuits. They subdued the natives and the opportunities of the missionaries for genuine conversion and instruction in Religion were limited.

The Dominican Friar Las Casas (1474–1566) had to work for decades in his fight for a more humane treatment of the native populations and still in the seventeenth century St. Peter Claver could do little to improve the treatment the natives and slaves received. And yet despite the tragic difficulties the missionaries brought many people to the faith and entire populations could gain respect for Christianity through their selfless efforts in the service of God and neighbor.

Especially in the Far East, India, Japan and China the missionaries gained more access through an approach called "Accommodation" It was refined by the Jesuit Robert de Nobili (1577–1656), when he lived as a Hindu among Hindus. The Jesuits had a similar way of accepting the native cultures and letting the people discover the truth of our faith on their own terms instead of receiving it through an indoctrination, which might remain alien to them. The great Jesuit Matteo Ricci (1552–1610) was very successful with his method in China; as an accomplished Astronomer and Mathematician he lived at the court of the Emperor of China and explained as a friend and a counselor the Christian faith. In the middle of the seventeenth century there were already 270,000 Catholics in China. The Jesuits accepted the faith of the people and acknowledged that they always had been faithful to God through their religious observances and that God was very pleased with them.

Christianity was not designed to introduce differences, but only to bring what they already had to its fulfillment in Jesus Christ. All the things the people valued should also be respected and accepted in their Catholic Faith. The Jesuits were accused in Rome as being unorthodox in their missionary efforts and Pope Innocent X declared the method forbidden and the Emperor didn't allow any further mission in China.

The Jesuits were expelled and persecutions of Christians began. Similar to the Reformation this was a tragic set-back for the Catholic Church. The missionary method called "Accommodation" was not a sales-trick, but had a theological intention. God accommodates himself to human beings in Jesus Christ who became man for us. In imitation of Jesus Christ the missionary accommodated himself to those he brought the message of salvation and from within he led them to the point where they were able to accept the Catholic Faith. Comparable to the Reformation which stressed the prerogative of God's Revelation in comparison to our response the missionary lets the example of Our Redeemer through his incarnation guide him in his work. Both set-backs in China and in regard to the Reformation shouldn't discourage us in our faithfulness to St. Peter and his successors. Sometimes Jesus lets St. Peter venture out to walk on water, and when St. Peter vacillates and doubts the power of the Lord, then Jesus lets him sink, only to have St. Peter show forth God's greater power and glory.

We can cope with such set-backs, but also wish that they hadn't occurred and later we can recognize where faith was lacking and pray that this may not happen in the future. In the twentieth century the Catholic Church was able to resume its missionary work in China and Pope Pius XI in 1939 and Pope Pius XII in 1940 allowed the Chinese Rituals for the liturgies there.

In other parts of the world, India, Japan and especially in the Americas the Jesuits and their methods were very successful. The discovery of the New World brought about many settlements of monks and religious there.

The transition to unknown territories actually made the code of prayer and contemplation even more acute, not only because people were more in need of God's intervention and protection, but even more on account of the surrender to God's plan for them. The migrant and particularly the migrant religious have this deep desire to discover not only new opportunities, but to find what God has in mind for them. When they have made this discovery, then they feel more blessed by God. Through the temporal God has shown something of his eternal consolation, for which there is no substitute. In India, Japan and the Americas the missionaries labored among the common people and they didn't have such a prominent position as in China and their efforts didn't receive such a derogatory label. And yet there they also had to suffer much as missionaries and often risked their lives and endured martyrdom in imitation of Jesus Christ. The challenge of the Reformation and the sudden worldwide expansion reminded the Church also that a less formal approach and yet one working from within the hearts of men may be the way God wants.

St. Philip Neri, Cardinal Berulle, and St. Vincent de Paul

Everyone Should Experience God's Love

In the case of St. Philip Neri (1515–1595) this approach found general acceptance and also influenced living in community of the clergy. Philip's father was a friend of the Dominicans in Florence and the example and the courageous death of Savonarola were still fresh in their memory. Already as a child he was happy to be in God's presence through the prayer of the psalms and those close to him recognized the grace of heaven in him. At age sixteen he helped his father's cousin who lived not far from Monte Cassino. Philip could visit a chapel of the Benedictines often and spend time in contemplation. Here at age eighteen he experienced heaven more closely and he felt its tremendous attraction.

He set out for Rome in 1533 and found the hospitality of a man from Florence, who asked him to tutor his two little boys for his lodging. The education he provided was excellent and apart from that he could pray and study. He studied philosophy and theology for three years, but was even more dedicated to the sanctification of his soul. Besides fulfilling his duties he visited the Churches and catacombs often and felt very close to God. His interior solitude was that of a hermit and he was open to God's inspiration, which took on the form of a miracle in 1544, when the Holy Spirit entered his heart in the form of a ball of fire. It was also the year when he became a friend of St. Ignatius of Loyola. Besides the miracle he also had to endure temptations and overcome these in God's name.

However, the morality in the Eternal City was in a deplorable state. Quite a few cardinals were descendants of the nobility of Rome and were able to live lives of luxury and leisure. They had become princes instead of men concentrating on penance and mortification. Part of this was due to the influence of the Renaissance. Pagan ideals took the place of Christian ones and the moral standards were low. This in turn led to a materialistic and hedonistic way of life and general corruption accompanied by indifference towards the Catholic traditions.

The saint accepted the challenge and began to preach on busy street corners, when people were coming out of the banks or the shops.

By endowment of nature and the miraculous gifts he had received he had a lovable personality and people were pleased to see him and to listen to him. He didn't preach fire and brimstone and threaten them that God would punish them if they went on living like that, but he simply called them to make a turn to the loving and holy God. There is a point when people can look through their infatuations with momentary pleasure and hold on to blessings surpassing everything. When the witness for these comes on the scene, then they can make the transition from one to the other rather naturally and the saint brings forth spiritual joy, which was latent within them. His preaching was marked by the simple question: "Well, brother, when are we starting to be good?" It called for the almost humorous response: "Why not? Let's try it."

When they were willing, then he was also ready to make it possible for them to practice their faith. He stressed the exposition of the Blessed Sacrament in the Church, so that people could remain in the presence of the Lord in quiet adoration. They could join processions to visit seven Churches and in each one spend some time in prayer. The pilgrimages were open to everyone and people discovered that they liked going for a walk of devotion together. Besides this, there were many poor and sick people in the city and they needed individual attention.

Once his hearers discovered the joy of helping others, they would also find the means to do so. As in other foundations there were first laymen who wanted to join together in a community following his instruction, which was begun in 1548. However, his activities were already those of a priest and people recognized this, so that in 1551 he accepted being ordained. He became even more effective hearing confessions and being more involved with priests, he encouraged them to also live in community like the laymen; he wrote a very simple rule for them, because basically they should only support each other. The simplest rule worked best and didn't need a lot of sophisticated policies and guidelines. Things worked out well for him and his brothers, because his heart was right and strengthened by the Holy Spirit. Contemplation also came easily for him, because of his great attraction to the love of God. A couple of hours in prayer seemed like nothing to him and people left him alone at these times, because they knew that they didn't have the same gift of being in God's presence as the saint did. He had the reputation to be the most unconventional of saints. When he was not at prayer, everybody could come to him for a visit and be with him for a while. This could even be a peak-experience for them, just to be for a while with this man, who was penetrated by God.

The example of St. Philip Neri was of great influence in France through Fr. Pierre Berulle (1575–1629), who after his ordination became chaplain of Henry IV. He became a cardinal two years before his death. He was very much interested in the contemplative life and supported Bd. Mary of the Incarnation in her efforts to bring about several Carmelite Monasteries in France, who followed the reform of the Order begun by St. Teresa of Avila. Pierre Berulle also believed that the clergy should be brothers together like the order of St. Philip Neri and founded an Oratory. Besides this, he was interested in good education of the priests and his "Ecole Francaise" became very influential for the high academic standard of the priests in France in the seventeenth century. He also was concerned about the conversion of the Protestants or Huguenots to the Catholic Faith. Love of God and of neighbor along with sound theological education should lead them to accept the Catholic tradition on their own, instead of being afraid of indoctrination and the use of power. Fr. Charles de Condren (+ 1641) continued his work.

Charles de Condren had a vision of God when he was twelve years old and this gave him the direction for his entire life. He and the efforts of the founder of the Sulpicians, John Jacob Olier (+ 1657) brought about a renewal of the clergy from within. When the heart is well adjusted to the grace and mercy of God, then the outward life will also find the right direction. By contrast modern psychology is often only concerned about behavioral guidelines instead of the inner disposition, which has the joy of eternal life as its goal. The spirituality of Philip Neri is basically happy and modern psychology often only leads to sadness.

This same basic conviction was at the heart of St. Vincent de Paul (1580–1660). His parents owned a small farm and they had four sons, Vincent was the third. His father was very much interested that Vincent received a good education, because of his intelligence. He did well in his studies and was ordained to the priesthood at age twenty. The Queen of Valois hired him as her chaplain and he received the income of an abbey, but when he stayed with a friend in Paris for some time this friend was robbed and accused Vincent. He bore this accusation in silence, because he believed slander and persecution sanctify the soul.

The real thief admitted his deed half a year later and Vincent was vindicated. This means that spiritually he upheld his conviction about his innocence and left the outward circumstances in God's hands. In humility he let God work for him and God did so at his chosen time. The inner depth, where God and the soul meet, was most important for him. As a young priest he was called to assist a peasant, who was at the point of dying. His visit with the man was accompanied by the gracious presence of the Lord and the man not only received the sacraments, but experienced true conversion and peace of mind.

The man represented the many marginalized and spiritually neglected people in the countryside of France and the saint developed a real mission about all these people. He saw in them brothers and sisters in Christ, who were in need of spiritual healing and the experience that God loved them and cared for them. The saint showed his genius with those who were left out of the common picture of society.

This is the trademark of the saint who felt like one of them and was able to renew their faith in themselves and in God. His missions among the country folks were very successful and those who witnessed them knew that God was at work in the saint. The people flocked to him and he had to ask other priests to assist him in hearing their confession. The same identity occurred when he visited the convicts in prison. The legend developed that he took the place of one for a while, but this story only explains how generous and loving he was in dealing with them. He became aware that entire sections of society had drifted away from the Church and lowered the standards of their morality, because there were no qualified priests to give them a Christian example and to model integrity and love for them. For him the misery of the people was connected with the lack of genuine priestly ministry for them.

In consequence he formed a congregation of secular priests, who had to follow the simple vows of poverty, chastity, obedience and stability. Almost automatically they came to understand, how much blessed by heaven's joy their lives became, when they served the poor country folks in remote towns and villages. With the help of St. Louise de Marillac he also founded the Sisters of Charity, also called Vincentians, who assisted the poor and the sick in the parishes. He even had time to pay attention to Christians who had been enslaved by Moslems in Northern Africa. It happened frequently that Moslems captured Christians and sold them into slavery. Historically we might again get to this point.

Those who were enslaved had to endure terrible hardships and were totally disconnected from the Christian world. It is hard to imagine their suffering, but St. Vincent felt it. Through his efforts over 1,200 such slaves were ransomed. Here also the story developed that he had been a slave once and therefore felt so much compassion for them. This story also shows his sanctity and how much love he felt for those who suffer, believing that Jesus suffers in them. Historically he is best known for his work for the poor, which has found acceptance and application in many parishes, especially in the United States of America, but we have to recognize his influence in other areas as well.

His great advantage was that he was recognized as a saint and supported by King Louis XIII and Cardinal Richelieu, who had him as a visitor several times and who gave him a house and substantial donations for his work with seminarians. The saint became famous and he put this fame to good use. The fame originated in his closeness to God and the invitation to new life, which emanated from him. He was appreciated and accepted as a gift from God on all levels of society and could create a unity, which people had lost sight of. The power of the Holy Spirit was at work in him witnessing to the holiness of his soul.

Along with Cardinal Richelieu's generosity towards the saint it is worthwhile to compare these two figures of the seventeenth century. Armand Jean du Plessis, Cardinal Richelieu's (1585–1642) claim to fame is that he laid the groundwork for the French absolutism in the seventeenth century. He became the main minister of Louis XIII in 1620, abolished the power of the Huguenots, directed his effort against the Habsburg Empire, joined Sweden in the thirty year war and declared war against Spain in 1635. We appreciate his love for St. Vincent de Paul and the support he gave to him, but we also have to acknowledge the difference between the two priests. It is either the power of the Holy Spirit as for the saint or the spirit of power as for the Cardinal. Only genuine Christian conversion can lead from the second to the first and only the impurity of the spirit creates a mixture between the two.

Richelieu's power came to an end and the loving example of the saint has endured through the centuries. St. Vincent de Paul's sentiment: "The demoralization of the clergy is the main reason for the ruin of the Church" was echoed by others like John Eudes and St. Charles Borromeo.

Cardinal Richelieu and Saint Cyran
Spirit of Power–or the Power of the Holy Spirit

The difference between Cardinal Richelieu and St. Vincent de Paul has become even more glaring in the case of the priest Saint Cyran, the successor of Berulle, who preached in the Reform-Monastery Port Royal and defended the spiritual independence of the Catholic Church. Cardinal Richelieu had offered this priest to become a bishop, but then in 1638 he changed his mind about him, because he felt uncomfortable about the way this priest defended the freedom of the Catholic Church from the intrusion by the State.

He declared Saint Cyran to be a heretic and put him in jail in 1638 and let a commission decide about his orthodoxy. The commission couldn't produce any significant evidence against the priest and the Cardinal decided to keep him incarcerated anyway. Even St. Vincent de Paul had a favorable opinion about Saint Cyran and other prominent people wanted Saint Cyran to be released, but the Cardinal remained harsh. Saint Cyran probably felt like some priests nowadays, who are sentenced by a bishop, an archbishop or a cardinal without any clear and decisive evidence against them. Saint Cyran came out of jail after the death of Richelieu, but he lived only a few more months, because of the devastating effects the incarceration had had on him.

This seems to be providential, because who would want to have a bishop, archbishop, or cardinal who treated you like a dog, at your deathbed? St. Vincent de Paul assisted at his funeral, expressing his love for the deceased. Especially after our departure from the world we believe that the Power of the Holy Spirit is different from the spirit of power so attractive for people throughout the ages.

The presence of the Holy Spirit is felt by believers through the joy they experience, even when they have to suffer. The Jesuit missionaries in different parts of the world were most remarkable in their skill and understanding of the people they wanted to bring to the faith. They discovered martyrdom as a source of joy, as for example St. John de Brebeuf, martyred in 1648 witnessed, "My beloved Jesus, because of the surging joy which moves me, here and now I offer my blood and body and life. May I die only for you, if you will grant me this grace, since you willingly died for me. Let me so live that you may grant me the gift of such a happy death."

Not only do we admire the willingness of the saint to endure martyrdom for God, his eventual death for the sake of God's kingdom, but also the way in which he expresses it.

He feels a surge of joy at the moment, when his earthly life draws to a close. Already in his heart his earthly life is totally absorbed in the Glory of Heaven. This is the result of intense prayer and contemplation. Whether it is achieved in the remoteness of a peaceful monastery or in an overwhelming wilderness, the same inspiration can be felt, because the same greatness of eternal life prevails.

St. John de Brebeuf and his companions were French Jesuits. They had brought the light of faith to people in the New World. Eventually the hard work and the sacrifices of these martyrs paid off, because many natives came to the conviction, that those who suffered so much had witnessed to the truth and we cannot do anything against the truth, but only for its sake.

Losses through the Reformation
Criticism can be Destructive

While there was some substantial gain in parts of the world there also came about unexpected losses not only for the Church, but also for monasticism. The Northern European nations joined the Reformation. To some extent it just happened, considering all the politics and the Thirty Year War involved. Many people were told that they were now Protestant and they didn't have a choice. By the same token we have to regret deeply all the neglect, lack of pastoral consideration, and the mere clerical stubbornness and arrogance, which favored this transition to the Reformation. It is very sad, when the Hierarchy of the Catholic Church has lost its touch with the very soul of countries and is virtually unfaithful to the gospel, even if they are on the side of theological correctness. It is easy to be correct, but very difficult to be on the side of truth. The martyrs were on the side of truth, although they were marginalized and labored among the poor of this world. The centuries lost in the Northern European nations cannot be brought back. This was very tragic for monasticism, because the Reformation had lost this sense for genuine contemplation, which is essential to sustain our contact with God's eternal love.

The secret code of the monk is always found in a very personal manner, because God loves human beings the way they are and leads them to how they should be, eventually to the beatific vision, which each and everyone enjoys in his or her personal way. Someone can be a monk even if his life could have taken a totally different direction.

Blaise Pascal and Jean Armand de Rance
New Life in Christ

We may look upon Blaise Pascal (June 19th, 1623–August 19th, 1662) in this way. One of the most gifted minds, especially in regard to mathematics and physics, in France of the 17th century. He grew up in a very Catholic home. His scientific research confirmed his faith in God. Only in God do we find the dignity and joy to which we aspire most in our hearts. We feel this in our hearts as well and therefore God calls us to entrust ourselves to him.

While he was still quite young, about 22 in 1645, he became more familiar with the convent of nuns in Port Royal, which had rooms for hermits, who joined them in prayer and contemplation. His sister, Jacqueline, became a nun there. He was a constant guest particularly after November 23rd, 1654 when he had his Jesus Christ experience, which he described in his memorial as follows, "The year of grace 1654, Monday, 23 November, feast of Saint Clement, Pope and Martyr, and of others in the Martyrology. Eve of Saint Chrysogonus, Martyr and others. From about half past ten in the evening until half past midnight. Fire. God of Abraham, God of Isaac, God of Jacob, not of philosophers and scholars. Certainty, certainty, heartfelt, joy, peace,

God of Jesus Christ. God of Jesus Christ. My God and your God. Thy God shall be my God. The world forgotten, and everything except God. He can only be found by the ways taught in the Gospel. Greatness of the human soul. O righteous Father, the world had not known thee, but I have known thee. Joy, joy, joy, tears of joy. I have cut myself off from him. They have forsaken me, the fountain of living waters. My God wilt thou forsake me? Let me not be cut off from him forever! And this is life eternal, that they might know thee, the only true God, and Jesus Christ whom thou hast sent. Jesus Christ. Jesus Christ. I have cut myself off from him, shunned him, denied him, crucified him. Let me never be cut off from him! He can only be kept by the ways taught in the Gospel. Sweet and total renunciation. Total submission to Jesus Christ and my director. Everlasting joy in return for one day's effort on earth. I will never forget thy word. Amen."

He kept this notice secret, sewn in his jacket, and it was found only after his death. We consider it his code. Like a monk he lived mostly in his cell in Port Royal. His focus on eternal life is convincing and even a challenge for many readers. We can say that the Memorial is a Catholic Document and doesn't show any influence of Jansenism. Blaise Pascal has encouraged many believers in their faith and his writings are a classical witness of what impact the greatness of eternal life should have on our earthly existence.

Pascal's personality also speaks in favor of his comprehensive approach to our Catholic Faith, in which we insist that grace goes along with nature, faith goes along with our reason and the Bible goes along with our tradition. He was a keen observer and admirer of nature, God's creation, used his reason to the max and accepted the tradition of our religion as it had been transmitted through the centuries up to him. And yet he was aware how much we are inclined to let things decline and go into disrepair, how much we neglect the proper use of the gifts, which God has bestowed on us, and that we can be very forgetful when our immediate interests prevent us from holding on to sacred tradition. Decline and renewal are part of the Church and of the contemplative life within it.

Entire religious communities can begin to soften their original rule and make life a little more convenient. It is so easy for an abbot to relax some discipline for the monks and they may even be grateful to him. The Cistercians had renewed the Spirit of St. Benedict in the eleventh and twelfth century and had become extremely influential, but then their influence waned, some historical changes took place and the lives of the monks had lost its original fervor. Those who should have protected the order and the individual abbeys used their position to take advantage of them and this was discouraging to the monks, who consequently were less interested to be devoted, zealous and god-fearing. This was true in the seventeenth century France, when people's attention had already shifted towards enlightenment instead of genuine love of God. On an individual basis Pascal's experience was designed to renew this love.

For the Cistercian Order this renewal had a lot to do with the conversion of Jean Armand de Rance (1626–1700). His family benefited greatly from the prebend system. For advocating the causes of monasteries and churches or for being concerned about them they received benefits or taxes. His older brother held many of these benefices and when this brother died Jean Armand became a Canon of Notre Dame of Paris in 1637 at age eleven. In a sense it was just a twist of history for a child his age to receive such a title and the huge income going along with it. However, he was very studious and published his first writing already in the following year and dedicated it to his god-father, the described Cardinal Richelieu. His studies didn't make him serious in regard to his religion, but he was serious about his intellectual advances.

Besides these he had lots of fun. His uncle was the Archbishop of Tours, who ordained him to the priesthood in 1651 and the following year his father died. Besides this loss it also increased his wealth, because of everything he inherited. His wealth was practically unlimited and he could live in luxury. One sort of entertainment of the French nobility was hunting. Blaise Pascal would have a lot of fun to describe de Rance's state of mind. Pascal truly enjoyed looking at the inconsistencies of human behavior and especially hunting caught his attention. He pointed out that people spend hours and hours to hunt a rabbit, but they wouldn't be interested to buy one when they saw it on the market and his adage was, that we prefer the hunt to the capture.

There is something entertaining about hunting, but the result of this entertainment is insignificant. The same would apply to gambling for example. People may have a lot of enjoyment to gamble for hours and hours and are very happy, when they come home having won a dollar. If they had worked for only ten minutes, they would have even more money, but they wouldn't have gotten it through entertainment. What was true for de Rance is still true today. Through his connections de Rance was elected as Deputy of the General Assembly, made archdeacon and the first chaplain of the Duke of Orleans. He did preach on occasion and administer some sacraments, but he was disconnected from the spirit of the gospel.

His conscience let him know what was going on, but he ignored this for some time, until yet another death of a friend made him pause and reflect. As he had played and enjoyed his life with a passion, so he now also went to the other extreme and realized the vanity of life. Here Pascal would join him. Our earthly existence is truly nothing in comparison to eternal life. In 1660 he assisted at the death, the Last Rites and the funeral of the Duke of Orleans and he dramatically changed his life around. He talked things over with his spiritual director and those whose judgment he trusted and he didn't take this step in isolation. He gave away all his possessions and kept only the Abbey La Trappe. He even asked for permission from the king. He truly decided to become a monk and he was firmly committed to do it well. He became the abbot of the monastery, which he intended to reform. He practiced great penance and deprived himself of anything that could be considered convenient or a luxury.

The food was very poor, hardly enough to keep someone alive and he and his monks were separated from the world and focused on God alone. Their intention was to be close to the original rule of St. Benedict and to recapture its spirit. In this tradition they stressed manual labor along with prayer and he wrote spiritual books about the monks in the abbey of La Trappe, about sanctification and about the true spirit of the Rule of St. Benedict. Even the penitential way of life of the monks became an object of suspicion, people thinking that they had become heretical, because of their strictness.

These concerns had also been expressed about the mentioned Monastery of nuns at Port Royal. Many sincerely devoted people accepted de Rance's example and many monasteries adopted his reforms. His conformity with God's will became even more pronounced when his health began to fail in 1695 and he resigned his office to his successor and showed and increased his humility until his death in 1700. The monasteries, who adopted his reforms, were called Trappists including new foundations like the famous Trappist Monastery in Gethsemani in Nelson Co, Kentucky, where Thomas Merton was a monk. We appreciate his conversion, his generosity to give away all his wealth and his sincere focus on eternal life. An early engraving shows him at his writing desk with his left hand on a skull, the sign of many monks to be mindful of the moment of our death. We can truly admire his insight that the feudal system of the Middle Ages had begun by giving protection to the faithful, but then turned against the true spirit of Christianity and had become a system of exploitation.

We may compare this to our modern banking system, which started to protect the investments of honest citizens, but then through risky exposure puts these investments at risk, needs help from the government and finally exploits the government and its own customers. In the case of the feudal system de Rance had first realized how much it had deviated from God's will and how sincere he and his monks had to be in order to return God his due. We also observe that on the whole only very few returned God his due and how much this falsified system continued until it finally led to the earth-shaking revenge of the French Revolution in 1789.

In their simple and sincere devotion the monks of La Trappe were a century ahead of their time and it could have saved a lot of suffering, hardships and bloodshed if their example had been followed on a larger scale, especially by the hierarchy of the Church. This didn't happen, but we have to be very realistic about the consequences of such neglect. We recognize the depth of contemplation creating a bond of spiritual freedom, equality and brotherhood in agreement with the gospel without the confrontation, which became so tragic in the eighteenth century.

Enlightenment and the Sacred Heart
One Should Lead to the Other, Not Away from It

One aspect of the spirituality of the seventeenth and eighteenth century was "Enlightenment". The word itself sounds plausible and convincing for us, because we like to be enlightened and to follow our insights and reasons. Our Religion also is a religion of light and not of darkness, "God is light and darkness is not in him". The sense for this light of God is even stronger than Enlightenment, because the light of God is more than anything created, including our reason, and because God is opposed to anything evil, which is the real darkness our salvation is concerned about. In these ways we can go along with "Enlightenment".

However, it was the very criticism created by Enlightenment, in which people became opposed to our religion. Those who believed to be enlightened didn't want to accept anything, which wasn't in the grasp of reason and therefore they didn't like the foundation of our religion, which is based on Revelation and the authority of God over us mere mortals. This dislike of religion turned easily into ridiculing those who believed. We may have to admit that some things could be subject to criticism at that time: superstition, hunger for miracles and being afraid of witches.

Believers of sound minds were willing to bring about the needed corrections. However advocates of Enlightenment went further and didn't want to respect the authority and the devotion as exercised in the Church. Arguments wouldn't help and the better reaction to this challenge was after the necessary correction to endure opposition, so that the enlightened may also have a chance to be converted and experience faith as a gift going beyond our mere reason.

The mentioned "monk" Blaise Pascal overcame our tendency to insist on reason alone by pointing out that our religion is a matter of the heart and the religious is willing to stay in touch with this inner voice. One of his contemporaries cherished this sense for the voice within, St. Jane Frances de Chantal (1572–1641). She married Baron de Chantal at age twenty. Her husband's household was in bad shape and she used her reason and common sense to bring it back to prosperity. In 1601 her husband was accidentally killed while shooting and she was left with four children. She had to live with her in-laws, so that her children wouldn't lose their inheritance. This was very difficult, because she wasn't treated well. She believed that instead of fighting she should endure, but she also needed some encouragement and asked God for a guide.

God responded with showing her the one who would bring her peace of mind and direction. She attended sermons of St. Francis de Sales and recognized him as the one who would guide her. As several times before we may believe in a private revelation, and that God's enlightenment is different from what we perceive as such. She believed herself to be called to become a nun and after she had sufficiently established her children she entered the Congregation of the Visitation. Her vision brought her closer to God and to the devotion to the Heart of Jesus so much promoted through Margaret Mary Alacoque (1647–1690).

Any argument or dispute in regard to "Enlightenment" wouldn't yield much, since the conviction of our faith has to grow in meditation and prayer. St. Margaret Mary was gifted as a mystic of the "Sacred Heart", which even grew when she was paralyzed for four years after her first Holy Communion. Her illness intensified her love of God and when she made a vow to St. Mary at age thirteen she was instantly cured. Her father's death left the family in severe poverty and she had to go along with all of them through a time of humiliation. She responded with silence and willingness to endure it. Jesus answered with his divine consolation. After three years the family's property was recovered and they could live a normal life. She later regretted some pleasures of her youth, but these were nothing to worry about. In 1671 she became a nun of the mentioned Congregation of the Visitation and lived out the mystery of the devotion to the Sacred Heart. This devotion is somewhat different from just spending more time in prayer. She was aware that God is willing to console us, but he is equally inclined to let us participate in his trials on earth.

Like many of the saints are able to experience God in the poor, the sick and the suffering, so also those devoted to the Sacred Heart of Jesus are willing to take on Jesus' abandonment and agony on the Cross. It is this mystical identity, which runs through their lives and gives evidence of their transition to eternity taking place within them. God has opened up this transition and in our own endurance we can express our love for him. There is no doubt for the saint that this takes place for his own and for other's salvation and sanctification. Even times when our meditation is dry can be turned into blessings by God's mercy and grace. It is almost natural for the Church to examine this approach to our faith, because it goes beyond our normal standards, but it is part of monasticism to do so. Her devotion and the revelations she received led to the Feast of the Sacred Heart. We can also look upon this piety as an appropriate response to the growing Enlightenment, because it connects to the seat of our emotions and experiences God as the one who comes to us with his divine love, not with an argument about how much or how little we should use our reason. We should use it as much as we can, but let it be embedded in the totality of our being and the always greater truth given to us by God.

Through the centuries the Franciscan Order has been very blessed with this loving encounter with God, in which our reason is just one portion of our natural and super-natural endowment.

St. Leonard, St. Gerard, and St. Alphonsus Liguori

Morality Should be in Balance, Not to the Extreme

St. Leonard of Port Maurice (1676–1751), received his early instruction in the Roman College of the Jesuits, but he entered the Franciscans when he was twenty-one and was ordained in 1703. In 1709 he took over the monastery in Florence, where the friars followed the strictness of the rule by living on what they got through begging, no endowments or stipends for Masses or preaching.

Through this poverty they flourished and their preaching efforts were most successful. The saint also established a hermitage in agreement with the intention of St. Francis, which he called a novitiate for Paradise. Here also the hermit relinquishes all his earthly concerns by leaving his soul in God's hands. Through this transition there was very little left for and of himself, except God in him. Through this sanctity he attracted people to God. Pope Benedict XIV asked him to preach on Corsica, where people were in a terrible fighting mode with constant feuds and vendettas. When the saint began people came to the gatherings with weapons. He was able to subdue them to the spirit of peace, but only temporarily. When he left the fighting started again.

He believed that the bishops failed to be permanently present among the people, which left them without the peace of a shepherd. He even said, "When I have an opportunity to meet the bishops I will tell them what I think." Who knows, bishops might listen to a saint. Good luck! Even the Pope was disappointed and wrote to the saint, "The Corsicans have become worse since the mission and it's no use for you to go back there." The saint was the main figure in promoting the "Stations of the Cross" and set them up in many places. The devotion is a way to be simultaneous with the actual Crucifixion of our Lord. In our eternal salvation the difference of time has been overcome and we can walk with Jesus as did the people at the time of his actual execution. Through the centuries the saints have discovered this simultaneity, which is one reason for their sanctity. In the Franciscan spirit the Stations prepare us for the eternal life that follows, both aspects are joined together.

This also applies to another Franciscan of this era, St. Gerard Majella (1726–1755), whose greatest love was to be in the presence of the Lord in the Eucharist and he spoke with God as with a brother, when for example he said to him, "Lord, let me go, please. I have some work to do". In an almost simple fashion the saint made it possible for people to also be in God's presence along with him. His short life of only twenty nine years, when he died of consumption, was no hindrance to be most effective in this service. This is significant because many conflicts erupt, because God's presence is missing in those, who have lost or denied their sense for it.

St. Alphonsus Liguori (1696–1787), the Founder of the Redemptorists, had a great respect for St. Gerard and favored his career in the Franciscan

Order. Alphonsus grew up as an extremely talented child of a noble family near Naples. His father saw to it that he received a very good education and he advanced very quickly. He was accomplished playing the harpsichord, loved music very much, but he had greatest success as a lawyer. He became a doctor of law at age sixteen, passed the bar three years later and won almost all his cases. Except in 1723 when he misread a document and had to admit defeat. This was a heavy blow for him, which changed his life. Although he could have looked upon it as just a human error, he wondered whether his humiliation was sent by God. When he visited a hospital a mysterious light surrounded him and a voice said to him, "Leave the world and give your life to me." Against the wishes of his father he decided to become a priest and he was ordained in 1726 at age thirty. He enjoyed preaching in the small villages of the goatherds in the mountains and he had a special love for animals. But he felt even more called to bring priests together, so that they could encourage one another in their ministry and in bringing people to the Church.

He was successful in his missions and became a bishop in 1762. His foundation of the Redemptorists was under attack by the anti-clerical policy of the Duke of Naples, who threatened it with suppression.

This was a blow for the saint, who was very sensitive and high-strung by nature. Even the Holy See expressed his displeasure. He was made bishop of St. Agatha in 1762, a small Neapolitan diocese with thirty thousand uneducated people, four hundred secular priests, of which some led scandalous lives and seventeen "relaxed" religious communities. His health was poor and during his life he received the Last Rites eight times. He worked as hard as he could and was permitted to resign his see in 1775 and he thought that he could go to his eternal reward, but God had other plans for him. A vendetta brought his foundation to court, alleging that it was an illegal religious congregation. In his old age the saint was betrayed at every turn by the local government, his friends, his brother priests and even his confessor joined the conspiracy against him. All he could do was to weep in silence. Even the Pope cut him off from his own Order, which the saint had established. He had to live in the state of expulsion and exclusion for seven years. During these years of the "Night of the Soul" he suffered from illusions, temptations, scruples and impulses to despair. Great, divine peace came over him when he could meet his Lord. The Pope, who had cut him off, declared him "Venerable". Besides his stressful life as a religious, a founder of an Order and bishop, he was a most accomplished Theologian of Morality, especially because he knew how to keep a middle ground between being too soft or too rigid.

Unfortunately, his example and his great insights into human nature didn't find a wide application in the century, which became very troubled at the end. We admire the experience of God's presence to him and his tenacity to endure everything in the belief that our redemption will succeed, even in the midst of great losses and set-backs. We can only wish that his vision had been successful on a larger scale.

Tragically, the attitude, which people assumed during the age of Enlightenment, prevented them from being in tune with the gentle and merciful ways of God's kingdom and the saint had to suffer for its sake. The "enlightened" minds insisted on their own decisions instead of looking up to God's plan for them.

In this tension the Jesuit Order came under pressure. We have to respect their admirable accomplishments as educators and missionaries. For the most part their dedication to God's cause in the world was impeccable and served the spread of the gospel tremendously. It would be unfair not to give them credit for the worldwide successes.

They implemented the theology of their founder, St. Ignatius very well and deserve their exemplary place in the history of Religious Orders. The pressure came from political powers being set against them, because of the influence they had achieved. Jansenism had become somewhat fashionable among the elite in France. For them it was a way of being more faithful to God's Revelation and often they didn't have any intention to oppose the authority in the Church. Five sentences of Jansenism were condemned and the question remained whether these had been taken out of context.

The Jesuits favored the condemnation, which only increased the confrontation. With the passage of time the tables were turned upon the Jesuits. They represented the Pope and various governments in Europe feared that they wanted to impose the wishes of the Holy Father upon them. The opposition to authority of "Enlightenment" only increased the dislike for the Jesuits, also in countries, which were little influenced by Jansenism. Individuals and national governments focused on their own power and wanted to do without the intrusion of the Papacy in their "own" affairs. "Enlightenment" took revenge and one of its victims was the Jesuit Order. In the case of Jansenism it appears that the Jesuits were asking for it.

The desire for influence is so appealing and they couldn't easily wean themselves away from it. We can ask the question: "What would have happened, if they had left everything on the level of gentle persuasion, instead of creating a challenge?" Considering St. Alphonsus Liguori of this same era, we conclude that this saint would have preferred gentle persuasion instead of confrontation, knowing that this will probably include greater suffering for the sake of truth and the ultimate victory of God's grace. The saint even had to wait until after his death for his work to bear fruit. In the eighteenth century the Papacy was no longer in a position to provide safety to the Jesuits and traditionally very Catholic countries, Portugal, France, Naples and Sicily waged a war against this powerful institution.

France even threatened the Holy See to occupy the Papal State, if the Pope didn't abolish the Jesuit Order. As a consequence of this pressure the Holy Father abolished the Jesuit Order in 1773. Fortunately, many individual Jesuits were able to go deeper in their faith and the vows they had made and remained priests even without the Order being there for them. They joined together in more or less private groups and continued their work as best they could. The suppression of the Order lasted forty years. Since God looks at us differently from what we often believe it could very well be that these forty years, in which the Jesuit Order was dormant, was a blessing. The Order officially did not exist during the French Revolution and later they could argue that they were not involved.

The French Revolution impacted the Church and Monasticism most traumatically and for the contemplative it is important to look at these events from a spiritual point of view. Enlightenment as mentioned had made its advances for almost two hundred years and it was easy to shrug it off as a mere intellectual endeavor. But this was not the case.

In its radical form it enabled human beings to take things into their hands without respect for historical developments up to that point. Thus it would reevaluate religion and admit for society only those aspects, which fit its format. It would assess the need or the use of the Church in general and also of the form of government. The French Revolution, beginning in August 1789 was an explosion of Enlightenment.

French Revolution

The Price of too much Enlightenment

At first those in power, the king and his ministers along with the authorities of the Church, believed that they could deal with the issue by granting some privileges to the advocates of change, but this didn't work. The longer it took the more radical did the action against the existing establishment become. King Louis XV had already confiscated all the property of the Society of Jesus in 1749 and the Assembly of the Revolution decided in November 1789 to close all useless convents and monasteries, which was followed three months later by the suppression of all monasteries.

All the privileges of the clergy were abolished and finally all the property of the Catholic Church was confiscated to cover the national debt. This was accompanied by an assault on castles, churches and monasteries and the effort was made to reduce the Catholic Religion to a format of Enlightenment. Religious were only tolerated, if they changed their vows and submit to the demands of the Revolution. The bishops as a body remained firm in their adherence to their basic Christian beliefs and most priest and nuns followed them. This led to bloody persecutions and about 40,000 priests were incarcerated, deported or executed. Finally King Louis XVI and the Queen, Marie-Antoinette were executed in 1793. Pope Pius VI was imprisoned and died in jail, alone and totally abandoned in 1799, in Valence, France.

The goal of this reign of terror was to substitute the "Cult of Reason" for Christianity. The persecution of the Church lasted until 1799, when Napoleon Bonaparte (1769–1821) took over.

However, it would be insufficient to just continue on the mere historical level. The Revolution had inflamed what had been brewing for many decades and probably several centuries. The leadership of the Church had sided with the nobility and had almost no interest in the lower classes of society. This neglect included the lower clergy, priests, who constantly lived on the level of poverty and mere subsistence and monasteries, which were being exploited.

Despite the deep faith of the French Catholics and their religious this had to lead to resentment, which finally broke loose and brought about an unexpected change. The scourge of the Revolution also led to a religious awakening, in which bishops, priests and religious rediscovered the simplicity and beauty of the gospel and the example of our Lord and Savior.

Once the shock had been absorbed people rallied their strength and their faith and renewed their commitment to God. Christianity proved not only stronger than the "Cult of Reason", but proved to be the only true response to our earthly existence. Napoleon was even interested to reinstate convents of nuns, who were dedicated to help the wounded. He needed them on the battlefields. This also indicates that he followed his own designs in regard to the Church. His aim was the extension of his universal realm and he didn't hesitate to incarcerate Pope Pius VII (1800–1823), who wouldn't hand over the papal state. The impression, which the secular powers continued to make upon the Church, continued to be devastating and increased the adherence to prayer and contemplation for believers, learning how much we are in God's hands and that without the real presence of Jesus Christ we can do nothing.

The drastic historical change also brought about a greater closeness between the faithful and the hierarchy. Bishops, priests and religious discovered how much all believers belong together as God's family, but this insight was purchased at a great price.

The Emperor Joseph II of Austria (1780–1790) had followed designs similar to the Enlightenment, through which many monasteries were closed. The Church in Germany was also reduced to poverty through "Secularization" and almost 300 monasteries were confiscated by the State. Here also the bishops, clergy and nuns reconsidered their position and became closer allies with the general population of believers.

The institutions of the Church, which had to rely on the support and the participation of all Catholics responded better to their spiritual and sacramental needs and in turn were renewed in the Spirit and the joy of the Gospel. If the hierarchy and the monks and nuns had remained close to the simplicity and basic demands of God's Revelation, many hardships and devastating events in history could have been avoided; but this didn't happen and the Church at large and the monks in particular had to renew their inner commitment through these experiences. However, despite these there was also growth taking place and new orders were founded. Wherever religious saw new social and educational needs they were willing to use their talents in response and their work was highly valued in these eras of change and growth.

The Trappists had been strong through the eighteenth century with over 300 professions renewing their fervor in the midst of an age dominated by materialism and hedonism. When they were beset by the Revolution in 1790, the abbot of La Trappe set out on a journey, accompanied by 24 monks. They first went to Switzerland and were able to make further foundations in Spain, Italy, Belgium and England. When the French invaded Switzerland in 1798 they had to leave again and settled in Poland, but they were called back to Switzerland in 1802. When they started a settlement in Genoa, Napoleon not only gave them permission, but even a grant of 10,000 francs. He wanted them to start more monasteries in the Alps, where they could serve as refuges for soldiers.

Later Napoleon changed his mind about them and the Abbot escaped to the United States of America and purchased a site in New York for $10,000, which was later sold to the Archdiocese of New York and used as the building site of St. Patrick's Cathedral. After the downfall of Napoleon they could come back to France. Through all of this their prayer and praise of God persisted and gave evidence of the strength of contemplation in the midst of the vicissitudes of history. The Congress of Vienna in 1815 created greater peace also for the Church and its institutions, so that monasticism could flourish and be renewed. The demand of "Enlightenment" to be more focused on the essential could very well be met and even contemplation could wean itself away from unimportant frills, which so easily enter monastic observances. God desires the pure and simple and the monks and nuns are very well equipped to fulfill God's desires through their way of life.

Abbot Prosper Gueranger

Joy of Salvation in Our Songs and Prayers

One of the most prominent monastic re-foundations happened in France through the young priest Prosper Louis Pascal Gueranger (1805–1875). His father opened a school in what had been the convent of Sisters and he, Prosper, was born there as the third of four sons. His father was rather serious, but his mother had a greater sense of humor and Prosper inherited her liveliness and playfulness, but he owed his strength and persistence to his father. These he needed for his extensive studies and his determination in pursuing his goals. He was baptized on the day of his birth and as a child he visited the deserted abbey of Solesmes.

This monastery had been founded by Geoffroy de Sable in 1010, the buildings and the Church had been renewed and extended over the centuries and they remained impressive even in their deserted state after the French Revolution. Prosper could go on meditative strolls as a child to this abbey, which was only two miles from his home. Everything made a great mystical impression on him.

A poetic word speaks of stones that sing, that they have a musical message. We imagine Prosper experienced it. The buildings, the empty church and the many statues within and around the cloister witnessed that monks had lifted their voices and their souls in praise of God there for many centuries. Couldn't this chant be renewed? Maybe this was just the dream of a child. And yet, wasn't he dreaming of heaven thinking of the monks, who had once been there? Those in heaven couldn't be brought back, but new ones could come and take their place on their journey to heaven. Who knows, the dream of a child could be a great awareness of the secret code of the monks.

Very likely he learned early from his father or his lively and faithful mother that the last prior of the abbey had been expelled only recently in 1791, been imprisoned for the faith and then died, because of all the hardships he endured. Prosper came to know Dom Papion, another monk of Solesmes, who exercised his ministry in his hometown, Sable, until 1819, when he died of old age.

A decisive aspect of Dom Gueranger's talents was his love of music and the liturgy of the Church. The sacred chant makes the monk sing along with the angels and the saints in heaven, already during his earthly existence. The liturgy lets him participate most intimately in the redemption brought about through the death and resurrection of the Lord. His dream was reinforced through his father's courage, which made it obvious to him that he should never be afraid to affirm his faith. The voice of God had found an echo in his young and fruitful soul and spoke to him of a vocation to the priesthood. He received his first Holy Communion in 1816 and his Confirmation the following year and in 1818 he entered the College Royal in Angers.

His favorite pastimes were poetry and reading. His friends called him "monk" and he accepted this cheerfully. Prosper entered the seminary of Le Mans and when he received his tonsure in 1823 he definitely felt consecrated to God. His extensive reading led him to focus on ecclesiastical antiquity. His experience of the Immaculate Conception on December 8, 1823 made his reason join his heart in total belief. He described his experience this way, "No transport whatsoever, but a sweet peace with a sincere conviction. It was one nature disappearing to make way for another."

For a short time he even became the secretary of the Bishop. He could make important contacts, which later helped him in his revival of Solesmes. He had also developed a great love for Rome and had overcome the prejudices of Gallicanism against the Holy See. Many bishops in France were prejudiced against Rome at that time and Gueranger proved his strength of mind and his faith by being committed to the truth. He was ordained Deacon in 1826 and Priest the following year.

He was quickly accepted and well liked for his sermons, because of his clarity, his direct and simple style, and for his enthusiasm. He advanced in his career as a priest and even made a name for himself as a writer. In 1831 he read a note in the newspaper that the Abbey of Solesmes was up for sale. His childhood memories came back to him and the monk was winning the upper hand in his soul. Everything about being a monk "suddenly sprang to life again" as he put it and never left him again.

At first glance the thought of purchasing the abbey and winning friends over to become monks along with him seemed utopian, but he couldn't dodge it. The idea took control of him. He reached an agreement about the purchase and in 1833 he arrived in Solesmes with five companions to begin monastic life there. Without personal monastic experience, relying on his studies and his great enthusiasm for the Benedictine tradition, he developed his program for the community.

There was joy for the new beginning, but there was also intense suffering. He knew how to atone for transgressions of his monks by making sacrifices for them. He waited on them at table, knowing what was at stake. From clergy and bishops he had to endure great opposition. He wrote about this as follows, "Nothing is harder for a Catholic heart than ecclesiastical persecution." Although he obtained permission from Rome, the local bishop suspended him for seven years and he had to endure this agony. He described the situation thus, "Our congregation suffers persecution, and the cruelest kind of all, for the authority of the Apostolic See is at the moment being exercised against her (Solesmes)." He remained faithful to Rome and its blessing finally succeeded. He became abbot and Solesmes was designated as Motherhouse of a French Benedictine Congregation. He returned to the original policy, in which each monastery is independent and exempt from the jurisdiction of the local bishop, elects an Abbot, who is in office for life. His association of Monasteries in France came about rather quickly.

Despite his own great influence he was not interested in any forceful centralization of the association. He also followed the rule of St. Benedict by asking the monks to renounce all involvement outside the monastery. In this way he emphasized contemplation and the foremost concern became the celebration of the Liturgy, prayer, music and the sacraments. He discovered and stressed through his interpretation the demand of the Rule of St. Benedict "that nothing should take precedence over worship". The daily routine of the monastery revolved once again around the recitation of the divine office in the Church together and the celebration of Mass.

The monks in Solesmes always pray and celebrate with great solemnity in remembrance of the display of liturgical beauty of the Cluny of the Middle Ages. The studies and the research of the monks also had to serve this purpose. Following Abbot Gueranger's great enthusiasm for music the monastery renewed the choral recitation of the divine office, which received great recognition, respect and publicity in the Roman Catholic Church. Gueranger wrote extensively about the history of liturgy, its importance and interpretation and laid the foundation for a worldwide liturgical renewal.

Gueranger helped form a new style of the Benedictine monk. Since the liturgy became the dominant factor it had its influence on the other aspects of monastic life. The dignity and elevation of prayer made the life of the monks also more dignified and somewhat aristocratic. This style witnessed to itself and didn't need any propaganda. Late in 1854 a new bishop took office in Le Mans, in which diocese Solesmes is located, and he publicly expressed his esteem for the monastery and its abbot. He had discovered in the abbot the joy of a father, who gives himself completely to his sons. In this joy Abbot Gueranger was always sustained by the glory of heaven.

When he died in 1875 at the age of seventy he had lived under six different political systems and saw his country shaken three times by revolution. The stability, which the Benedictine cherishes, is coming from the source above human history and Gueranger lived with extraordinary strength from this source. For many he renewed this awareness that the Church is principally a society of divine praise, which the monk is privileged to reflect through the particular code entrusted to him. Dom Prosper Gueranger was focused on this code, but he was never free from risks, uncertainty, false steps and suffering.

Søren Kierkegaard
Forged a way for the Freedom of Being a Child of God

One of the greatest contemporaries of Abbot Prosper Gueranger was the Danish Philosopher and Theologian, Søren Aabye Kierkegaard (1813–1855). Unfortunately the two never met during their earthly journeys of faith. If they had Prosper could have surrounded the eight years younger Søren with the loving care of an older brother. As a thirteen year old he could have taken him on a walk to Solesmes and in his typical joyfulness he could have brought the empty church, the courtyard and the sacred ground to life through his lively explanations and with Gregorian chant he could have lifted the melancholy of the child. Later he could have strengthened his trust in God's grace residing in his heart, not through any counsel given with the air of superiority, but by singing the psalm with him, "How good it is when brothers live in unity".

Throughout his adult life he could have been his friend, since both lived in the awareness that the truth of Christianity is something given to us by God and that this God is independent from our mere human minds. Abbot Prosper survived Søren Kierkegaard by twenty years and as the fifty year old monk he could have helped him to prepare for death. This preparation could have assured Søren that heaven is the community of saints around the Throne of God and that he would follow him when God decided to call him as well.

We believe that Søren Kierkegaard would have been grateful and would have gone to his reward with even greater confidence, accompanied by the prayers of a friend. But the two countries, France and Denmark, were too far apart by way of history, culture, and religion and Søren Kierkegaard had to live through even greater isolation and give hints for the secret of the heart. If the two had met in life they could have encouraged one another in a bond of friendship, which faith can establish as Jesus makes clear in his Farewell Discourse, "I have called you friends." When human beings are friends of Jesus, then they can also be friends with each other like monks in a monastery.

Instead, Søren Kierkegaard had to fend for himself and discover the secrets of his soul, which became a striking model for philosophy and theology. He was brought up in a very Christian household, which was probably even stricter than a monastery. Instead of the freedom of the gospel the disciplined Lutheran family lived with a sense of guilt on their consciences, because we all have sinned in Adam and Eve.

Especially his father instilled in the child that God is our judge and we must render him an account. He also let him grow up with some isolation. Instead of permitting him to go and play with other children, he talked with him at home and explained to him that our imagination can substitute for a lot and save valuable time, which might be wasted on childish games. Søren could invest all his willpower and intelligence on learning and he was fond of it. His study of our Christian faith, his regular observance of our religion, Eucharist, Confession and prayers, were part of his schooling and he took these very seriously. His talents for languages, literature, poetry, the Bible, philosophy and theology were extraordinary, on the level of a genius. In a double sense he was isolated.

Like a monk isolates himself away from the world in order to form a more intimate bond with God, so also Kierkegaard accepted this isolation as a cross and as an opportunity to let the Spirit take hold of his existence. He compared this situation of his soul to a Chinese puzzle of box within box. Hidden from the world the soul takes on a meaning, which ultimately is accessible and blessed only by God. Bonds of friendship and love can rightfully only be established with God in view. Without him they dissipate and dissolve into nothing.

When Søren Kierkegaard was twenty eight years old in 1841 he was engaged to the strikingly beautiful 17 year old Regina Olson. He dissolved the engagement, choosing instead his "monastic" existence. Monastic here has to be taken in the sense of being alone. This step was a great sacrifice for him and ultimately only God can judge its weight and quality. We are convinced that he didn't take it lightly. It weighed heavily on his mind, but it was in and through this sacrifice that his responsibility before God was confirmed and became settled.

The insights it set free have become a source of inspiration for many people serious about their faith ever since. He made it clear that God has given a dignity and a value to the human soul, found in and through the gospel. But human beings have to be willing to endure his training, without it their lives remain on the surface. We have to discover that we can be trapped by mere appearance and in a Spirit of Irony we have to uncover the appearance and remain firm in the spirit. A little philosophy is useful for everybody, who wishes to engage in the reflection about his life.

Our very existence as human beings requires a life which is either guided and supported by the Spirit or led astray by something of an ephemeral nature. There is anxiety in every human heart, through which it is focused to give the "object" of its attention its proper designation or to fall under its "spell" and be overpowered by it. Anxiety is a great educator, who teaches us to discount, what doesn't bring eternal happiness and to become stronger in faith; finally anxiety teaches a person to rest securely in God. Of course, everyone, who wants to be with God, has to cope with the end of our earthly life, following our Savior, who not only died for us, but who also invites us to die for and in him. The greater glory of God comes close to those, who entrust themselves ever more fully to him. Trust in God can require actual martyrdom, if God wants it.

Søren Kierkegaard didn't become a monk, because of the situation of the State-Church in Denmark, but his life resembled that of a monk very much. For him everything revolved around the truth of our religion. He witnessed publicly to this in his talks: *Love covers a multitude of sins, About Faith, Encouraging the inner man, Job, For the occasion of confession, At a grave, and The power of God in the weakness of man*. He regretted that the Reformation had brought monasteries to an end and we assume that he had felt at home for example in Solesmes in the presence of such an inspiring monk like Abbot Prosper Gueranger.

Both had such a clear awareness that we believe in heaven as the goal of our faith journey and therefore Søren Kierkegaard deserves to be counted among the monks and their close bond with God. He died very young at age 42 and the legacy, which he left behind in his extensive writings witness to the fact that his mind like that of every religious was set on God, who would be his reward. His experience of God's grace gave him the assurance that his earthly ordeal was not in vain, but in God's hands.

Theologically he also paved the way for citizens of countries of the Reformation to be able to renew their interest in this hidden life of the contemplative. He knew that there is no substitute for it. It can be quite natural for the scholar to discover the great value of prayer.

During the first half of the nineteenth century there were also opportunities for the renewal of monasticism. It was also the time when more Abbeys established daughter houses in the United States of America, which proved to be very fruitful territory for monasteries, because of the prevalent religious fervor of the immigrant populations.

King Ludwig I and Improvements for Monasteries

Strengthened Monasticism

In Bavaria religious institutions found a strong advocate in King Ludwig I (1825–1848). He was born in 1786 and had witnessed the events in France already in his youth, the rise and fall of Napoleon and the ensuing spread of the revolutionary movement in Europe. We understand some reasons for this historical progress, but we also are aware, that it was purchased at great costs of human lives and sufferings. Instead of really integrating "Enlightenment" the emphasis on reason grew and developed into "Rationalism", which would show its greatest destructive power in the two World Wars of the twentieth century. King Ludwig I was an accomplished intellectual and had recourse to our Religion.

He called some of the most prominent Professors of Philosophy, Theology and Literature to the University of Munich, who could lead their students and parts of the general population to be aware of the dangers of mere rationalism and that it needs to be balanced through God's Revelation and the mysticism of our Faith, in order to create peace in our soul and in our world. Many monasteries in Bavaria were reopened and others were built in Bavaria during the reign of King Ludwig I. He favored the cause of contemplation even against great opposition. His world-famous grandson, King Ludwig II, the fairy-tale king of Bavaria shared some of his grandfather's sentiments, but they were turned towards the Romanticism of Music (Richard Wagner) and his enchanting castles. He didn't interfere with monasticism, but it didn't play any significant role in his life either.

Austria also experienced this revival of religion, in which the monasteries always were important centers of meditation, prayer and pilgrimages. The promulgation of the Dogma of the Immaculate Conception by Pope Pius IX in 1854 and the Apparitions of the Immaculate Conception to Bernadette Soubirous in 1858, who later became a nun, also increased devotion and the focus on our Salvation of religious and lay-people.

St. Therese of Lisieux
Let God Take Over

The most glamorous witness of the code of the monks or in her case the code of the nuns of the 19th century was St. Therese of Lisieux, born on January 2nd, 1873 and died on September 30th, 1897. She was the youngest of five living children of Louis Martin and Zelie Guerin, who both have been declared saints of the Church. Her four older sisters also were nuns. She had some health problems as a child and was taken care of and nursed away from home for over a year.

The very devoted atmosphere of the family always penetrated her to the depth of her heart and she virtually recognized God's call for her at the age of three. When she heard at that time that her older sister was going to be a nun she exclaimed, "I also will be a religious". She didn't really know what that meant, but the sentiment in her heart was real; she was aware of God's love for her and wanted to respond. She was very intelligent and by nature given to contemplation and prayer. Sitting for a long time by herself, she felt God close even though there is the separation between heaven and earth. Intuitively she hit the nail on the head: The world seemed to her a place of exile and she longed for heaven. This mapped out the secret code of the nun for her. Being away from everybody and by herself was her secret, known to God alone. This indicated to her the shortest route to heaven, which had to be in the cloister. By the same token she recognized the immensity of eternal life, which a tiny human being is unable to comprehend and has to trust that God knows.

A visit to the Atlantic Ocean increased this recognition and feeling for a greatness, which is not in our grasp. She didn't want anything to stand between herself and God, whom she held close, even when she was studying or doing things. She was brought up on truly Christian fare, regular in her prayers and the attendance at Mass, when she was of age. The family read daily passages from the gospels or the lives of the saints and she was able to internalize these teachings well. She liked poetry and later composed some poems herself.

She also liked drawing and painting and did it rather well. She had a natural dislike for anything evil and remained pure as a simple matter of fact, without any compulsion or exercise of abnegation. If God had called her to get married, she would have fulfilled her role as wife and mother without any restraint. She didn't have any pride of the nun over the married women, because she was convinced that both these vocations come from a loving God.

Both are of equal value to him and she exclusively wanted to fulfill God's wishes. When she was old enough to go to confession she exercised this fulfillment of God's will and she wasn't so much preoccupied with herself as eager to please the beloved Jesus. She cried when she was afraid that she had disappointed him in the least. She not only extended her relationship with her father to Jesus, but intensified it in the awareness that nothing can match the loving heart of Jesus Christ. But Jesus imposed trials on her like moving to a new home or having a vision about her father's later illness.

She spent five years as a student in a school run by Benedictine nuns, which were the saddest in her life. Other girls bullied her, because she was so good in school. She did receive her first Holy Communion at the Abbey in 1884, which she experienced in the most loving way as a kiss of love. God as the master-artist creates mutuality along with our relationship with him, which she described as follows, "I felt myself loved, but I also said: I love you and I give myself to you forever." For her it was a mystical experience.

After her first Holy Communion she was free from interior trials for a year, but later she became sick with nervous trembling and hallucinations without losing the use of her reason. Her father took her home in 1886. She was miraculously cured by the Blessed Virgin Mary and resumed her normal daily routine. This grace brought her closer to God, as did the feeling of conversion on Christmas of that same year.

Although God calls each and everyone in a unique way he wants us to help others on their way to salvation. He solicits our sacrifices for others and we can trust in his power to do so. In 1887 she put this truth to the test. The assassin Pranzini was sentenced to death and she prayed and made sacrifices for him. Before his execution he kissed the crucifix three times, which was a sign of his conversion for Therese. This also affirmed her trust in God's great mercy. Jesus came after all to save sinners. This shows an even deeper side of the secret code of the nun. Something done hidden from everybody is seen and rewarded by God. We have to believe and trust that he turns our sacrifices into favors for others and it will happen even if nobody else besides him should know about it. Her intense struggle to enter Carmel at the age of fifteen is a masterpiece of this secret code. She knew that it had to happen, but nobody else was able to see it from the hidden angle from which God was calling her.

The superior of Carmel and the bishop believed that she was too young to make this decision and commitment. She was too weak to overcome their resistance. The secret had to remain in her heart. However, her father had made plans for a pilgrimage to Rome, which included an audience with his Holiness, Pope Leo XIII. These audiences were very structured and nobody was supposed to talk to the Pope. People knelt down in front of him, kissed his ring and moved on. Therese thought, "If I tell him that I want to enter Carmel at the age of 15 then it will be granted." She knelt down before him and said, "Most Holy Father, I have a particular favor to ask of your. Please, permit me to enter Carmel at age 15." The Pope responded, "Do, what the superiors tell." And she talked back, "If you gave permission, everybody would agree."

We have to admire her presence of mind and her courage. The Pope had remembered this incident and gave his consent, which was then transmitted to the authorities in France. Therese had won. She had also deepened her conviction about the power of God and the mysterious strength, in which he acts. She was exceedingly delighted when she entered the cloister knowing that her life would contain more thorns than roses, but she wanted to suffer everything for Jesus alone. Her secret mission intensified. Without any contacts with the world outside she trusted that God would turn her prayers and sacrifices into great blessings for others. It is this introversion, which belongs to the Catholic Religion. Without it our religious practices would easily become flat.

St. Therese of Lisieux is most remarkable in the way she prayed and made sacrifices. We admit that devotion in her intensified so much that it gained a new quality. For the observer it is just a nun praying or making some sacrifices. For her there is a marked difference. She had given herself so totally to God that she became aware that God was praying and sacrificing in her. She quoted the words of St. Paul, "It is no longer I who live, but Jesus lives in me." All of a sudden something very normal is done by God himself and she–so to speak–only has to let him do it. Her discovery of spiritual childhood is a breakthrough to the simplicity and unparalleled originality of the gospel, "If you do not become like little children, you cannot enter the Kingdom of God." This is not any false humility, because she has come to the point, where God is acting in her. Nothing can interfere, which would not agree with him.

The baby is so to speak an extension of mom and dad, who have given him life. The child is like the family, into which he was born and in the same way the child is brought or comes to Jesus, happy to become just like him. Jesus therefore says, "Let the children come to me, for theirs is the kingdom of God." Therese has acquired this simplicity and the barriers between a human being and God have disappeared; consecration has taken place. By the same token she has to suffer like the Messiah had to suffer for mankind. It can take on a playful note. She has become like a little ball, which the child Jesus uses to play with. Jesus was a well behaved boy and he would use the ball as a ball appealed to him, kicking it, throwing it against the wall and let it bounce around. Therese enjoys the games the child Jesus is playing and the times, when he totally forgets the ball, are the hardest for her. He is preoccupied with other things and she has to wait patiently and endure, when nothing is happening.

When waiting has come to an end, then this time, when nothing was happening, is also like nothing and the surprise of Jesus' enduring love prevails. Whenever Jesus wishes he can assure her of his greater love and mercy and she can renew her trust in him.

She has to remain little and become even smaller, so that Jesus can lift her up all the easier. Even the ball is just an extension of the child's playfulness. This does not mean that salvation has become a game. Therese has offered herself as a sacrificial victim and the consequences are real and very painful. She is ordered to sit at the table with real sinners, people who are turned away from God, and people who have turned against him. As an extension of Jesus' sacrificial love she has become one of them. "He was made sin for us" St. Paul wrote and the saint also has to endure this bitter situation.

She doesn't know any longer, whether she is an object of love or hatred. Her prayers and sacrifices for sinners are not performed from a spiritual distance, but from among them. Physically she is removed from them, but spiritually God has made her one of them. This is paradoxical and faith is a paradox. In line with this awareness of God's unfathomable grace the Pope declared her to be the patron of the universal mission of the Church, although she always remained in the monastery, hidden as a sacristan, a teacher of novices, gardening, cleaning, helping an older sister to walk from the refectory to her cell and serving bread and water. Jesus saw her selfgiving and turned it into blessings.

This enabled her to bridge the gap between saints and sinners, leaving the final outcome in God's hands. It also made it possible for her to bridge the gap between priesthood and sisterhood in the Catholic Church. Asking herself about her ultimate vocation it would have been possible for her to ask the question, whether she was called to the priesthood.

She had found out that priests are weak, and that the salt of the earth has to be protected. In her fully developed spirituality she didn't seek the priesthood, because in the depth of the heart of the Church the various vocations are united. This heart is burning with love and assigns the different tasks. The priests are inspired from the love of the heart of the Church and Therese has found her place in this heart. She didn't feel deprived of anything by not being permitted to become a priest. On the contrary, she felt privileged to lodge deeper in the heart from which the priesthood springs.

She was able to respect and cherish the difference established by God and didn't have to accept this difference only by way of authority. She was able to accept the difference between men and women and between priests and nuns. She didn't have to look for equality, where God has given clear distinctions. This also means that modern advocates of equality cannot claim her as one of their own. By the same token she is in full agreement with the gospel. She didn't want to say, "If Jesus had lived today, then he would have called me to be a priest." She had no inclination to be smarter than Jesus. We can admire and imitate her childlike trust in God.

Her physical illness of tuberculosis and her early death at the age of twenty four years and nine months are also an expression of co-redemptive suffering. This gives an insight into her great love for the Blessed Virgin Mary, the Co-Redemptrix. St. Mary is so much neglected in the piety of the modern Church, because people don't like to suffer anything and especially not for others. St. Therese of Lisieux was able to extend her involvement in the salvation of mankind until the end of the world.

This enlarges our view of the saints, who are not only in heaven, but have a real interest in our faith. St. Therese of Lisieux deserves not only a special place in the history of the contemplatives, but also in Theology. We cannot engage in the Mission of the Church, in the priesthood, in sisterhood or in the married state, without this inwardness given by God's design.

Overall the nineteenth century closed with some confidence in regard to the monks. They received greater recognition and respect. The industrial revolution opened many opportunities for people to make a living and often they had to relocate. Many religious were willing and happy to live among them and to support them in their challenges.

Through the advances in science and technology we so easily devalue human beings and they become mere material in the machines of progress. The monk stands up against this mentality, which threatens the integrity of the human soul and he renews the awareness of the purely spiritual and the joy of the gospel. For him the workers behind machines are first of all brothers and sisters in Christ and he affirms their value in God's eyes, even if he affirms this value "only" in prayer and silence.

Charles de Foucauld

Saint in the Desert

A remarkable monk in this struggle and a witness for it was Charles de Foucauld. He was born in 1853 and was murdered by a group of Moslems in 1916, although many Moslems love him deeply. He grew up as the son of a military family in France and became an Officer himself. Rather well situated and independent he was able to enjoy being a playboy for a while. Even his traditional Catholic Faith didn't mean much to him for some years. Along with his youthful escapades he had acquired a real interest in the desert, personally and as an object of research. He explored some mountain ranges of the Sahara desert in Morocco and received a prominent reward for his maps from the Geographical Society of France. There is something timeless about the solitude of the desert, giving human beings an impression about the Creator, who is above time. Human life is being renewed for him, who is able to connect with this Creator and Redeemer. For Charles de Foucauld the scientific research was accompanied by spiritual longing. Fortunately he came to know an Augustinian Abbot in Paris, who opened for him this transition from temporal truth, goodness and beauty to eternal truth, goodness and beauty.

Like everybody else Charles de Foucauld also had to go to confession and receive forgiveness. He realized that penance is part of our return to God and yet his attitude towards God was not morbid, but filled with confidence in the overwhelming greatness of our Creator and Redeemer. In and through this confidence he became a monk, willing to endure whatever God wanted him to go through. He joined the Trappists, but thought that this discipline was too light for him, so he went to Nazareth and then into the desert among the Tuareg tribe in the Sahara. He believed his mission to be among them.

He had been ordained to the priesthood in 1901 and his love for Jesus Christ impelled him to proclaim the gospel, but he couldn't do it among the Moslems by preaching, because this would have led to arguments instead of conversion to the truth. His Catholicism was firm and he used his loneliness, his hardships of desert-life, his private prayer and the celebration of the Eucharist as means to witness to Jesus.

His contemplation before the Blessed Sacrament assured him of God's love, but also of God's call to co-redeem through his suffering. This is probably the hardest thing for anybody to grasp and yet Charles de Foucauld had become intimately familiar with this mixture of love and suffering of believers on their journey. He also held out the appeal to the Moslems to be converted to the Truth. Without this appeal our faith would be weak and the monk, Charles de Foucauld, was not weak in faith.

His quiet presence among them solicited cooperation and understanding, not arguments and confrontation. He described his attitude as follows,

"If a person is able to suffer and to love, then he can do a lot; it is the most we can do in the world; we always feel when we suffer, we do not always feel that we love, which makes our suffering even harder; but we know that we would like to love, and this is already loving. We believe that we don't love enough and this is true. We are never able to love enough; but the loving God knows of what we are made of and he loves us even more than a mother loves her child. He, who never dies, told us that he will never refuse anyone, who comes to Him."

Charles de Foucauld's secret code of the monk was this contact with our Savior Jesus Christ and his silently courageous way to give witness to this contact. Also Moslems, who came to know him, loved him and respected him as the monk among them. From a missionary point of view his is an achievement and he has found many adherents, who believe his insights. They share his inspiration of a different Christian life in a world, which has brought about new and unheard of conflicts. The First World War had its impact also in the Sahara desert among the Tuareg.

A few of them thought that Fr. Charles de Foucauld was a spy for the French and they murdered him in 1916. His silent witness to the truth led to martyrdom, bringing to fulfillment his insight that Christian love may have to go all the way, even to give one's life for the gospel. This final witness made his efforts all the more convincing and worthy of imitation. We assume that the death Charles de Foucauld endured was a somber and confusing moment. Many years of suffering, endurance and prayer were coming to an end and he had to entrust these to God, who had called him.

The people whom he loved and served had turned against him and he was not personally responsible for their animosity, but had to experience it nonetheless. Only God could unravel these entanglements. His legacy gives evidence that he was right and that monasticism had found a new expression in a very complicated modern world. This applies even more to the beginning of the twenty first century, in which the contact and possibly the conflict between the Christian and Moslem world, is growing.

The contemplatives like Charles de Foucauld look upon this encounter from God's perspective. God may let it happen, because so much in our Christianity has become superficial and needs to be cleansed. God may let it happen, because our religion has become a mere matter of convenience or a mere matter of our interests. God may let it happen, because our disregard for human lives through abortion is atrocious in comparison of the value, which Moslem believers assign to it. God may let it happen, because our

Western hedonism and cynicism no longer have anything in common with his Revelation and we have to face the consequences.

As pointed out, Rationalism of the 19th century continued to increase and along with it the insistence on our power and the inclination to use it, even when it would lead to great destruction. This is the dark side of Rationalism, which brought about the First and Second World War. This does not mean that we have the right to just blame all the people of this era. Often they were caught in a situation, which was not in their control. For the contemplatives it took a lot of soul-searching and prayer to entrust themselves even more to God as it may take for us dealing with modern hedonism and cynicism. And yet we can be confident that insistent prayer will bring us to the point of finding God's answer.

Edith Stein
Intellectual Belief in God

An extraordinary contemplative of the first part of the 20th century, Edith Stein, found God's answer. She was very much familiar with the modern secular society, its "independence" from Christianity and the need for this society to be brought back into the Christian realm and the sacrifices involved in this process. She was born October 12, 1891 on the Feast of Yom Kippur of a Jewish family in Breslau, Germany. Her father died, when she was only two years old and she didn't have any personal remembrance of him. Her mother ran the family business, selling wood-products for construction. This gave Edith an example for the strong and industrious modern woman.

She, as the youngest, was the favorite of her mother, not only because of her intelligence, but also because she was born on this high holiday of atonement. As a four year old, Edith was able to recite poems and received the nickname "the clever Edith". She had a very lively imagination and any reports of evil deeds affected her and she suffered spiritually along with those, who had been victims of crime, even to the point of screaming in the middle of the night. She displayed the same intensity in school and excelled. By nature she had a great aversion to arguments and outbursts of anger, which she had to witness as a child.

These experiences made her even more reserved and she kept things to herself. Her introversion led her to be inwardly calm and children felt attracted to her. On account of her lively imagination she could provide a lot of material for their games. When she was ten and eleven she had to deal with the trauma of the suicides of two of her uncles. She believed that they had been unable to endure tragic losses because of the absence of belief in the immortality of the soul. Her faith didn't include this conviction, but was only directed towards our earthly existence. This led easily to practical atheism, but her decisions welled up from a spiritual depth almost unknown to her. She was able to wait until a decision was ripe.

For a number of years she was an atheist and culture became a substitute of religion. However, she was convinced that morality has to demand sacrifices from our emotions. Without these sacrifices human beings lose their dignity. If they are willing to make these sacrifices then they gain an even greater dignity and peace. Edith Stein was willing to make these sacrifices even as an atheist and discovered their value all the more, when she became a Christian. The discovery of spiritual values made her curious in her studies, especially when she opted to pursue philosophy as a career. Her choice was puzzling for her family, but an inner drive mapped this out very clearly to her. After finishing High School in 1911 she was able to go to the University. The Phenomenology of Edmund Husserl brought her to appreciate truth as something given to us, which we are bound to accept as a gift from a power not in our grasp.

On account of this gift from above she also became critical of psychology, which turns human beings very quickly into mechanisms of instinct. She wrote her doctoral thesis, "About the concept of Empathy" in 1916 and was able to begin a teaching career. Edmund Husserl had made a very personal impression on her as she put it, "It seemed to me that never before had I met a person, who had such a good and pure heart as he." As a teacher she wanted to imitate his example.

The First World War had caught everybody off guard and she volunteered as a nurse for wounded soldiers. When the war was lost, she was devastated and realized that ultimately only religious values can renew our strength, if we want to cope with disaster. She found solace in a circle of like-minded friends and some of them witnessed to their Christian faith unabashedly. This prepared a turning point for her. She taught in a Catholic High School, studied Catholicism and finally the writings of St. Teresa of

Avila like "The Interior Castle". She converted, became a Carmelite out of her sense of contemplation, knowing that God is setting our lives on a path towards eternal happiness.

This takes place in and through Jesus Christ and as he was crucified, so we must endure the same. He gives us strength to wear our cross like a crown, as she put it in her "Science of the Cross". As a nun she received the religious name: Sister Teresia Benedicta a Cruce, probably also expressing her conviction that the Cross contains this blessing for her.

Edith Stein had come to know our modern secularized society, made her way through the prejudices towards religion and discovered genuine contemplation and in it her access to God. Some impressions had guided her along the way. At one time she saw a woman in Frankfurt visiting the Cathedral for a time of prayer during the busy time of the day in the city. She learned that this woman combined daily life with transcendence in contemplation. Edith Stein put it as follows, "She went away from her business and entered the empty Church as if coming for a friendly conversation." Looking at this impression from the viewpoint of modern society we observe that the very business virtually demands contemplation as a counterpart of the otherwise too mundane occupations.

Edith Stein was also very impressed by a piece of art depicting the Crucifixion of our Lord and his everlasting love. God's love doesn't come to an end and we only gain, when we look up to him. The rift of our modern dichotomy seeks healing and Edith Stein recognized God's healing presence in a Double-Church for Catholics and Protestants.

God is bringing people together, who are otherwise separated from each other. In prayer we participate in God's grace and we make our contribution for the healing of mankind. The Holy Ghost Church in Heidelberg became for her a symbol of hope for the unity we seek and which has to be given by God. Once again she discovered that the Crucified Savior has identified himself with every suffering.

Her conversion had changed her values, or as she wrote, "We shouldn't despair, when things turn out differently from what we expected. We should think about what remains and that we are only visitors here and that everything, which seems such a burden at the present isn't all that important in the end and that it will acquire a totally different meaning from what it is today." Her insights didn't make her "other-worldly" in a bad sense, but let her see the present in the light of eternity. Her contemplation taught her to hold up the Cross like a banner in battle, to endure danger and even defeat in humility, aware that greater blessings are to come. Carmel was not a secure haven away from danger, but the place where everything of an earthly nature is being purified and lifted up to God, who accepts it in a most glorious way. Her sacrifice in contemplation was also the attitude, in which she accepted her arrest by the Nazis in 1942.

The transport from the time of her arrest on August 2, 1942 took about a week until August 9, 1942. Edith and her sister Rosa showed their composure by helping infants, whose mothers had become totally apathetic and were not able to help their children. We can also observe through these actions, how focused she was at this most tragic time of her life. She met her end with inner dignity in the awareness that a greater life had taken hold of her. We also have to appreciate her philosophical writings in this light. She had discovered that society, governments, education, advances in science, the role of women and so forth have to be ruled by ideas, which are expressions of timeless truths.

If this is not the case, then human beings will always fall prey to ideologies, which in turn will end up in narrow-minded confrontations and the accompanying clashes of interests. This confirms our conviction that she had acquired the freedom of spirit, which is given in and through Jesus Christ and his sacrifice for mankind. This acquisition of the freedom of spirit is her witness to the faith. As pointed out, she and her sister Rosa, died on August 9th, 1942 in the Concentration Camp Birkenau, close to Auschwitz. Her death was that of a martyr. She was beatified in 1987 and canonized in 1998 by His Holiness, Pope John Paul II.

Secular Institutes, Fr. Josef Kentenich, and Fr. Alfred Delp

Struggle and Victory of Our Faith in the Modern World

The New Code of Canon Law describes the option for lay-people to be even more closely associated in "Secular Institutes", where also religious join, who follow the evangelical counsels, but do not necessarily wear any garb designating them as such. Their intention is to be a leaven of

Christianity in the world without the traditional outward appearance. When entire societies drift away from God so easily, then it is urgently needed that as many people as possible come together in prayer groups and communities to strengthen each other in their faith and their witness to God being at work among them.

One of the more prominent of such associations, besides the Opus Dei Movement, is called Schoenstatt.

The founder of this movement, Fr. Josef Kentenich, was born in a Catholic environment in the town of Gymnich, close to Cologne in 1885. Being very intelligent he not only took his religious instruction for granted, but had the gift of real prayer already as a child. On occasion people observed him in contemplation and knew intuitively that his closeness to heaven was filled with grace. Prayer was imbedded in his heart and he kept his inner eye set on heaven throughout his entire very difficult life. Because of economic hardships he had to live in an orphanage from 1894–1899.

He then entered the Novitiate of the Pallotine Order in Limburg. He suffered from tuberculosis from 1906–1908, but was able to be ordained to the priesthood in 1910 and became Spiritual Director for students in 1912 and founded the Brotherhood of Schoenstatt two years later. He was well liked as a teacher and retreat master. The experiences of his own existence had set him on this path of a heroic trust in God's Providence in the face of overwhelming vicissitudes and opposition.

For him human life is this drama, in which God's greater love and power are always under the most serious attacks, but always triumphant in the end. In this struggle he always wanted to be on God's side and made himself a tool in God's hands. Through his devotion he was able to be engaged in the most active apostolate. He was very forceful as a teacher and preacher of the truth and yet willing to suffer for his conviction at the same time. His childlike trust in God was disarming and remained firm along with his sense of humor. Everything about him made him very successful in his priestly career, especially because he was a very serious opponent of the Nazi-Regime.

As a consequence of his opposition to the Third Reich he was arrested on September 20, 1941 and sent to the Concentration Camp of Dachau until the end of the war. He was not a quiet victim, who endured to get it all over with, but a vehement fighter for the truth. The guards of the camp knew, what he stood for, and they couldn't really shake the truth even though they didn't believe in it. Even if they had executed him, he would have kept his conviction, "You can kill a man, but you cannot kill the truth". For him heaven was in control, whether this meant death or the continuation of his apostolate. By God's design he was called to survive this ordeal.

He had faced death during these four years and increased his conviction in God's triumph over sin and mortality. He proved willing to be a martyr, but he was equally happy to continue his apostolate after the war. His heroism was accompanied by a childlike confidence in the gentle role of the Blessed Virgin Mary, who continually watches over our well-being for the sake of our salvation. Her motherhood is a permanent feature and we would miss the point, if we didn't accept the truth through her loving hands. He believed that this applies to everyone and therefore his institute was open to everyone, who wanted to accept the challenge of a more intensely apostolic life. Like the Blessed Virgin Mary he also wanted to live the truth in love. This enigma of truth and love is challenged not only in society, but also in the Church.

The hierarchy became suspicious in regard to his orthodoxy and he was expelled from Germany and had to live in Exile in Milwaukee, USA. He lived there from 1952–1965, but he was permitted to continue his ministry. His Holiness, Pope Paul VI, lifted the decree against him in October 1965 and he had the honor of an audience with the Pope and returned home on Christmas Eve of that year. These trials and tribulations made the movement only stronger and increased the enthusiasm of the members. The Blessed Virgin Mary had triumphed even in the Church. He died in his beloved chapel of Adoration on September 15, 1968 and the process for his beatification was begun in 1975.

The Schoenstatt movement includes, besides many lay-people priests, brothers, sisters and those more strictly dedicated to contemplation. The founder has made it clear that the serious impasse Christianity had to endure during the Third Reich will continue, even if the form of such an impasse changes. This is part and parcel of Christianity and it would be unhealthy and unrealistic to look for a golden age in this world.

Similar to Fr. Josef Kentenich in his opposition to the Third Reich was the Jesuit Fr. Alfred Delp. He was born in Mannheim in 1907, converted to Catholicism, taught Sociology and joined a circle of dissidents. He also saw the need to take a stand against evil, in his case from a sociological point of view. He was apprehended and sentence to death. There was some time for him between his trial and his execution on February 2, 1945 to describe his spirituality. He called it, "In the face of death". Everything is taken away from a man and he has to look up to God in total surrender.

Right from the start Fr. Delp saw through his trial, knowing that the dice had fallen and that the hearings and the sentence were just a mockery. He didn't have any illusions about his fate, but he experienced that his inner strength was coming from a different source. The Advent season of 1944 became most significant for him. One of his descriptions goes like this, "The comfort of the season of Advent is that the Announcement of the Angel found the heart of Mary ready for him, that the Word became flesh and found room in the heart of the mother and it was in her that the earth grew beyond itself into the world of the God-Man. Our awareness and our experience of difficulties do not do us any good, if there isn't a bridge between heaven and earth."

Both Fr. Josef Kentenich and Fr. Alfred Delp had a certain understanding of the occurring catastrophe. They had to ask, "Why does God let this happen?" They concluded that Christianity had neglected those on the margin too much and needed this wake-up call. Both perceived the events in the train of thought of St. Augustine that God hates the sin, but loves the sinner and knows how to bring good out of evil. Fr. Kentenich was very fond of the idea that God is a Master-Artist. Yes, we can conclude that there is something artistic about the contemplative, which enables him to pull through occasions of despair and find a new beginning in God's greater grace. Even the tragic events of the Third Reich didn't destroy religion, but brought it into a new light and made it even more intense. The contemplatives knew that God remained close to them and to all those, who were willing to be inspired by him. Fr. Alfred Delp realized the great need that the different denominations and Churches join together as one family of believers having faced this enemy, who didn't distinguish between them at all, but treated them all alike. He stated that we cannot afford to present to the world once more a divided Christianity.

In this light we can also appreciate the Ecumenical Monastery of Taize in France, founded by Roger Schutz during the Second World War. It emphasizes a universal need for contemplation in our modern world.

The contemplatives have been very keen to pinpoint the lop-sidedness of our mere scientific world and that it is in dire need to find the balance given in prayer and meditation.

Henri de Lubac and Contemplation Today
Believers Cannot Ignore Science nor Should it Dominate the Soul

he Jesuit Priest, monk, and scholar, Henri de Lubac (1896–1991) had to go through some struggles to discover the validity of the gifts from heaven, but also to find out that these gifts are not in our grasp like a recipe. We are familiar with the fact that our era has posed a very serious challenge to the faith through science, a challenge, which is still very strong and vibrant in our 21st century and will still remain with us. Science has given evidence about the millions of years, since the beginning of creation.

Believers have to face these findings and try to reconcile them with their faith. Henri de Lubac believed that we have to feel comfortable with science and trust that God's creation and our salvation in Christ belong together in his bond of love. Along with this expansion of our time-line with regard to creation and salvation he was firm in his Catholicism and didn't think that we should try an easy ecumenism with other world-religions, especially Islam and Buddhism. If we don't have an interest to convert them, then we are weak in our faith. Jesus Christ is the Lord of the entire history of the human race and ultimately all people should have access to him. If we don't have this strength of faith, then we only provoke greater conflicts. Islamic people may very well consider us to blaspheme, since we believe man in Jesus Christ to be God.

Buddhism has given mankind a tremendous insight into the difference between time and eternity, which is above time, but there remains a void in their eternity, which has to be filled through our belief in the Blessed Trinity. If we don't stand ready as missionaries to fill this void, then we leave them spiritually in the lurch and we haven't done our duty. Any kind of soft tolerance may only show disinterest and indifference.

Both world religions, Islam and Buddhism, require the witness of Christians, which may have to go to the point of martyrdom. St. Francis of Assisi was willing to give this witness to Islam in the thirteenth century and Charles de Foucauld gave his life in witness for it in the twentieth century. Henri de Lubac was a Jesuit and a scholar, who took this witness seriously and we have to regret that people didn't learn more from him. We have to regret this, because this neglect on the part of Christians only leads inevitably to greater conflict.

Henri de Lubac had explained his view through teaching, preaching and writing. The superiors of his Order became suspicious about him and believed he had become heretical and was no longer faithful to the Church. He had to experience the harshness of religious superiors. As if hit by lightning he was singled out as the main scapegoat of the "Novelle Theologie" and those, who blamed him to be an innovator, believed that they had to root out this evil and they took action. Spiritually he was bound to the pillar of the Praetorium, scourged and he had to endure this way of the cross for about ten years (1947–1957).

He had taught theology for a number of years in the Jesuit Seminary in Lyon, had enjoyed the academic advances of his students, their interests in the faith and in research. Suddenly, his teaching credentials were withdrawn, and he wasn't permitted to have any contact with his students and almost no contact with brother priests of the order. We can hardly imagine the impact this must have had on his sensitive nature. He hadn't incurred any personal blame and yet he was ostracized. The next step against him was that he was expelled from the city of Lyon and he virtually had become homeless. His publications were suppressed, taken from the shelves of the libraries and withdrawn from the market. We can ask, "Was it God, who humiliated him or did God let him endure this as atonement for others and for those, who caused him this pain?"

He reported his suffering in this way, "Never have I been questioned during all these years, never did I get a chance to talk with someone in Rome about the issues, neither in the Curia nor in the Society of Jesus. I wasn't informed what the accusations were and nobody asked me to retract something or to clarify a point." He only knew that he had been shunned and reduced to complete isolation.

It is most remarkable that he kept his peace of mind and focused on the spiritual values, which are the essential bequest of our faith. Contemplation kept him on the right track in the midst of what he had to endure. He remained faithful to the tradition of the Church. An improvement of his plight came slowly. His Provincial allowed him to continue his research and publish them after they had gone through the censure of the Curia. The Confessor of the Pope, Fr. Bea gave some of his books to Pope Pius XII, who expressed his gratitude. Archbishop Montini also encouraged him. Finally His Holiness, Pope John XXIII, named him consultant of a theological commission in preparation of the Second Vatican Council and Pope Paul VI (the former Archbishop Montini) asked him to be a main speaker. We can say that the code of contemplation worked admirably in his lifetime. Henri de Lubac also makes the point that a religious order is of a timeless quality and will only disappear, when there are no more members left, who are inwardly connected with eternal life.

In our appreciation of Monasticism we include the many Monasteries in the Eastern Orthodox Churches. Their tradition of contemplation is a permanent source of strength for them and their mystical union with God has remained constant through the ages. Often the monasteries have suffered plunder, destruction and confiscation of their property and they have returned to their observances, liturgies and prayers. This was particularly the case after the Russian Revolution in 1917. At that time the Blessed Virgin Mary appeared in Fatima and asked for prayers for the conversion of Russia and pointed out that otherwise Communism would spread their errors. She also promised that Russia would be converted and there would be a time of peace. At the beginning of the 21st century we can look back on the many decades of Communism and a renewal of monastic life there.

This shows on the one side that Christianity has a greater depth than materialism expected and on the other that the amount of dedication, prayer and sacrifices needed is immense and demands a lot of contemplation for the renewal of the Spirit. The 20th century was a very drastic reminder of how devastating the modern world is becoming without this link between heaven and earth, made possible by all people of faith and goodwill and especially by the contemplatives.

As always it would be premature to just rejoice and celebrate that a difficult era like Communism has drawn to a close. For the contemplatives in countries, who have suffered through modern materialism, the end of an era is the beginning of a long process of renewal and rebuilding.

Conclusion

The monks and the secret code, in which they operate, are not only an essential aspect of the Church, but also a trademark of genuine Christianity. It would be an error to conceive of Christianity without this impact of genuine contemplation, which we find particularly in those, who devote their entire life to prayer and meditation. At times this aspect seems to be subdued and almost lost in the business of the Churches and their many activities. Then almost as if out of nowhere it stands out and everybody has to acknowledge that this aspect was actually indispensable.

A genuine contemplative like St. Bernard not only bore the twelfth century on his shoulders, but as Henri de Lubac described it, the struggle of several centuries lodged in his heart and he brought it to a conclusion in the awareness of the security of salvation we have in Jesus Christ through the protection of the Mother of God. His devotion centered in this mystery and he was able to draw Christendom to a closer participation in it. He was a simple monk and yet paradoxically he was connected with all the people of his age and their concerns.

A modern Benedictine monk, Raphael Hombach, experienced his call from God in the universal sense of being lonely for everybody. Alone in his cell he knew that no one is excluded from his call from God and that his single life has the intention from the Lord to benefit everybody. He was almost astonished and surprised to discover that God not only acted in him in this way, but that God continued to unfold his plan of salvation through the individual, who has time for contemplation.

By the same token he had to face the fact, how seriously God was taking him and all those devoted to his cause. He described it as follows, "Monk! You have prayed: Accept me, Lord! Why do you wonder that God is granting your request and is accepting you? Why do you wonder, when you feel that you have been accepted? Monk! You have prayed: Accept me, Lord! Be happy, because God is granting your request and is accepting you! Even at the cost of your life he is accepting you. Don't be afraid. Your worst days are your best. These are the days, when God placed his entire burden on your shoulders."

As the monk and the nun are surprised, when God is close to them in prayer and contemplation, so may these pages assist the reader to let himself be surprised by God. May God bless all efforts to follow the path, which the monks have mapped out for so many centuries, making it possible to renew our bond with the Lord.

Chronology

Index

About the Author

Fr. Otto A. Koltzenburg was born in the town, Rohr, in the Eifel-region in Germany in 1950. This village was first mentioned in documents dating back over 1,000 years ago when the town received its spiritual and political guidance from the Benedictine Abbey of Pruem. The Patron Saint of the village is St. Wendelin, a hermit of the Middle Ages. Through centuries the population of this town remained faithful to the religious customs and to the Catholic Faith. Fr. Otto was happy to grow up in this strong traditional environment with his three brothers. He studied Theology in Wuerzburg and was ordained to the Catholic Priesthood in Spokane, WA in 1981.

Also available from San Juan Publishing

The Light on the Island by Helene Glidden
Once Upon an Island by David Conover
Andrew Henry's Meadow by Doris Burn
Springer's Journey by Naomi Black and Virginia Heaven
Gloria's Miracle by Jerry Brewer
Areté *Again* by Tobin Wilson

SAN JUAN PUBLISHING
P.O. Box 923
Woodinville, WA 98072
425-485-2813
sanjuanbooks@yahoo.com
www.sanjuanbooks.com